CAUSING, PERCEIVING AND BELIEVING

PHILOSOPHICAL STUDIES SERIES
IN PHILOSOPHY

VOLUME 6

PETER H. HARE and EDWARD H. MADDEN

State University of New York at Buffalo

CAUSING, PERCEIVING
AND BELIEVING

An Examination of the Philosophy of C. J. Ducasse

D. REIDEL PUBLISHING COMPANY

DORDRECHT-HOLLAND / BOSTON-U.S.A.

Library of Congress Cataloging in Publication Data

Hare, Peter H
    Causing, perceiving, and believing.

    (Philosophical studies series in philosophy; v. 6)
    Bibliography: p.
    Includes index.
    1. Ducasse, Curt John, 1881–1969. I. Madden,
Edward H., joint author. II. Title.
B945.D84H37   191   75–4899

ISBN 90 277 0563 1

Published by D. Reidel Publishing Company,
P.O. Box 17, Dordrecht, Holland

Sold and distributed in the U.S.A., Canada and Mexico
by D. Reidel Publishing Company, Inc.
306 Dartmouth Street, Boston,
Mass. 02116, U.S.A.

Printed in The Netherlands by D. Reidel, Dordrecht

CONTENTS

ACKNOWLEDGMENTS

We have been aided by many people in writing this book and wish to express appreciation especially to the late C. J. Ducasse for making his unpublished manuscripts and letters available to us, and for advising and guiding us in many matters through the years; to James Humber and Barry Cohen for contributing substantively to the topics of causality and metaphilosophy, respectively; to Roderick Chisholm, Frederick Dommeyer, Vincent Tomas, and James Wheatley for reading the manuscript and making many helpful suggestions; and to Carol Breitenbach for typing the manuscript, managing correspondence, and, in general, assisting at every stage of preparation of the manuscript.

For the encouragement necessary to put together a book, even a moderate size one, we are indebted, in addition to the above, to family, friends, and colleagues who often knew our needs better than we. Our warm thanks to Daphne and Marian, most of all.

Finally, we express appreciation to the National Endowment for the Humanities and the State University of New York Research Foundation for their support and to the editors of *Ratio, Philosophy and Phenomenological Research, Transactions of the Charles S. Peirce Society, The Personalist*, and the *Southern Journal of Philosophy* for previous publication of several sections.

CHAPTER I

INTRODUCTION

I

Although a succession of fashions swept the American philosophical scene, C.J. Ducasse was throughout his long career an effective practitioner of analytic philosophy in the classic tradition. As he explained in 1924 "[i]t is only with truths about such questions as the meaning of the term 'true', or 'real', or 'good', and the like . . . that philosophy is concerned."

Such truths are to be discovered *inductively* by comparing and analyzing concrete cases of the admittedly proper *use* . . . The pressing problems of philosophy are thus in my view primarily problems of definition, and moreover, problems of framing definitions which must be in formal terms, under penalty of not being otherwise understandable by or acceptable to one or another philosophical school, since the formal elements of thought and they only are common to all schools. These definitions, of course are not to be arbitrary; their relation to the facts of admittedly meaningful linguistic usage is the same as exists between any scientific hypothesis and the facts which it attempts to construe.[1]

When Ducasse first formulated this method, he contrasted it with such methods as Russell's logical atomism and pointed out that Russell's own practice in his discussion of our knowledge of the external world is best described, not as an exercise in logical atomism, but as a skillful attempt "to define accurately the meaning of the terms 'external world' and 'the mental world' in a manner that will check with the undoubtedly meaningful use made of these terms in practice."[2]

A generation later, when another method became influential, that of logical positivism, Ducasse effectively criticized Carnap's claim that philosophy should concern itself only with the syntax of the language of science. "[T]he language of science," Ducasse suggested in his 1939 Presidential Address to the Eastern Division of the American Philosophical Association, "is not the only language there is." There is also "the language of art, the language of religion, the language of law, of morals, and so on; for man is not exclusively a cognitive, science-building animal. And these other languages too have their respective syntaxes."[3] Moreover, Ducasse argued, though the study of logical syntax may be useful for some philosophical purposes, Carnap's claim that philosophy is properly the study of logical syntax rests on the mistaken assumption that the relevant philosophical statements in the material mode can be strictly translated into the formal mode.

Still later, when ordinary language became an influential method in the 1950's, Ducasse acutely criticized this newest fashion in analytic philosophy, though for more than twenty-five years he had been insisting that language-facts constitute the basic data of philosophy. He concluded that "the terms 'correct' and 'incorrect', as applied to the use made of a given word by a given person, imply nothing as to whether or not that use is 'ordinary'." [4]

Painstaking application of his "knowledge-yielding" philosophical method, without being taken in by the analytic extravagances of logical atomism, logical positivism or ordinary language philosophy, is what made possible Ducasse's lasting contributions to areas of philosophy as diverse as philosophy of science, metaphysics, epistemology, aesthetics, theory of action, ethics, and philosophy of religion. Indeed, Ducasse's contributions are too wide ranging to admit of brief summary. In the body of this book we will critically examine Ducasse's philosophy in detail. By way of introduction we can only mention a few of the areas in which he has important things to say.

Ducasse himself regarded his analysis of causation as the cornerstone of his philosophy, and his defense of a non-Humean concept of causation should be regarded as one of his most distinctive and significant contributions. Even staunch Humeans recognize Ducasse's critique of the Humean position as a model of philosophical analysis, and the defense in recent years of the non-Humean position by such able philosophers as Rom Harré, Peter Alexander, Nicholas Maxwell, and Richard Taylor promises a degree of recognition of Ducasse's contribution that was impossible while Anglo-American philosophy of science was entirely in the grip of Hume and his followers.

Ducasse's analysis of perception is hardly less significant. His adverbial theory, first developed in the early 1930's, culminated in a fascinating exchange with G. E. Moore in the 1940's. The cudgels were then taken up by his student Roderick Chisholm, whose *Perceiving* is one of the most widely read works in recent epistemology. Also noteworthy is the fact that

Chisholm's much discussed views on both incorrigibility and the ethics of belief are largely developments out of Ducasse's views. However, of greater significance than the special aspects of epistemology we have mentioned is the general epistemological stance that Ducasse took. The adverbial realism found in Ducasse's theory of objective reference has recently been influentially defended not only by Chisholm but also by Wilfrid Sellars and his students.

In metaphysics Ducasse's chief contribution has been in philosophy of mind. His critique of behaviorism and defense of interactionism are widely respected. His critique in the early 1940's of Charles Morris' behavioristic theory of meaning, for example, exerted a strong influence on Chisholm, who is a leading anti-behaviorist in contemporary metaphysics. Ducasse was still having interesting exchanges concerning philosophy of mind in the 1960's. After one such exchange with Antony Flew, he was so pleased to have Flew concede that, contrary to the views of Gilbert Ryle, there is an irreducibly experiential element in the analysis of mental words he joked to Flew that "[y]our philosophical soul will be saved yet!"[5]

Although Ducasse's work in metaphysics and epistemology is perhaps the most widely known and influential part of his philosophy, his work on many other philosophical problems is in some respects equally important. It has been justly said by Vincent Tomas that his aesthetics is the "most ably defended version of the emotionalist theory of art and aesthetic appreciation that has been written."[6] His writing on the standards of criticism and the nature of expression continues to be widely discussed and reprinted. Although hitherto unknown because unpublished, Ducasse's discussion of normative ethics is also fascinating. His articles on the philosophy of education are widely known in the field, but they can be appreciated fully only when they are understood in the context of his unpublished normative ethics. In philosophy of religion Ducasse's contribution to the tradition begun by William James is also impressive. At the heart of his views on religion is his ethics of belief, an ethics of belief presented most forcefully in correspondence with Dickinson Miller. This, however, is only one of the many parts of his philosophy that is illuminated by reference to his extensive correspondence with other philosophers.

Without further attempt to summarize Ducasse's philosophical contributions, let us turn now to the man himself since biographical knowledge of him will shed light on our subsequent detailed analysis of his philosophical writings.

II

Born on July 7, 1881 in Angoulême, France, Ducasse left for Bordeaux in 1893. First enrolled in the *Lycée* of Bordeaux's classical curriculum, he later turned to mathematics and science in preparation for admission to the engineering program at the *École Centrale*. In 1897, however, an illness incapacitated him for a year and led to the abandonment of his plans to become a civil engineer. After regaining his health, he attended the Abbotsholme School in England for a year. In later years when Ducasse looked back on his early education in France and England a number of things seemed to have been important to his intellectual development. He remembered:

the vivid impression of the moment when, in my study of Latin, I first realized in myself an appreciation of sentence structure. I also remember becoming clearly conscious some years later that the mathematical, and in particular the geometrical, modes of thought were to some extent colouring my reasoning processes in other subjects, inclining me to seek order, clearness, and objectivity. Again, I recall that the habit I eventually developed, of beginning every systematic inquiry with the most definite statement possible of the matter in doubt, had its origin in the constant question, 'What are we trying to find out?' asked in class by one of my teachers in England, Dr. Cecil Reddie.[7]

In 1899 he returned briefly to France and then travelled widely for a few years experimenting with a variety of occupations. Shortly before his 19th birthday in 1900 he took a job in one of the foreign outlets of the Parisian firm for whom he had wrapped packages, a dry goods store in Mexico City whose owners were French. After a few months of carrying bolts of cloth upstairs and putting them on the proper shelves, he was promoted to the job of cashier downstairs. Not allowed out except on Sunday afternoons, he slept on the counters and ate in the clerks' refectory on the top floor. Next he took a job with a firm of window glass contractors for whom he cycled all over Mexico City measuring window frames. After switching briefly back to work with another importer of French dry goods, he decided in 1901 to go into business for himself. With a stock of Mexican lace, he went to New York to open a lace shop on Fifth Avenue, but business was bad and the would-be entrepreneur soon took an office job with an importer. Later he handled the Spanish correspondence of a music publisher who sent him back to Mexico as their representative. After travelling all over Mexico as a salesman of music publications, he went back to work for one of the importers in Mexico City for whom he had worked before going to the U.S. But this job, too, he kept only briefly, and soon he went back to New York City to work as a steno-typist in the foreign department of an insurance company. After three years, salaries in the insurance company were cut, including his, so in the fall of 1906, having heard that Seattle was booming, he left New York to become secretary to the chief engineer in the Seattle office of a railroad under construction.

While living in New York City, he had taken a short trip to France to visit his family. On this trip a family acquaintance showed him a little book which acquainted him with the views of the theosophists. When he returned to New York, he joined the Theosophical Society and was for some time in charge of the library of the New York branch. It was during this period that he stumbled upon what he later considered the first philosophical book to come into his hands, *The Science of Peace*, by Bhagavan Das (Theosophical Publishing Society, London, 1904). The book, Ducasse remembered,

dealt with the relation of the Individual to the Absolute, and contained a chapter, beyond which I think I did not go, in which the author brought into his discussion the thought of various European philosophers, and in particular of Fichte and Hegel. That I found such a book rather hard to understand goes without saying; but the reading of it at least made me realize the existence and the general nature of the questions that philosophy asks, and revealed to me at the same time the intense interest that such questions had for me.[3]

It was not long before the views of the theosophists came to seem "too doctrinaire" to Ducasse, and he discontinued membership in the Theosophical Society.[9] In Seattle in the fall of 1907, finding his "dislike of business pursuits growing at the same rate as [his] preoccupation with philosophical questions," [10] and having come into a little money, he entered the Philosophy-Psychology Department at the University of Washington with senior standing because of the work he had done at the *Lycée* in Bordeaux years before. He was graduated *magna cum laude* the following June, 1908, with an A.B. degree and received his M.A. degree at Washington in 1909. During the academic year 1909—10 he was a graduate assistant. Two of his teachers at Washington were especially important to his intellectual development: Professor W. Savery in Philosophy and Professor H. C. Stevens in Psychology. Savery was "a constant incentive to logical watchfulness" and set "an exacting intellectual standard." [11] Stevens, whom he assisted in research and with whom he later published his first paper, taught Ducasse what is meant by "tireless patience, painstaking care, and scrupulous scientific honesty" in empirical investigations.[12]

In 1910 Ducasse became a naturalized citizen, and in the fall of that year went to Harvard where he received his Ph.D. in 1912. At Harvard most of his work was done under Josiah Royce. Ducasse later described his contact with Royce:

> His unaffected and kindly but impressive personality, his powerful constructive intellect, the extraordinary range and thoroughness of his learning, and the genius which enabled him to find for even remotely abstract logical considerations the most concrete and living illustrations, all made upon me a profound and lasting impression, the effect of which, although not easy to analyze in detail, has been far-reaching.[13]

When Ducasse arrived at Harvard, he was "thoroughly convinced" of the essential soundness of Schopenhauer's philosophy.[14] He had arrived at that position by a route which started at Berkeley and led him through Hume and Kant before his arrival at the idealism of Schopenhauer. This interest in classical modern philosophy, especially in Schopenhauer and Hume, stayed with him for the rest of his career. Schopenhauer and Hume were the two philosophers he chose to be examined on in detail for the Ph.D. and his later teaching showed that, though sharply critical of them in many respects, he never lost his interest in and respect for these philosophers. His subsequent publications also were affected by early study of these philosophers. He wrote that he was first awakened to causality's "great importance by my study years ago of Schopenhauer's 'Fourfold Root of the Principle of Sufficient Reason'," [15] and much of his work on causation, even at the end of his career, was a detailed critique of Hume and his followers.

It was not long, however, before Ducasse's idealism was challenged by the neorealism of Ralph Barton Perry. In Perry's seminary he read his first paper, and

> On that, to me, memorable occasion I defended my idealistic positions fiercely, and remained unconvinced of any unsoundness in them. On the other hand, I could not at the time clearly perceive the defect which I believed existed in the position of Professor Perry, and I resolved to examine his published articles with care before the next meeting of the seminary.[16]

A few days later Ducasse had a dramatic experience that was the origin of his relativistic views on the nature of philosophy.

> I was at home quietly reading some book . . . when suddenly a most vivid and luminous insight came to me that neither idealism, nor realism, nor any other metaphysical

position could, in the very nature of things, be either refuted or proved . . . For nearly two days, with hardly any sleep or food, and in a state of the highest exaltation, I wrote feverishly . . .[17]

Although many would agree with Brand Blanshard that Ducasse's "rigorous practice" in philosophy was "better than his permissive theory," [18] there is no question that Ducasse's conviction that metaphysical positions are logically arbitrary and represent only taste, whim or temperament led him to the view that the proper business of philosophy is the analysis of value predicates, and this view, in turn, led him to consider predicates and language-facts in general as the basic data of philosophy. It was his vivid Harvard experience of the need for tolerance in philosophy that led to his semantical conception of philosophical method, a rigorous analytic method which, as we have seen, made possible numerous non-relativistic contributions admired by philosophers who, like Blanshard, are unwilling to accept what Ducasse called, following Royce's suggestion, his "philosophical liberalism."

Having received his doctorate, Ducasse returned to the University of Washington where he taught between 1912 and 1926. Although he published nothing before 1924 (with the exception of the article in psychology co-authored by Stevens), he was actively writing on a variety of philosophical topics during his early teaching career. For example, in 1914 he wrote his father in France: "j'ai tout de même fini mon article sur l'Individualisme, et l'ai transcrit à la machine . . ." [19] Among the other areas in which he was teaching and doing research were aesthetics and logic. In the latter area one of his prize pupils was Charles A. Baylis. This was the beginning of a long and fruitful association with Baylis. In 1934 when both Ducasse and Baylis were teaching at Brown, they organized the meeting at Harvard that led to the establishment of both the *Journal of Symbolic Logic* and the Association for Symbolic Logic. The meeting was attended by A. A. Bennett, P. Henle, E. V. Huntington, H. S. Leonard, Wm. T. Parry, W. V. Quine and H. M. Sheffer as well as by Ducasse and Baylis. A. N. Whitehead and C. I. Lewis were unable to attend but sent word of their support. Ducasse, who did much of the work between the time of the Harvard meeting and the election of the first officers in 1935, was elected first president of the Association.

It was during his Seattle period that Mabel Lisle, a painter, was a student in Ducasse's aesthetics class. In 1921 he married his former student. Having a wife who was a widely exhibited painter must have encouraged Ducasse in his work in aesthetics, and it was during the first years of their marriage that he did his most significant work in that area culminating in *The Philosophy of Art*, published in 1929. In 1945 he was elected President of the American Society for Aesthetics.

We have already mentioned Ducasse's later role in organizing the Association for Symbolic Logic. It should also be mentioned that during this early period of teaching at Washington he was instrumental in organizing another important philosophical association, the Pacific Division of the American Philosophical Association. In April 1924 he wrote his wife: "I have just returned from Berkeley, where I had lunch with Adams and Loewenberg. The latter suggested that we organize a Pacific Division of the American Philosophical Association, and we constituted ourselves a committee of organization, with myself as chairman." [20] Upon his return to Seattle, Ducasse wrote to a number of influential philosophers on the West Coast, and the Pacific Division held its first meeting at the University of California in November, 1924, with Ducasse serving as the Division's first Secretary.

1924–26 was an academic watershed for Ducasse. Although in 1924 he was 43 years old and had published nothing in philosophy in the twelve years since receiving his doctorate, during this brief period of three years there appeared in print (in a major book and no less than ten articles!) most of the philosophy that was eventually to receive its fullest statement in *Nature, Mind and Death*. It was at this time also that Ducasse was appointed Associate Professor by Brown University, the university with which he was to be so closely associated until his death 45 years later. It cannot have been difficult for Brown to recognize his promise.

Of Ducasse's numerous services to the academic world after 1926 we can mention only a small number beyond those we have already mentioned in passing. Some of the most notable offices he held were: President, American Philosophical Association (Eastern Division), 1939; President, Philosophy of Science Association, 1958–61; Chairman, Philosophy Department, Brown University, 1930–51; Acting Dean, Graduate School, Brown University, 1947–49; Member, Executive Committee, American Council of Learned Societies, 1939–41; Fellow, American Association for the Advancement of Science, 1938; Member of Council, American Academy of Arts and Sciences, 1954–58; First Vice-President of the American Society for Psychical Research, 1965–67, and Chairman of the Society's Publications

Committee, 1959—67. He had visiting appointments at such distinguished institutions as the University of Michigan, University of California at Los Angeles, Columbia University, Cornell University, Radcliffe College, and the University of Chicago. He published nine books, nearly 150 professional articles, and about the same number of book reviews and newspaper articles.

Having sketched his academic history, we now have the pleasant task of saying something about Ducasse's personality. In Ducasse's philosophical work it is immediately apparent that he had an amazing capacity for taking pains to clarify his own ideas and those of others. Among the aphorisms he loved to compose but never published are many that concern this quest for clarity.

> Most intellects don't bite into facts, but only suck.
> Six inches of muddy water looks as deep as the ocean.
> The name often wholly insulates us from the thing.
> To be definitely wrong is usually better than to be vaguely right.[21]

We will see in later chapters how this "master of the English language" (as C. D. Broad called him) made his own ideas clear, but something should be said here about his desire and ability to make clear the ideas of others. "[T]here is one particular quality," Broad wrote, "which Ducasse seems to me to have possessed to a degree unsurpassed in all other writers. This was his power of giving, in his own words, a lucid, fair, and comprehensive account of highly complex matters treated by an author whose work he was reviewing ... It was a very great and very rare merit." [22] Needless to say, Ducasse's students benefited from this trait as much as the readers of his reviews.

In some ways even more striking than his quest for clarity was his impish wit, a wit that was given free rein, for example, in his popular discussions of art. Declaring the independence of the consumer of art from the tyranny of art criticism, he loved to poke fun at critics who write intimidating tomes filled with "pussyfootnotes." [23] In a series of dialogues he published in a Providence newspaper, Ducasse cast himself in the role of Dr. Wiggins and the oppressed and gullible consumer in the role of Adrian. The following concerning a book on post-impressionism is a typical exchange:

ADRIAN. But what about the skill of the painter? Isn't that worthy of praise? Some of the post-impressionists are said to have had not only the courage of their feelings, such as they were, but the skill to express them with extraordinary force and accuracy.

DR. WIGGINS. No doubt. It takes great skill to hit a man across the street in the eye with an egg. But to admit this leaves open the question whether the result is as praiseworthy as the skill of the technique.

ADRIAN. Yet it seems that after a while one gets to like some of the queer pictures that shocked one the most at first. The writer of the book recites for instance his experience with the pictures of Matisse. He had to try a long time before he got to like them, but finally he made the grade.

DR. WIGGINS. Yes, critics are often like the loggers of the Northwest, who pride themselves on being able to drink anything. I was told that after five attempts they manage to make rubbing alcohol stay put. That makes me think of Steffansson's feathers.

ADRIAN. His feathers?

DR. WIGGINS. Yes, I heard him say that once he found himself at a place where there was no food at all except oil – fish oil I think it was. Well, it seems that if you swallow that by itself, your interior decorations go on strike. But it occurred to him to sop it up in some feathers and fur that he had so there would be something to chew on, and that worked. He said that after a while he almost got to the point of looking forward with pleasure to his next meal. [24]

Ducasse's wit is also ever present in his aphorisms:

Life is just one damned thing after another. Love is two damned things after one another.

Keeping one's virtue is one thing; hoarding it is another; and investing it yet a third.

College students should be either married or single.

Love that has to work miracles outlives but few of them.

The most useful of domestic animals is not the cow, but the husband. [25]

Always game for a harmless prank, Ducasse, before he decided that hypnotism was too potent and might be misused, hypnotized friends and told them their chairs were hot, whereupon they would jump in alarm, and a hypnotized friend he told to sneeze twice at breakfast next morning, did just that. He even succeeded in hypnotizing his friends over the telephone.

Arthur Murphy, for some years a junior colleague of Ducasse at Brown, nicknamed him Jack Oakie (from John, his middle name and the cask supposed to be in "Ducasse") and was one of many fellow philosophers who enjoyed bringing out the imp in Ducasse. Antony Flew recalls that even in his later years "Ducasse just naturally gravitated toward the liveliest members of any group; and these, equally naturally — even when the liveliest happened also to be the youngest — accepted him as another of themselves." [26]

Ducasse's wit, however, was warm and destructive only of pretentiousness. Gardner Murphy recalls that it was because of Ducasse's "informed heart" that he was asked to be Chairman of the Publications Committee of the American Society for Psychical Research. [27] Among philosophers perhaps the best illustration of the warmth of Ducasse's personality was his friendship with Dickinson Miller. Miller was a gifted former student and friend of William James who found the world of professional philosophy extraordinarily threatening, so threatening that in some of his most important articles he felt compelled to use the pseudonym R. E. Hobart. During the last twenty years of Miller's life Ducasse was his closest friend; they had a fascinating correspondence on a variety of fundamental philosophical issues and exchanged visits until Miller's health prevented his coming to Providence and Ducasse then made special trips to Boston to cheer his friend.

Camping was among the non-philosophical activities Ducasse enjoyed. He and his wife camped in mountains and woods all over the West, from the Canadian Rockies to the Grand Canyon of Arizona, between the Rocky Mountains and the Pacific Coast. He recalled "many pack-sack trips in the Cascade Mountains in Washington Sate" and liked "few things better than sleeping under the stars in sage brush desert, or in the virgin timber of the Siskiyous or Cascades or on the matchless coast of southern Oregon." [28]

Although in the world of art he usually played the role of aesthetician, he also liked, in a minor way, to create his own art. He took pride in his handicrafted jewelry, and in his earlier years wrote a series (unpublished) of melancholy romances entitled *The Lovestone, and Other Dream-Spun Tales*. His artistic activity extended to his clothes, usually a symphony of blues and sometimes topped, perhaps incongruously, by a green eyeshade. Certainly his most satisfying artistic activity, however, was the writing and speaking of beautiful English laced with slang. Although traces of his French accent remained, he had no interest in fine food and drink. "Meals," he said, "are nuisances to be got out of the way. I look forward to the time when we can feed ourselves with pills." [29] He found a nicely balanced sentence, a thought well turned, more exciting than the most perfectly concocted salad or the rarest of vintages.

His most characteristic non-philosophical preoccupation was with cats and other small creatures. In 1930 a cat he named "Cockroach" amused Ducasse by refusing to drink out of anything but a bathtub. Later Ducasse and his wife were slaves for twenty-one years of Chichibu, a Siamese cat. As Ducasse quipped, "I call that cat mine, but I have no doubt that she, too, calls me hers when she discusses me with her friends, and with better reason, since I work for her, while she does nothing for me." [30] Chichibu was often to be found curled around Ducasse's neck, forming a living collar. Chipmunks in their garden were tamed with peanuts and sunflower seeds. Even field mice were given loving attention. He built a special trap in which to catch them without hurting them and liked to tell the story of Conrad. "We caught Conrad, whom we identified by a kink in his tail, 176 times in our cellar. Even when we took him a couple of blocks away, he was back as soon as we were, and we never could find out where he came in." [31]

Antony Flew remembers that when Ducasse and H. H. Price first met, they "delighted one another and everyone else present by discovering that they shared not only an interest in philosophy and psychical research, but also a liking for owls, for cats, and for mice," though they apologized "that this combination of animal loves was 'in a way almost self-contradictory'."[32] Apparently Ducasse's liberalism, whether philosophical or temperamental, extended even to the lives of little animals. His sympathy for all living things was unbounded.

NOTES

[1]   C.J. Ducasse, *Causation and the Types of Necessity* (New York: Dover Publications, 1969), p. 120. Originally published in 1924 by the University of Washington Press.
[2]   *Ibid.*, p. 124.
[3]   C.J. Ducasse, "Philosophy and Natural Science," in *Truth, Knowledge and Causation* (London: Routledge & Kegan Paul, 1968), p. 220. Delivered in 1939, published as an article in 1940, and reprinted in 1968.
[4]   Letter to Roderick M. Chisholm, September 7, 1951. Professor Ducasse's unpublished letters and manuscripts are in the archives of Brown University, the John Hay Library.
[5]   Letter to A.G.N. Flew, May 2, 1963.
[6]   Vincent Tomas, "Ducasse on Art and Its Appreciation," *Philosophy and Phenomenological Research* 13 (1952–53), 69.
[7]   C.J. Ducasse, "Philosophical Liberalism," in *Contemporary American Philosophy* (London: Allen and Unwin, 1930), p. 301.
[8]   *Ibid.*, p. 302.
[9]   Letter to Dale Riepe, March 5, 1968.

[10] "Philosophical Liberalism," p. 302.

[11] *Ibid.*, p. 303.

[12] *Ibid.*

[13] *Ibid.*, p. 303f.

[14] *Ibid.*, p. 304.

[15] Letter to Paul Edwards, June 14, 1957.

[16] "Philosophical Liberalism," p. 304.

[17] *Ibid.*, p. 304f.

[18] Brand Blanshard, "A Tribute to C.J. Ducasse," *Journal of the American Society for Psychical Research* 64 (1970), 139.

[19] Letter to Jean Louis Ducasse, May 28, 1914.

[20] Quoted in Frederick C. Dommeyer, "Introduction and Biographical Data," *Current Philosophical Issues: Essays in Honour of Curt John Ducasse* (Springfield, I11.: Charles C. Thomas, 1966), pp. xxiii–xxiv.

[21] C.J. Ducasse, 5 page untitled and undated typescript of aphorisms.

[22] C.D. Broad, "A Tribute to C.J. Ducasse," *Journal of the American Society for Psychical Research* 64 (1970), 142.

[23] C.J. Ducasse, "Taste, Training and Blue Ribbons," *The Providence Journal*, March 2, 1927.

[24] C.J. Ducasse, "Post-Impressionists, *et al.*," *The Providence Journal*, April 20, 1927.

[25] C.J. Ducasse, typescript of aphorisms.

[26] Antony Flew, "A Tribute to C.J. Ducasse," *Journal of the American Society for Psychical Research* 64 (1970), 143.

[27] Gardner Murphy, "A Tribute to C.J. Ducasse," *Journal of the American Society for Psychical Research* 64 (1970), 147.

[28] C.J. Ducasse, "Biographical Notes Concerning C.J. Ducasse," 2 pages, undated typescript.

[29] Interview, *The Evening Bulletin* (Providence, R.I.), June 13, 1930, p. 14.

[30] C.J. Ducasse, "Taste, Training and Blue Ribbons."

[31] Interview, *The Evening Bulletin* (Providence, R.I.), June 26, 1958, p. 18.

[32] Antony Flew, "A Tribute to C.J. Ducasse," p. 143.

CHAPTER II

CAUSALITY AND NECESSITY

For over forty years C. J. Ducasse effectively criticized Humean views of causality, though he was never content simply to be a critic. We owe to his ingenuity and precision one of the most attractive non-Humean alternatives to be found in twentieth-century philosophy. *Causation and the Types of Necessity* was the first published statement of his views, and this book, long out of print, has been republished recently with more recent articles appended.[1] His second major statement, changed in details but essentially the same, appears as Part II of *Nature, Mind, and Death*, his contribution to the Carus Lecture Series.[2] His later articles on causality are included in the recently published collection of essays *Truth, Knowledge and Causation*,[3] where he thoughtfully answers the questions raised by serious-minded critics of his two books.

Professor Ducasse's contributions to the analysis of the concepts causation and nonlogical necessity are considerable, and are, as we shall see, contributions from which Humeans and non-Humeans alike have much to learn. This holds true for method as well as substantive results. His analyses of causal concepts provide models of precision and clarity rarely achieved by those who most ardently declare their devotion to these virtues. Ducasse had that rare genius of *being* clear, as well as stressing the need for it. Not only did Ducasse have something important to say and say it clearly, but what he said is relevant to contemporary discussions. A close study of his work will throw considerable light on the new directions that discussion of causality has recently taken. We will proceed in the following way:

(1) state his analyses succinctly, yet hopefully with the same precision found in his own work;

(2) give reasons for rejecting his analysis of causality and nonlogical necessity, at the same time indicating what we find of lasting value in it; and

(3) indicate briefly the direction in which we believe a more successful non-Humean analysis must proceed — a direction already implicit in certain elements of Ducasse's own analysis.

I

First, only an event, and not an object, thing, or substance, can be a cause or an effect. It is the exploding of the gasoline in the cylinders that causes the car to move and the running out of gasoline that causes it to stop on the highway. It is the lightning striking the tree that caused the forest fire, and the snapping of the beam that caused the bridge to collapse. Whenever we say that an object caused something to happen that is only an elliptical way of referring to an event causing something to happen. Thus when we say that the carpenter caused the table to exist what we must mean is that certain movements of the carpenter caused the table to exist. These examples are all intuitively clear, for what we ordinarily mean by an event is a "happening," which, in turn, means a change in a state of affairs. Clearly this is what Ducasse means by 'event,' but he also intends something more. A change of a state of affairs is an event, to be sure, but, according to Ducasse, so is *the continued existence of a state of affairs* an event. The question "What happened then? " can be answered reasonably either by saying "He got up," a change in a state of affairs, or "He remained seated," an "unchange" in a state of affairs, and hence the latter qualifies as an event just as much as the former. Thus Ducasse defines 'event' inclusively as 'either a change or unchange in a state of affairs'.[4]

Second, Ducasse identifies the causal relation between events as that which holds between the three terms of any strict experiment. Usually he describes an experiment only in terms of a change in a state of affairs. An experiment, he says, is a state of affairs S in which only two changes occur: one, C, occurring in S at t_1, and the other, E, occurring spontaneously and immediately following C in S at t_2. The first change may be introduced by human beings or by the natural course of events as in an eclipse. The only change at t_1 must be the *total* change, and C, consequently, may be either simple or complex. Since the elements of S and the changes at t_1 and t_2 are all observable (or insofar as they are all observable), the causal relation itself can be said correctly to be directly perceivable and, upon occasion, directly perceived. The strict experiment, Ducasse continues, is what the logician calls the method of single difference and, like the other "experimental methods," is usually construed as a way of discovering or confirming causal relations. However, it is not in fact simply a method for discovering causes in some other sense of 'cause' but itself constitutes the *definition* of that concept. The principle provides a method for identifying a cause only in the sense in which the description of a fugitive from justice can be said to be or to provide a method for identifying him. Ducasse's last and most concise definition of the causal concept is this:

> Causation is the observable relation which obtains between the three terms of any strict experiment: If, in a given state of affairs S, *only two* changes (whether simple or complex) occur during a given period, one of them E occurring immediately after and adjacent to the other C, then *eo ipso*, C proximately *caused* E, and E was the proximate *effect* of C.[5]

From this definition of 'cause' various important consequences follow.[6] (i) Causality is an irreducibly *triadic* relationship between C and E *in* S. The analysis of 'cause' as 'whole set of necessary conditions' is necessarily mistaken, since such an analysis is dyadic in nature. It collapses the common-sensical distinction between cause and condition by making the whole of S C of E. Commonsensically, Ducasse says, we distinguish between dry under-brush as a condition for the occurrence of a forest fire — a condition without which the effect would not occur — and the striking of the tree by lightning as the cause of it — that change in a state of affairs sufficient to bring about another single change in the same S. When the string by which a weight is suspended is cut and the weight falls, it was the cutting of the string that caused the weight to fall and not the attraction of the masses of the object and the earth. The attraction was just as much a fact before the string was cut as after; hence while it is a condition for the occurrence of the effect it is not the cause of it.

(ii) If the total change C at t_1 is simple, the only point in repeating an experiment is to check that all the factors in the control and experimental groups were indeed held constant. If the total change C is complex, how-ever, repetition is required to discover if $C(a,b)$ was just sufficient to E or more than sufficient. Another experimental set-up would be needed where $C(a)$ is repeated without $C(b)$ in a state of affairs otherwise identical to S. If E did not occur at t_2, then we are in a position to say that $C(b)$ is just sufficient to E while $C(a,b)$ is more than sufficient. According to Ducasse, when we now say that $C(b)$ is the cause of E we are using a "generalized" concept of cause and cannot be said to directly perceive causes in this sense. This generalized sense has important practical functions and is the sense usually involved in ordinary usage. However, it still remains true that in perceiving the concrete, unique $C(a,b)$ in S one perceived the only change in

S prior to E at t_2 and hence observed the causal relation. To perceive what was more than sufficient to E was also to perceive what was sufficient to E.

(iii) Regularities are causal when each individual case subsumed under the generalization is causal. Relations are not causal simply because they are regular; they are regular because they are causal. Causality explains regularity, not the other way around. A sequence could be unique in the history of the world and still be causal, while a regular recurring sequence, like that of night and day, might not be causal at all.

(iv) To ask how one given event caused another can only mean, "What other intermediary causal steps were there?" Such a question if asked of proximate instead of remote causes is absurd — implicitly self-contradictory. It makes sense to ask why taking a pill removes the symptoms of an illness. Such a question amounts to asking for a specification of the in-between steps between taking the pill and the disappearance of the symptoms. The answer consists in specifying certain chemical changes brought about by the dissolution of the pill and the distribution of its ingredients throughout the system. But it does not make sense, except in terms of a higher-order chemical theory, to ask why the chemical ingredients have the power to remove the symptoms — as if there were still further in-between processes which, by hypothesis, there are not.

(v) The causal relation is wholly neutral about whether cause and effect events are physical or mental, or whether one term of the relation is one type while the other is the opposite. Ducasse eventually claims that all possible combinations of cause-and-effect relationships occur: (1) physico-physical (the snapping of the beam caused the bridge to collapse); (2) physico-psychical (the stimulation of the central nervous system caused the person to have a percept of the table); (3) psycho-physical (his desire for the orange caused him to pluck it off the tree); and (4) psycho-psychical (his intense interest in things past caused him to write his memoirs).

(vi) One might be mistaken in believing that C at t_1 was the only change in S prior to E at t_2, and hence mistaken in ascribing C as cause of E, but one cannot be mistaken about this: if C was the only change prior to E then it was the cause of E, for this is precisely what is meant by saying that anything is the cause of anything else.

When any philosophically pure-minded person sees a brick strike a window and the window break, he judges that the impact of the brick was the cause of the breaking, *because* he believes that impact to have been the only change which took place then in the immediate environment of the window. He may, indeed, have been mistaken, and acknowledge that he was mistaken, in believing that impact to have been the only change in the environment. But if so he will nevertheless maintain that *if* it had been the only change, it would have been the cause. That is, he will stand by the definition of cause, and admit merely that what he perceived was not a true case of what he meant and still means by cause.[7]

The precariousness of causal assertions, however, should not be over-emphasized. They are no more precarious than any universal negative proposition established through observation. It is admittedly difficult to make sure that no other change than C occurred at t_1 in S, but it is also difficult to make certain by observation that at any given time there is no mosquito in a given room or no flea on a given dog. "All we really know in any such case is that we have searched and not found any; that our method of search was one capable of revealing cases of the sort of thing we were looking for; and that the more thorough and careful was our search with such a method, the less likely it is that a case of what we look for would have escaped our observation."[8] That the experimental methods of science are excellent methods of search is attested to by the imposing achievements of modern science. Certainly experiments performed under strict laboratory conditions help ease the precariousness of causal judgments. And in cases of the direct perception of causality there are times when it would be strange indeed to insist upon the precariousness of such judgments: "I submit that, when Charles I lost his head, it would have been mere silly perversity on the part of the executioner or of other close spectators to maintain that the blow of the axe was not certainly but only probably what caused his head to come off."[9]

II

Ducasse's definition of causality and its implications raise almost every substantive issue that has been debated by Humeans and non-Humeans, and we cannot hope to consider even all the major issues here. We will limit ourselves to what seem to be four of the most fundamental and interesting issues and will show where we think Ducasse is wrong. Our criticisms will in no way depend upon Humean assumptions, but will reflect either inconsistencies in Ducasse's view or our own brand of non-Humean commitments. Other crucial issues will be discussed later when we consider Ducasse's analysis of nonlogical necessity. There our own positive views will become increasingly evident.

(i) There is an initial difficulty with Ducasse's inclusive definition of an event as a change or unchange in a state of affairs. The first half of the definiens seems faultless, but the latter half strained and difficult to justify. What we ordinarily and intuitively mean by an event is a "happening," and this meaning can be formulated technically as a change in a state of affairs, this concept referring in turn to objects (or particulars of any other justifiable sort), properties of objects, and relations among them. Examples of an event would be the snapping of a beam, the breaking of a glass, the exploding of gasoline, and the recalling of a forgotten name. Ducasse, however, extends this intuitively clear notion of event to "unchanges" in states of affairs as well. According to Ducasse, the question "What occurred then? " or "What happened then?" could be answered equally sensibly either by "He got up," a change in a state of affairs, or "He remained seated," an "unchange" in a state of affairs, and hence the latter qualifies as an event just as much as the former.[10]

This argument seems weak, however, since it gives unusual meanings to the words occur and happen while supposedly using them in ordinary ways. These words have the general dynamic sense of "to take place" or "to come about," which suggests the basic notion of change in a state of affairs rather than unchange. The same suggestion is involved in the colloquial exclamation, "That was some event!" where 'event' means 'some change in routine of a dramatic sort.' So there is something quite artificial in saying that the man's continued sitting is an occurrence or happening and hence an event. It would seem more reasonable to say that in this case the man did nothing that could be construed as a happening and, in fact, nothing happened to him. To the question asked after a severe storm, "What happened to the barn?" it is correct to say that in spite of what happened to it, the pounding rain and hurricane-force winds, the barn still stands intact. The continued standing of the barn, then, in spite of what happened to it, is not a "happening" itself, but the continued existence through time of certain particulars, their properties, and their relations.

The strangeness of Ducasse's definition of 'event' can be brought out in yet another way. On his view, one may legitimately ask, "What is not an event?" 'Event' must be construed as including everything, for there is nothing with which it may be contrasted. It is as though one defined a new color "brello" as being 'blue or non-blue'; of what use is such a concept? So too with the supposedly empirical concept event; if it is to have any utility it must mark off some distinction. But it does not. When this fact is taken in conjunction with the fact that ordinary usage contrasts an event with an unchange in a practicable and serviceable manner, one cannot help but feel that Ducasse has uselessly redefined 'event.' We are forced to conclude that if unchanges can properly and meaningfully be designated causes and effects, as Ducasse maintains, then he should really give up the view that only events can be causes.

(ii) There seems to be no good reason for insisting that a cause is always an event, as distinct from a standing condition, and that Hume, Mill, and their modern counterparts are simply flying in the face of commonsense when they define 'cause of y' as 'whole set of conditions necessary for occurrence of y'. That commonsense supports his claim and not theirs is, in fact, the only reason Ducasse ever gives for the correctness of the former and the falsity of the latter. In spite of his commitment to ordinary contexts, however, Ducasse unfortunately is not sufficiently attentive to the complexity of such contexts. Paying attention to such complexity quickly convinces one that there is no point in looking for *the* meaning of 'cause' supported by ordinary usage as if the term were somehow being used in the same sense throughout. There are numerous occasions when we do usefully refer to an event and only an event as the cause of y, and the reasons for doing so are usually practical, prudential, or legal in nature. We say that running out of gasoline caused the car to stop and removing the center beam caused the barn to collapse. Such talk makes perfectly good sense by drawing attention to a change in a situation which was under the control of human intelligence, and the point of drawing attention to just these conditions is prudential in nature: check the tank before starting next time, and learn something about construction before you try your hand at remodeling. Sometimes the point of such ascriptions is to assert legal responsibility; the guide on a desert tour whose car runs out of gas and the contractor who pulls the wrong beam may well be liable for damages. There are, however, numerous other occasions, both scientific and commonsensical, when we usefully refer to what Ducasse calls a "standing condition" as a cause, or to a whole set of conditions, including both events and standing conditions, as the cause of y. For example, we sometimes ask "What was the cause of y?" when what we want is an explanation as complete as possible of this particular occurrence of y, an explanation which shows, without taking anything for granted, why it is that y had to occur at t_1 rather than something else. In response to such a question as this one it would not be enough to mention either those conditions alone which have prudential or legal significance or those which have scientific significance, but it would be necessary to mention the set of conditions without which the effect at t_1 would not occur. To explain why the car stopped it is necessary to mention both that the car ran out of gasoline and that friction was no longer over-ruled, just as it might be necessary another time to mention both that the driver put on the brakes and that friction was reinforced.

The first context is the one that gives rise to the ordinary distinction between cause and standing condition (though the distinction is not always or necessarily made by using these specific words), and Ducasse is rightly sensitive to this important distinction. He errs, however, in elevating the concept of cause involved in it into *the* meaning of the concept cause — claiming, as he does, that only changes in S (whether introduced by a person or simply occurring in nature) count as causes — and then justifying this claim by reference to usage as if it were the only sense used.

The second context is the one that gives rise to the definition of 'cause', given by Hume, Mill, and their modern counterparts, as 'whole set of necessary conditions'; and they are rightly sensitive to *this* explanatory sense of the word.[11] They err as much as Ducasse, however, by elevating *this* definition of 'cause' into *the* definition — claiming, e.g., that it is always arbitrary and capricious to single out one necessary condition and call it the cause of y. That such selections are far from arbitrary and capricious should be abundantly clear from the examples and contexts given above.

(iii) Strangely enough, Ducasse and Hume both seem to fall victim to the same error, though, of course, not in identical ways. They both confuse the *reasons* we have for saying that two objects or events are causally related with the *meaning* of the term cause. They both mistakenly presuppose that if we discover how causal statements are verified we would automatically have discovered the meaning of such assertions. (This claim refers to the positivistic and not the skeptical interpretation of Hume's work.) Hume sees the method of agreement as the primary way causal propositions are verified and so interprets the meaning of 'cause' as 'constant conjunction'. Ducasse, on the other hand, sees the method of single difference as the primary way causal assertions are known to be true (that is, *identified* as causal asser-tions) and hence interprets the meaning of 'cause' as 'the only change in S immediately prior to E'. No doubt both methods provide upon occasion perfectly good reasons for saying that x is the cause of y, but in that case they cannot also be construed as definitions of the concept cause. If I say that John is Carol's brother and someone asks how I know this, what reason I have for saying it, the reply "because John is Carol's male sibling" would be rejected as either irrelevant or enjoyed as a jest. Specifying a definiens and giving a reason are not only two different things but are incompatible. If x is used as one, it cannot be used as the other, and vice versa. The confusion between giving the meaning of x and giving a reason why x is the case could never be more beautifully signalled than in the conflict between Ducasse and Hume. Both operate on the assumption that meaning and verification are intimately connected and, operating on this assumption, produce two incompatible definitions of the concept of causality. Indeed, this anomaly points up nicely how the meaning of a proposition could not possibly be the sum total of its experienced consequences or effects, since such consequences in the case of causality would lead to incompatible elements in a generalized definition.

(iv) Ducasse seems mistaken in claiming that when we perceive what was more than sufficient to E we have nonetheless directly observed the causal relation. The situation referred to, it will be recalled, is this: The complex change $C(a,b)$ is the only change perceived in S at t_1 while later experiments show that $C(b)$ was just sufficient to E and $C(a,b)$ more than sufficient to E. Now the question is, in perceiving the complex change $C(a,b)$ in S at t_1 and then perceiving E at t_2, did we directly observe the causal relation? Ducasse answers "yes" because we experienced what was in fact sufficient to E, even though what we experienced was more than sufficient. It seems to us, however, that the correct answer is "no" because there is a difference between experiencing the cause of E and experiencing something *as* the cause of E. Ducasse confuses the two notions. He is right in saying that one has perceived what is the cause of E but wrong in thinking that one thereby has perceived x *as* the cause of E. Given any complex change, one cannot claim to have experienced the whole of it or any part of it *as* the cause of E because what the cause of E is can be known in such cases only inferentially. Take the case of a football player being hit by tacklers on both sides and falling to the ground. Being hit by the two tacklers is the only change in S immediately prior to the player's falling, and we directly perceived this (complex) change in S. Consequently we perceived what in fact made the runner fall to the ground, though we did not perceive anything as making him fall. The runner may have fallen because of one impact or the other, or their combined impact; and since we cannot know which is the case we cannot be said to perceive $C(a,b)$ *as* the cause of E. The case might be otherwise for the runner. He may have felt the impact of the second tackler knocking him to the ground just a second after he weathered the impact of the first. Being hit simultaneously by both, however, he might be in no better position than an observer to know if this complex change in S was just sufficient or more than sufficient to knock him to the ground.

III

Thus far there has been no mention of Ducasse's concept of nonlogical necessity, certainly one of the most interesting strands of his causal theory and one which takes us to the heart of current discussions of causality. Having cleared the ground, so to speak, we can now proceed to an examination of this crucial concept and can indicate the direction we think a more adequate non-Humean analysis than Ducasse's must take.

Ducasse's analysis of 'causal necessity' is not as clear and unambiguous as most of his writing. Even so, certain facts are undeniable. It is clear that Ducasse's notion of causal necessity entails the view that necessity is not limited in its meaning to logical necessity. Logical necessity, by definition, is found only between logical entities; it dictates the relationships which concepts or propositions may or may not have to one another. Causal necessity, on the other hand, holds only between *events*; it dictates the relationships which events, whether physical, physiological, or psychological, may or may not have to one another. Thus 'causal necessity', as understood by Ducasse, cannot have 'logical necessity' as all or any part of its meaning. In order to distinguish causal necessity from logical, and in an attempt to make the term broad enough to cover its presence between events of dissimilar types (e.g. the blow of the hammer physically necessitates the breaking of the vase, chopping off a man's head physiologically necessitates his death, and thinking of "two plus two" psychologically necessitates some people to think of "four"), Ducasse refers to such necessity as *etiological*. He introduces this concept through the prior one of etiological sufficiency. When one perceives a situation in which C at t_1 is the only change prior to a second only change E at t_2, he has perceived a situation in which C was etiologically sufficient to E. Conversely, he has perceived a state of affairs in which E was etiologically necessitated by C in S.[12]

Now the above facts are helpful but fall short of telling us what Ducasse takes to be the precise meaning of "etiological necessity." Scattered throughout his works there is evidence to support either of two possible interpretations. The first interpretation is that Ducasse sees this concept as denoting some perceivable "power" or "force" which is present in the cause, thus *making* the effect occur. Certain examples tend to indicate that such is his meaning, not the least of which is the reference to King Charles I losing his head. Recall that telling quotation:

> I submit that, when Charles I lost his head, it would have been mere silly perversity on the part of the executioner or of some other close spectators to maintain that the blow of the axe was not certainly but only probably what caused the head to come off.[13]

In this passage it would certainly seem that Ducasse is taking 'etiological necessity' to mean 'a perceivable power present in the axe-swing which *forced* King Charles' head to separate from his body'.[14] To the objection that it is conceivable that the science of the future might discover some way of preventing decapitation from killing a person, Ducasse aptly replies that the assertion about the death of Charles is no universal proposition and what the science of the future might discover is irrelevant to both its meaning and truth. All that commonsense asserts about his death is that "in the circumstances *that were present at the time* (which included the fact that no such surgical feat occurred), the beheading did suffice to cause his death." [15] In the most recent statement of his views, Ducasse writes that "the spectators *perceived* the blow's *making* the head come off." [16] Scattered elsewhere throughout his writings on causality are similar statements that lend themselves to the same interpretation. " 'Produces' is substantially synonymous with 'causes', and has no more anthropomorphic implication than has the latter term." [17] And the plain fact is that "every person has *perceived* – and I say *perceived*, not *inferred* – that, for example, a particular tree branch was *being caused to bend* by a particular bird's alighting; that a particular bottle was *being caused to break* by the fall on it of a particular rock; that a particular billiard ball was *being caused to move* by a particular other billiard ball's rolling against it; [and] that a particular match was *being caused to ignite* by friction of it on a particular rough surface . . ." [18] And, the favorite example again, "To say that the movement of the axe *made* the head come off means that *causation not logical entailment*, of the second by the first is *what occurred then*." [19]

Ducasse's examples and statements lend themselves to an interpretation of nonlogical necessity interestingly akin — though superior — to that taken by the otherwise divergent philosophers William James, F. C. S. Schiller, G. F. Stout, A. N. Whitehead, Charles Hartshorne, and W. R. Boyce-Gibson.[20] They all agree that 'causal necessity' is undefinable but denotatively meaningful from the direct experience we have of it in volitional contexts. Then they (or most of them) extrapolate this relationship to the physical world and say it holds between physical objects also, thus getting involved in a panpsychism which is wholly objectionable to most contemporary philosophers. Some writers avoid volitional contexts, thus hoping to avoid panpsychism, though they retain the person as one term of the causal relation: we directly experience the hurricane wind bending us, the falling boulder crushing our leg, and the waves tumbling us smartly into shore. But it is not clear how this strategy successfully avoids panpsychism, since it also extrapolates the relation to physical contexts where neither term refers to a conscious being. The significance of Ducasse's statements and examples is that they suggest we are directly aware of causal necessities in the physical world itself and hence that there is no need of projecting anything whatsoever onto the physical world. According to Ducasse, we directly experience the blow of the axe severing Charles' head from his body, the alighting of the bird bending the branch, the falling rock breaking the bottle, and the hitting and moving of the second billiard ball by the first.

Ducasse's examples of the striking of a match on a rough surface causing it to burst into flame and the gasoline exploding in the cylinders causing the car to move also suggest a second interpretation of the concepts power and nonlogical necessity, wholly compatible with the first, which has been increasingly advocated in recent literature.[21] Scratching the match on a rough surface is what made the phosphorus sulfide tip burst into flame at that moment and thus exhibit the power of igniting it always had by virtue of its nature. The chemical structure of phosphorus sulfide explains why it has the power to ignite under certain conditions, and chemical theory, in turn, can explain the structure of phosphorus sulfide. Turning on the ignition, etc., is what made the gasoline exhibit at that moment the power of exploding it always had by virtue of its nature. The chemical structure of gasoline explains why it has the power to explode and chemical theory, again, can explain why it has that structure, though it is not necessary that a particular have *its* nature explained before that nature is capable of explaining the powers and capacities of that particular. The weight of the air and the pressure of the atmosphere explain why water goes up a pump when air is evacuated from the cylinder even though the weight of the air is not explained, in turn, though it could be, by gravitational attraction. Again, the weight of the bird, the weight of the stone, and the pressure of the deep water — all characteristics of the nature of some particular — explain why the bird's alighting makes the branch bend, the stone break the glass, and the pressure crush the submarine — where 'bending', 'breaking', and 'crushing' are causal verbs expressing powers to make certain events occur under specific releasing occasions of alighting, falling, and submerging.

Though Ducasse's examples and use of phrases like 'x produces y', 'x makes y happen', and 'causal necessity is directly perceived' suggest the above analyses, he draws back from their implications. There are two reasons for this, one which he explicitly gives and one which hovers in the background and needs to be made explicit. Any "power" analysis of causality, Ducasse charges, introduces a mysterious, ineffable element into causality and thus must be rejected. It would do no good simply to add such a concept to the definition of 'cause' as an unanalysed element, since such a procedure would guarantee nothing about what it supposedly referred to. We need no St. Anselms in the philosophy of causality![22]

It is also necessary for Ducasse to reject power interpretations of etiological necessity because they sometimes lead to ascriptions of causality incompatible with his claim that causes are always events and never standing conditions. Instances of this conflict are not difficult to find. If a car runs out of gasoline and comes to a halt on the highway, the question arises of whether the disappearance of the gasoline or the friction of the tires on road surface was the cause of the stopping (assuming that one is not holding that the whole set of necessary conditions was the cause). Given his definition of causality, Ducasse would have to say the event consisting of the disappearance of the gasoline, as distinct from the standing condition of friction, was the cause, for this was the only change in S prior to the occurrence of E. However, as one critic points out,

There is strictly no causal connection between the absence of something and the failure of an event to happen ... [T]he friction of the moving car with the surrounding air and the road down which it was proceeding caused the car to come to a stop.[23]

Ducasse, however, was unmoved by his critics and resolutely and finally equated 'etiological necessity' with his formal definitions of 'sufficient to' and 'necessitated by' and insisted that necessity in this sense was directly perceivable. If C is the only change in S at t_1 and E the only change at t_2, and the times are immediately successive, then C is causally sufficient to E in S, and anyone who has perceived this only change has perceived causal sufficiency. Conversely, if C *was* the only change in S immediately prior to E, then E was necessitated by (as distinct from necessary to) C in S, and anyone who had perceived this only change and its result had perceived causal necessity.

This definition of etiological necessity, it should be clear, runs into all the difficulties of the definition of causality pointed out earlier, but the claim that etiological necessity is literally perceivable raises additional fascinating epistemic problems. There is no problem in saying that changes C and E are directly perceived in some cases at least, like the snapping of the beam and the falling of the bridge; nobody would reject this contention. The problem, however, is to make sense out of the claim that we can directly perceive C as the *only* change in S immediately prior to E. There is clearly inference rather than perception involved here: we infer, e.g., that C was the only change in S at t_1 because we observed it and did not observe any other change even though we were alert and looked carefully. Surprisingly enough, Ducasse would admit that this description precisely fits the case, but nevertheless would claim that it still counts as perception. The reason for this is that he thinks some sort of inference is involved in all perception as distinct from a sensory given.[24] When one perceives a bird, one's "perceiving" consists not only in having certain visual sensations but in addition in *interpreting* these sensations, semiotically, as *signs* of the existence, at that time and place, of all that being a bird includes (being tangible, having blood, beak, wings, feathers, etc.). The same is supposedly true in the case of perceiving etiological necessity. When one perceives C as the only change in S at t_1, one's "perceiving" consists not only in having visual representations of C but, in addition, in interpreting these visual sensations as referring to the only change in S at t_1 by virtue of the fact that no other change was observed, etc.

Fascinating as this view may be, there seem to be fatal difficulties with Ducasse's claim that etiological necessity is directly perceivable. The immediate objection to his theory of perception, and all such examples like "perceiving" a bird, is that we are never aware of any inferential dimension in perceiving. Always and in every case we seem directly aware of the

attributes of physical things, though the grounds for retrospectively justifying such perception may well refer to specific ways the object appeared to
us. Ducasse's reply is that such inferences are automatic, telescoped, non-
discursive, and unconscious, and hence pass unnoticed. To an ear un-
prejudiced by theory, such a reply is unconvincing since rejecting all the
ordinary criteria of inference seems to amount to the admission that there is
not any inference present after all.

The situation is even more problematic in the case of perceiving etiological
necessity since a discursive element seems genuinely involved. I may perceive
C and no other change at t_1 but not go through any inferential process to
the effect: "I saw C; I did not see any other change; I was alert and looked
carefully; hence C is (probably) the only change in S at t_1." If the answer is
given that the inference went unnoticed because it was automatic, telescoped, nondiscursive, and unconscious, the previous reply is again appropriate — such a response seems to deny any inferential nature in the process
of ascribing it. Moreover, a person *may* go through a genuinely discursive
process to establish this causal claim. A person may observe C in S at t_1 and
really say to himself, "look around carefully," do so, find nothing, and
conclude that C is indeed the only change in S at t_1. But then we have a case
of actually inferring that C is the only change, in which case, however, we
have not perceived C's being the only change in S.

It is particularly difficult to see how Ducasse can claim that etiological
necessity can be directly perceived when the paradigm case for his very
definition of causality requires that such necessity be inferred. The experimental method of single difference provides Ducasse with his definition
of causality. Now the whole point in equating all factors except one in the
control group and the experimental group is to have good reason for saying
that C in S at t_1 was the only change in S and hence must be the cause. But
great precaution and expert knowledge is required in setting up such a
controlled experiment; the whole procedure is elaborately inferential and
renders the claim that C is directly perceived as the *only* change, even in
Ducasse's extended sense of 'perceive', completely untenable. Ducasse might
admit that in such a case the inference genuinely is too long-drawn-out to be
accommodated even within his extended sense of 'perceive' but still insist
that in other cases etiological necessity can be directly perceived. We have
already thrown doubt on this latter claim, and the point we would urge now
is this: Ducasse's claim that etiological necessity can be directly perceived

cannot apply where it crucially needs to apply, namely, in the paradigmatic case that gives his concept of nonlogical necessity its very meaning.

Another fundamental difficulty with Ducasse's discussion of nonlogical necessity centers around his assumption that 'x caused y in S' simply entails 'y is necessitated by x in S'. Whence the justification of his identification of the causal relation with necessary connections between matters of fact? The main reason Ducasse gives for identifying the two is that there are perfectly good examples of causal talk in everyday life which imply nonlogical necessity. These expressions are clear and precise and serve perfectly good purposes. Hence there is no point in flying in the face of such usage as Hume does by insisting that all necessity is conceptual or logical in nature. Such a performance misses the whole point of philosophy. The job of the philosopher is to frame definitions which fit the ways in which crucial terms like cause are actually used in ordinary life and not invent prescriptive senses of such terms that satisfy the needs of ontological commitments which are, in principle, indefensible.[25] Ducasse offers many examples of ordinary usage to support his view: "When, for instance, we speak of 'the necessities of life' we mean certain physical things — food, water, etc. — without which life ceases; and the impossibility of its being maintained without them is not logical — not a matter of contradiction in terms — but physiological."[26] Again, we would say, and correctly so, that it is physiologically impossible for a man to live after his head has been severed from his body; it was physically impossible for the stump to be unmoved by the explosion of a certain amount of dynamite; and that it was psychologically impossible for Smith to hear fingernails grating on a blackboard without shivering. It would simply be flying in the face of linguistic facts to insist that the necessity meant in all these cases was conceptual or logcial in nature; rather the sufficiency and necessity involved here are relations between matters of fact.

The trouble with Ducasse's argument is that it contains little which a Humean need deny. The Humean willingly admits that we employ nonlogical concepts of necessity in ordinary discourse, but he offers a very simple and powerful argument to show that it is impossible to take these usages at face value. It is in principle impossible, he says, that C and not E be self-contradictory because it is always logically possible that nature might change its course. Then he has the problem of explaining why we mistakenly think there are necessary connections between matters of fact.

Hume offers the projecting-habit-onto-events explanation, a poor one, to be sure, and one which contemporary Humeans reject, though they are no more able to produce a convincing explanation than he. But poor as these explanations are, the in-principle argument of Hume remains and nothing Ducasse writes even tends to rebut it. And unless the Humean argument is rebutted, Ducasse's contention that 'x caused y' entails 'y was etiologically necessitated by x' collapses. Moreover, as far as we can see, Ducasse's event ontology has no resource whatever for rebutting the Humean argument. Had he followed the lead of his examples and phrases and analysed the concepts of power and capacity in terms of the natures of particulars, he would have had the ingredients for an adequate reply to the in-principle argument. We shall return to this point later and discuss it in some detail.

IV

While we have been critical of Ducasse's philosophy of causality, we believe that he has made contributions of permanent value to this topic. Though he never countered Hume's in-principle argument against nonlogical necessity, he criticized the positive doctrines of the Humeans in numerous incisive ways. His claim that any adequate analysis of 'cause' must leave the meaning and truth value of ordinary causal assertions unchanged is sound and crucial, even though, in the face of Hume's argument, he does not show how such an analysis is possible. It should be pointed out that Ducasse advocated this sort of analytical metaphilosphy long before it was fashionable to do so and continued to insist upon it even though it became fashionable.

Moreover, Ducasse's distinction between cause and condition is more precise and sophisticated than any previous one and can usefully be accepted by one who nevertheless rejects the absolute nature of the distinction. His insistence upon the fact that we are sometimes directly aware of causal necessity, that we genuinely *perceive* upon occasion the causal relation, is also useful in drawing attention to the neglected non-Humean views of James and Whitehead, though, of course, the nature of the causal necessity allegedly perceived in all these cases is different. Ducasse's examples, in fact, suggest a way in which James' interesting view could be rephrased so that it would avoid the panpsychistic consequences James dreaded.

While we believe strongly that the non-Humean view of causality held by

Ducasse has its virtues, we also believe that the view he almost held — the one suggested by his examples and phraseology — has far greater merit. We had a brief glimpse of this view in the previous section and will not amplify it much more in the present one. We have given detailed explanations and defenses of it elsewhere.[27] Suffice it to show here that, unlike Ducasse's view, it yields a fundamental answer to Hume's in-principle argument against the possibility of nonlogical necessity.

Recall Ducasse's examples of a match brusting into flame, gasoline exploding in the cylinders of a car, the branch bending, the glass breaking, and the crushing of the submarine. The atomic structure of phosphorus sulfide and gasoline, the weight of the bird and the falling stone, and the pressure of the deep water — all characteristics of the nature of some particular — explains why scratching the match on a rough surface made it burst into flame, turning on the ignition made the gasoline explode, the bird's alighting made the branch bend, the stone's falling made the glass break, and the deep water crushed the submarine — where 'igniting', 'exploding', 'bending', 'breaking', and 'crushing' are causal verbs expressing the powers that particulars have by virtue of their natures to make certain events occur under specific releasing occasions like scratching, alighting, falling and submerging.

The question immediately arises of what sort of relationship there is between the nature of a particular and the powers and capacities this nature helps explain. It cannot be a contingent one in the sense that particulars could lose all their powers and capacities, or special sets of them, and still be said to remain the same particulars in the sense that they still have the same nature. A liquid that smelled like gasoline but would not explode no matter what means of ignition were applied would not count as gasoline any longer, since a cluster of interrelated concepts and explanations would have broken down; just as a bird that was so diaphanous as never to bend a limb, or twig, however small, would not count as a bird any longer, but would necessarily turn out to be something seen in an animated cartoon or the inhabitant of our dream world. The claim that atmospheric pressure failed to raise water in a pump, given the appropriate condition in the cylinder of the pump, but nevertheless that air has weight and the atmospheric blanket remains, is simply self-contradictory, just as the claim that falling stones left all glasses in their paths unbroken even though the stones retained their weight and motion, and the glasses were not reinforced, is self-inconsistent. To talk about the nature of a particular remaining the same even though p loses the powers and capacities this nature helps explain, is to assert and deny at once that p has nature N. There is, in short, a relation of natural necessity between what a thing is and what it is capable of doing and undergoing, and it is this relation of natural necessity that the conceptual necessity of the concept of cause reflects.

While a relation of nonlogical necessity exists between N of p and the powers and capacities of p, there is nothing self-contradictory, it is true, about the possibility of a change in N of p. Some changes in N of p, of course, do not count, since they occur in a theoretical structure which explains the identity of p through change. Such a theoretical structure, however, presupposes certain fundamental p's which do not change themselves since these p's constitute an explanatory frame of reference (S). These p's are the ones that count. Now the crucial point is that there is nothing self-contradictory about the notion of change even in these fundamental p's, since no actual or possible S's entail the falsity of each other. Though there is a necessity corresponding to the nature of the actual, this necessity does not imply that the actual is itself necessary in the sense that its meaning implies its existence. We happen to have the universe we do, though within any possible universe certain things would be bound to happen.

Now we are able to see the crucial fact that Hume's in-principle argument against the possibility of nonlogical necessity is mistaken. The argument, again, is this: "If there were a necessary connection between C and E, then the conjunction of $C \cdot \sim E$ would be self-contradictory; but clearly it is not so, since there is nothing self-inconsistent about the concept of a change in the course of nature. Hence there can be no nonlogical necessity between C and E." However, it follows from our analysis that the conunjction of $C \cdot \sim E$ is self-inconsistent even though there is nothing self-contradictory about the notion of a change in the course of nature when this phrase is taken to mean a change in the nature of a fundamental p. There *is* something self-inconsistent in the conjunction of $C \sim E$ unless one puts double quotes around C to indicate that while "C"$\cdot \sim E$ is not self-contradictory the concept of x as C of E has been relinquished. It would simply be self-defeating to say that x has nature y which helps explain the occurence of E, and hence is part of C of E, and yet x still has nature y when C occurs without E. This would be equivalent to saying that x at once both has and does not have nature y. The great error of Hume was to think mistakenly that

' "C"$\cdot\sim E$ is never self-contradictory' entails '$C\cdot\sim E$ is never self-contradictory'. Or saying the same thing in a better way, and one that is closer to the historical facts, he never saw the ambiguity of the phrase "change in the course of nature" and so erroneously thought that because it is logically possible for nature to change at all it is impossible for there to be any nonlogical necessary connections in the world.

NOTES

[1] C.J. Ducasse, *Causation and the Types of Necessity* (New York: Dover Publications, Inc., 1969). This new edition has an introduction by Vincent Tomas. The book was originally published by the University of Washington Press in 1924. All references in this chapter are to the Dover edition.

[2] C.J. Ducasse, *Nature, Mind, and Death* (La Salle, Ill.: Open Court Publishing Company, 1951).

[3] C.J. Ducasse, *Truth, Knowledge and Causation* (Londen: Routledge and Kegan Paul, 1968).

[4] *Nature, Mind, and Death*, pp. 108–9.

[5] C.J. Ducasse, "Minds, Matter and Bodies" in *Brain and Mind*, ed. by J.R. Smythies (London: Routledge and Kegan Paul, 1965), p. 84. Cf. *Causation and the Types of Necessity*, pp. 51–61; *Nature, Mind, and Death*, pp. 101–49; and *Truth, Knowledge and Causation*, pp. 1–14.

[6] All these implications are to be found in the material cited in the previous footnote.

[7] *Truth, Knowledge and Causation*, p. 8.

[8] *Nature, Mind and Death*, p. 119.

[9] *Ibid.*, p. 120.

[10] *Ibid.*, pp. 108–9.

[11] Cf. S. Gorovitz, "Causal Judgments and Causal Explanations," *Journal of Philosophy* 62 (1965), 695–711.

[12] *Nature, Mind, and Death*, pp. 113–21.

[13] *Ibid.*, p. 120.

[14] Sterling Lamprecht clearly understood Ducasse in this sense at first but through an interchange of notes came to realize that Ducasse really meant something quite different. Cf. *Causation and the Types of Necessity*, pp. 131–36.

[15] *Nature, Mind, and Death*, p. 116.

[16] "Minds, Matter and Bodies," p. 84.

[17] *Nature, Mind, and Death*, p. 144.

[18] *Truth, Knowledge and Causation*, p. 26.

[19] *Ibid.*, p. 31.

[20] Cf. E.H. Madden and P.H. Hare, "The Powers That Be," *Dialogue, Canadian Philosophical Review* 10 (1971), 12–31.

[21] E.H. Madden, "Scientific Explanation," *Review of Metaphysics* 26 (1973), 723–43. Cf. E.H. Madden and R. Harré, "In Defense of Natural Agents," *Philosophical*

Quarterly **23** (1973), 117–132; and "Natural Powers and Powerful Natures," *Philosophy* **48** (1973), 209–230.

22 C.J. Ducasse, "Of the Nature and Efficacy of Causes," *Philosophical Review* **41** (1932), 397, and *Causation and the Types of Necessity*, pp. 131–36.

23 Sterling Lamprecht, "Causality" in *Essays in Honor of John Dewey*, ed. by John Coss (New York: Henry Holt, 1937), pp. 201–2.

24 C.J. Ducasse, "How Literally Causation is Perceivable," *Philosophy and Phenomenological Research* **28** (1967–68), 271–73, and *Nature, Mind, and Death*, pp. 304–99 (especially pp. 332–33). Cf. Nani L. Ranken, "A Note on Ducasses' Perceivable Causation," *P. and P. R.* **28** (1967–68), 269–70.

25 *Nature, Mind, and Death*, pp. 3–87; *Truth, Knowledge and Causation*, pp. 238–55; and *Philosophy as a Science* (New York: Oskar Piest, 1941).

26 *Nature, Mind, and Death*, p. 114.

27 Madden and Hare, "The Powers That Be."

CHAPTER III

HUMAN AGENCY

As Roderick Chisholm had remarked, the classical formulation of the view that desires and beliefs are causes of human action is due to C. J. Ducasse.[1] However, soon after he had carefully formulated his position, a reaction against any causal analysis of action set in under the influence of the later Wittgenstein, Ryle, and Austin. According to the adherents of this new philosophy of mind, it is a simple category mistake to apply the concept of cause to human action. Countless articles and books later, the tide began to turn and it became respectable once again to hold a position closely akin to Ducasse's. It is well known that one force helpful in turning the tide was Donald Davidson's justifiably esteemed paper "Actions, Reasons, and Causes."[2] What is less well known is that Ducasse himself in his later publications and in correspondence with Richard Taylor ably defended his view against contemporary criticisms and effectively attacked, in turn, the assumptions from which they emanate. Ducasse, then, not only elegantly formulated the classical view of volitions as causes but also contributed arguments that are useful in its current rehabilitation. The point of this chapter is to articulate these arguments and, in hope of further rehabilitation, to strengthen and extend them.

I

Ducasse's classical analysis of action in terms of causation is this: 'x is an action of P' means exactly the same as '(i) P wants or desires y; (ii) P believes that if he brings about x then he will bring about y; and (iii) this belief and desire jointly cause P to bring about x'.[3] Both wants and beliefs are essential to calling x an action and so explaining why P did x. P's going to the refrigerator is explained by the fact that he wants food only on the assumption that he believes food is to be found there. Again, P's searching for the water hole is explained by his belief that there is one in the vicinity only on the assumption that he wants water to drink for himself or someone else, wants to irrigate the land, or whatever.[4] The above analysis, it must be kept in mind, is a mere sketch. While a belief and a want are always involved in calling x an act, it is not usually the case in human behavior of any complexity that only one belief or one desire is involved in any x. Both dimensions of an act can be quite complex in ways easily imagined by the reader. The limiting case occurs where not all wants can be mutually satisfied and deliberation is necessary about what to sacrifice, or where the correctness of what is believed is in question and deliberation is necessary about the relation between it and evidence.

According to Ducasse, simple actions like going to the refrigerator are justifiably called voluntary even though not deliberately willed. Such acts may be habitual responses to certain cues none of which is articulated at the time, but they are still under P's control since they are inhibitable. Ducasse defines a voluntary act inclusively as either those which are "permitted," because inhibitable, or those which are deliberately willed. A man's moving up his arm may not be "a *willed* act, but . . . nevertheless a *voluntary* act. It is voluntary in the sense that volition by him that his arm *not move up then* – or, if the arm is then moving, that its upward motion *cease* – would cause, or would anyway facilitate, nonoccurence or cessation of the motion. Hence, *absence* of such volition at the time by him constitutes *permission* of the motion. Thus upward motion of his arm is *voluntary* if it is either *willed*, or *permitted*, by him . . ."[5]

Ducasse analyses deliberation along the same lines as simple actions. "To deliberate is to seek such reasons as there may be for, and against, one's doing A; and in then noticing that the reasons on one side motivate one more strongly than do those on the other side. If and when such noticing *terminates* one's process of seeking and comparing reasons in respect of their motivating force, then termination of it *in this manner* constitutes what is called 'deciding'."[6]

Ducasse's correspondents object to his causal analysis of action on two main counts. (i) One is never introspectively aware of desires, intentions, choices, and so on causing one to do anything but only of oneself deciding, intending, or choosing to do x and (ii) one cannot describe a desire, belief, or volition independently of the nature of the action involved and hence the relation between the two is logical or conceptual in nature rather than empirical as it would have to be were the relation causal. We shall consider each of these objections in turn together with Ducasse's replies.

(i) Typical of the introspective objection in various letters are the following comments: "If a decision, for instance, is an event that occurs at a certain time, and if that decision is supposed to literally raise my arm up for me when I decide to raise my arm, then I'm certain I've never experienced a decision to raise my arm, which is of course consistent with saying that I have often decided to, e.g., raise my arm, and forthwith done so."[7] ". . . I feel quite certain that no such internal events, which are allegedly responsible for my bodily voluntary motions, exist. I'm sure I've never *felt* any such internal cause, or "introspected" it, or otherwise been acquainted with it."[8]

Ducasse writes that he is "bewildered" by such comments. "Do you really mean to say that your decision or resolution, made on a certain day a few months ago, to quit smoking henceforth, had no causal responsibility for your subsequent smokeless behavior? If good resolutions, whether at New Year or on Sunday mornings or at other times, were inherently totally devoid of causal efficacy, how strange it would be that people should ever have come to urge us to make such resolutions!"[9] The point Ducasse is making is a crucial one. It is a hallmark of a causal relation that by manipulating x we can control y, a mark, however, which is also found in the case of human action. The acts of a person can be controlled either by himself or by others by changing or manipulating his wants, desires, beliefs, and choices.

Another rejoinder follows from a cardinal point in Ducasse's meta-philosophy often expressed in his published writings.[10] No philosophical claim is acceptable if it entails the falsity of a well-formed sentence in ordinary life correctly held to be true. The introspective argument, however, entails just such a consequence. When we ask "What caused him to leave the office early?" the specification of his reason "because he promised his wife he would cut the grass" counts as an appropriate and no doubt true response. The introspective argument, however, in denying that we are ever aware of causes of acting entails that such correct ordinary locutions are in fact inadmissible.

Other rejoinders follow from Ducasse's distinction between voluntary acts that are habitual but inhibitable and those that are deliberate. Naturally there is no introspection of volitional causes in the former cases, since one cannot introspect the absence of an event permitting the act and cannot introspect the fact that if there were a certain kind of volitional event it would inhibit the action. Moreover, in the case of inhibitable behavior even when a cause *can* be introspected it is not a volitional sort of event. "If, for example, the man perceives a baseball about to hit his face, his *perceiving* this will usually cause his arm to move up automatically."[11] Again, in contexts of deliberation it is a mistake to look in introspection for a mental event that takes the form of a resolve and is in that sense a volitional event. Rather it is the mental event of the termination of comparing reasons that is introspectible and causes action or abstaining from action.[12]

(ii) Typical of the "logical connection" objection are the following comments: "I take it that, whenever there is a genuine cause-effect relationship . . . , the cause can be described without any mention of or reference to the effect. For instance, if I know what causes a particular match to ignite at a particular moment, then I can give some description of that cause without mentioning the igniting of the match. As Hume rightly insisted, cause and effect are logically independent, and each can be conceived and described independently of the other."[13] "I'm afraid I still feel that the difficulty I raised [of supposing that a desire, or a volition, might be a cause] . . . still remains . . . Now the difficulty, at least for me, is in rendering a description of such an alleged cause, without making any implicit or explicit reference to its alleged effect . . . If someone suggests that some event, *A*, is, within a given set of conditions *C*, the cause of another event, *B*, then it is surely fair to ask him to describe *A* for me in such a way that I can know which he is referring to, but to do this *without* making any reference whatever to *B*. In section 6 of the article you kindly enclosed with your remarks, I find that I cannot do this."[14]

Ducasse replies to this argument by writing that it evaporates automatically as soon as one realizes that the possibility of describing a cause without any mention of or reference to the effect is not an intrinsic part of the causal relation itself but only of those instances of it which are mechanical in nature.[15] This claim is certainly true if one considers Ducasse's analysis of the causal relation. As we have seen in the previous chapter, causation, for Ducasse, is the *triadic* relation which obtains between the three factors that together constitute an experiment. They are: (1) a concrete *state of affairs S* in which only two changes, whether simple or complex, occur; (2) one of these a change *C* occurring at a time *T*; and (3) the other a change E that begins to occur after change C has begun to occur. This triadic relation is *not a sign* that causation, in some mysterious sense, is occurring, but is *causation itself*, and is perceived by the performer or observer of a well-conducted experiment.[16] This definition, it is clear, is wholly neutral about the nature of the events which are causally related. It leaves open whether they are both physical, both mental, or either one of them physical and the other mental. Likewise it leaves open the question of whether or not there can be any conceptual relation between C and E.

It might seem that Ducasse's answer depends wholly upon accepting his particular analysis of causality, but this is not the case. If one does accept it, there is no problem, but even if he rejects it he can profit from Ducasse's point that as long as there are *two* events it is possible for them to be causally related whether they are conceptually related or not. The only way they would cease to be causal candidates would be to have the conceptual relation so close that there are not two entities involved but only two different descriptions of the same entity. But certainly no one would want to claim that wanting to do x and doing x were simply different ways of describing the same event.

However, there is a stronger way of rejecting the logical-connection argument than Ducasse uses. He agrees with the critic that there are no conceptual connections between events in the physical world, and this agreement is a pity since if one could show that there are such connections even there the whole ground of the logical-connection argument would be undercut. And it is not hard to show that there are such connections in the physical world. Brittleness and instability, for example, are logically or conceptually related to the ideas of breaking and of collapsing, and yet these physical concepts can be invoked legitimately in causal explanations of particular happenings. According to a recent commentator, "Thus (to use Urmson's example), in saying how the wing of the airplane came to break off, one might say, 'The (unusual) brittleness of the wing caused it to break off.' Similarly, one can say 'The (unusual) instability of the structure caused it to collapse under the first load'." [17]

II

In his publications and correspondence Ducasse stresses the point that the critics of desire-and-belief-as-causes are remiss to begin with, since they never indicate what sense of 'cause' they are using in their arguments.[18] Since this is the case, it is clear that one cannot say responsibly whether anything at all qualifies as a cause. As we have seen, Ducasse offers an analysis of 'cause' which he believes is correct in itself and which shows that conceptual independence is not a part of the analysans of 'cause'. Also he tries to show that 'Every event (including human actions as events) has a cause' analytically follows from his definition of 'cause' and hence that the libertarian is necessarily wrong in denying it (unless he provides an alternative sense of 'cause' which does not have this consequence).[19] Ducasse, in fact, believes that his sense of 'cause' is the only admissible one, but we have tried to show in the previous chapter that there is at least one other admissible sense of the term, which, again, would allow us to count desires and beliefs as causes. In what follows we will briefly develop those features of our theory most relevant to the present discussion and show how the theory extends and refines the "brittleness" point of the previous section and yields rebuttals of still other criticisms of Ducasse's "determinism." As we shall see in Section III, there are interesting intimations of our theory in Ducasse's own later work.

We must avoid Ducasse's assumption that there is only one *correct* sense of 'cause'. The concept is used in many ways, and there is no point in arguing which is *the* right way. The different senses serve various useful purposes. Sometimes one factor is singled out from a whole set of necessary conditions and called the cause of E because a person can be held responsible, either morally or legally, for its occurrence. The point of such causal claims frequently is to help prevent the reappearance of such E's in the future. Other times the set of necessary conditions sufficient for E is called the cause of E. This occurs when a more complete explanation of why E occurred is needed. This concept of cause approximates the traditional concept of a *ratio essendi*, but since the relationship between the set of conditions and E may remain opaque it does not fully capture the concept. It is this concept which is at the heart of our notion of causality. To understand it requires analysis of the pivotal concepts of power and capacity that figure prominently in explanations in science and ordinary life.

We say that the atmosphere has the power to crush a container that has no air inside, the sea the power to crush a submarine that goes too deep, dynamite and gasoline the power to explode when ignited, electric current the power to heat a resistance coil that is wired-in, an avalanche the power to crush the houses in its path, a wind the power to bend the trees in its way, and the swinging axe the power to split the log it hits. Correspondingly, we say that the can with no air inside has the capacity or disposition to be crushed by the atmosphere, the submarine with a shell of a certain strength to be crushed by the deep water, the resistance coil to become hot with increased movement of molecules, the houses to be crushed by the avalanche, the trees to be bent by the wind, and the log to be split by the swinging axe. There are, in short, both forceful and passive p's in the world, though it is unlikely that any p plays wholly one role. A landslide crushes the tractor that furrowed the earth.

Such ascriptions of power and capacity are causal promissory notes. They tell us that the natures of the p's are such that specific manifestations of the powers and capacities must occur under the appropriate releasing conditions. Supplying the cause of such manifestations consists in specifying the nature of the p involved along with the appropriate releasing condition. Explaining the collapse of the can (E) consists in specifying that the atmosphere has weight and so exerts pressure and that the equalizing air has been pumped out of the can (C). Explaining the heating up of a resistance coil (E) consists in specifying the molecular structure of the current and the fact that the resistance coil has been wired in (C). And so on for all the other examples. The general formula is this: N of p plus appropriate condition constitute the cause while the particular manifestation of a power or capacity constitutes the effect.

In applying this concept of cause to the present issues, we must note first that the relationship between a cause and effect is no longer opaque even in the physical world. Here the use of the word "appropriate" for the releasing condition is no accident. There is a conceptual connection between the nature of a p and the condition that releases some power of p, and, more important, between both of them and the manifestation on a given occasion of that power. The conceptual connection can be seen clearly if we realize that 'power or capacity of p' is involved throughout both C and E and hence that N of p is also involved, since 'power of p' and 'N of p' are intimately related conceptually.

The conclusion is inescapable that Ducasse was mistaken in agreeing that C and E are conceptually independent in physical causation and insisting only that they are interdependent in telic causation. We can now see that they are interdependent in both cases. Moreover, it is now clear that it is not necessary to search diligently for isolated examples like brittleness and instability (where we are confined to the level of causal promissory notes) in order to undercut the claim that there is no logical or conceptual connection between a C and E. On the contrary, conceptual connections are involved as a matter of principle in causal explanations. If there is no conceptual connection, there is no genuine case of a causal connection. Hence the major criticism of Ducasse's analysis of desire and belief as causes is eliminated entirely, since one of its essential assumptions is demolished.

Our concept of causality is useful in rebutting other arguments against a Ducasse-type analysis of human agency. Following Ryle, many authors have argued that only events or "happenings" are the right sort of things to count as causes. Since a desire, motive, or belief is not a happening, therefore, it cannot count as a cause of anything. However, it should be clear from our above discussion that N of p plus releasing condition is one admissible sense of 'cause' and that N of p, at least, does not bear the slightest resemblance to an event. Therefore the assumption of this argument that all causes are events is mistaken and the argument completely collapses.

Also it has been argued that reason explanations cannot be causal in nature, since we generalize the latter but not the former. Causal explanations are implicitly general; reason explanations not. This argument, however, again depends upon an inadequate conception of causality. Causal explanations in fact refer to generative mechanisms which *explain* generalizations rather than imply them. It is silly to think of causal statements like ours as implicitly general in nature. It makes only truistic sense to say that anything identical in structure with dynamite will explode upon ignition. The point of a causal statement here rather is to *explain* the lawful and general connection between ignition of a certain substance and its exploding. Again, since one of the assumptions of this argument is mistaken, the argument collapses along with the others.

III

In one of his later publications Ducasse defines the concept of capacity, and here he seems to be very close in principle to our analysis of 'cause'.[20] He ascribes capacities to what he calls "substants," and this unusual word requires explanation. He uses it to refer to substances in the ordinary sense rather than a metaphysical one. His notion of (physical) substance is the commonsensical one in which glass, lead, and water, for example, are called substances. They are substances in the sense of integrated sets of capacities, and not in the sense of underlying "stuff" in which properties inhere.

Ducasse, then, defines "capacity" as follows: "That, in circumstances of kind K, a substant S has a capacity x means that S is such that occurrence then of an event of kind C in a relation Q to S causes occurrence of an event of kind E in a relation R to a substant Z, which may be the substant S itself or may be a distinct substant."[21] In an effort to be consistent with his long-standing theory of causality, he still speaks of the cause of any event as another event, and yet he holds that it is the *substant* that has the capacity which is *causal* in import. It is clear that this theory though not identical with ours is similar in describing N of p or nature of substant as part of the cause. The crucial phrase is "S is such that." In distinguishing different kinds of capacities, Ducasse also has the equivalent of our distinction between powers and capacities. There is the capacity of a substant S to *affect* directly or indirectly a substant Z — indicated by such terms as "abrasiveness," "corrosiveness," and "toxicity" — and the capacity for a substant Z to be affected directly or indirectly by a substant S — indicated by such terms as "abradibility," "corrodibility," and "intoxicability." Ducasse clearly looks upon capacity concepts as causal promissory notes, though he never elaborates upon the nature of a substant as making good the note. Most significantly of all, in discussing human capacities Ducasse finally forgets his efforts to keep his cause-event ontology intact and explicitly refers to the agent as the cause of his action. According to Ducasse, "When, however, an agent is a purposive agent, then the behavior through the instrumentality of which *he causes* [our italics] the effect he intends is termed specifically *an act*, and the effect intentionally caused by that act is termed specifically *a deed.*"[22]

If we follow Ducasse's lead and apply our concept of cause to human agency, we find an instructive new way of looking at the issue between the determinist and libertarian. The application, briefly, is this: P has the power to do Z means that the nature of P (his character, personality, and so on) together with some releasing mental event (perceiving x, wanting y, believing p, and so on) causes P to do Z (and explains why P did Z). Let us call this view our rendition of "determinism." The libertarian view, then, in our schema, would amount to the claim that P's power to do Z is unrestricted by any N of P. It amounts to saying that 'power of P' is basic and unanalysable into anything else. It is, to use a favorite term of the libertarian, a case of immanent, as distinguished from transeunt, causation.[23] The crucial point is how far the libertarian and determinist are prepared to push their respective claims. Clearly character and personality traits (N of P) are often relevant in explaining why P did Z, so an unrestricted version of the libertarian view must be false. However, character and personality do not always explain an action, so it is by no means obvious that unrestricted determinism is true. There is a crucial difference between power statements applied to a physical p and to a human P. If there is an N of p plus a releasing event, then the power of p to do Z must be actualized. However, if there is N of P plus a releasing mental event, it is not always necessary that the power of P to do Z be actualized. P may "deliberately" choose not to exercise the power he possesses. Whether unrestricted determinism is justifiable, then, depends upon the determinist's ability to account for *deliberation* along causal lines. He must show that deliberation modifies the nature of the person and that it is this modified N of P that inhibits Z. Deliberation, in short, must be shown to be synonymous with the power to edit one's habits, traits, and character. If he fails to do this then it follows that there are some cases — namely, those that are genuinely deliberative — where 'power of P' rather than 'N of P' is basic. Whatever the outcome of debate on this level, it seems likely that Ducasse's analysis of deliberation in terms of motivation (noticing that the reasons on one side motivate one more strongly than those on the other) is an inadequate one. However, if the claims of this chapter are sound, there is no doubt that outside deliberative contexts beliefs and desires do function as causes of human action.

NOTES

[1] Roderick Chisholm, "Freedom and Action," in *Freedom and Determinism*, ed. by K. Lehrer (N.Y.: Random House, 1966), p. 30, n. 16.

[2] Donald Davidson, "Actions, Reasons, and Causes," *Journal of Philosophy* 60 (1963), 685–700.

[3] C.J. Ducasse, "Explanation, Mechanism, and Teleology," *Journal of Philosophy* 22 (1925), 150–55; *Nature, Mind, and Death* (La Salle, Ill.: Open Court, 1951), pp. 174–216; "Determinism, Freedom, and Responsibility," in *Determinism and Freedom*, ed. by S. Hook (N.Y.: New York University Press, 1958), pp. 160–69; "Life, Telism, and Mechanism," *Philosophy and Phenomenological Research* 20 (1959), 18–24; and "Naturalism, and the Sense and Nonsense of 'Free Will'," in *Phenomenology and Natural Existence: Essays in Honor of Marvin Farber*, ed. by D. Riepe (Albany: State University of New York Press, 1973), pp. 213–16.

[4] Cf. W.D. Gean, "Reasons and Causes," *Review of Metaphysics* 19 (1966), 667–688.

[5] Letter to Richard Taylor, April 26, 1962. Cf. letter to Taylor, March 30, 1960.

[6] Letter to Taylor, November 26, 1962.
[7] Letter from Taylor to Ducasse, January 25, 1960.
[8] Letter from Taylor to Ducasse, July 13, 1960.
[9] Letter to Taylor, January 30, 1960.
[10] Cf. particularly *Nature, Mind and Death*, 3–87, and *Truth, Knowledge and Causation* (London: Routledge and Kegan Paul, 1968), pp. 238–55.
[11] Letter to Taylor, April 26, 1962.
[12] Letter to Taylor, November 26, 1962.
[13] Letter from Taylor to Ducasse, November 25, 1962.
[14] Letter from Taylor to Ducasse, December 3, 1962.
[15] Letter to Taylor, November 26, 1962.
[16] Cf. *Truth, Knowledge and Causation*, pp. 1–35.
[17] Gean, *op. cit.*, p. 679.
[18] Letters to Taylor, May 13, 1959; January 30, 1960.
[19] *Nature, Mind, and Death*, pp. 150–60; and *Truth, Knowledge and Causation*, pp. 29–35. Cf. *Nature, Mind, and Death*, pp. 174–216.
[20] "Substants, Capacities and Tendencies," *Review of Metaphysics* 18 (1964), 23–37.
[21] *Ibid.*, p. 33.
[22] *Ibid.*, pp. 28–29.
[23] Chisholm, *op. cit.*, pp. 17–21.

CHAPTER IV

SENSING AND OBJECTIVE REFERENCE

The question of how it is possible to have knowledge of the external world is a perennially favorite topic of philosophers, and Ducasse was concerned with this question throughout his career. He considers the problem in various early articles (including the crucial one "On the Attributes of Material Things"), in his contribution to the Moore volume in *The Library of Living Philosophers* ("Moore's 'The Refutation of Idealism' "), and in correspondence with Moore where they continue their debate about the status of sensations and sense-data. His analysis of this question forms a major part of *Nature, Mind, and Death* (Chps. 12-16), and important articles in this area are reprinted in his recently published *Truth, Knowledge and Causation* (Chps. 6, 7, 9, 13).

We believe that Ducasse's contribution to the discussion of this issue is of major importance and constitutes the best answer yet given. He saw that naive realism founders on the issue of false appearances (as do most philosophies), but he also saw more clearly than other philosophers that all subsequent efforts to go beyond naive realism made the fatal mistake of saying that the only thing we are directly aware of are our own sensations. This substantive interpretation of sensation is made alike by idealists, phenomenalists, sense-data theorists, representative realists, and critical realists; and in different ways in the various cases it leads to disastrous consequences. By contrast Ducasse formulates an "adverbial" analysis of sensation. Sensations are not entities but ways of being appeared to. "Sensing" rather than "sensation" is the appropriate word to use. Given his initial insight, Ducasse criticizes in an effective way the sense-data theories of Broad and Moore and presents in a detailed way his dispositional view of properties and the way they are related to sensing. The result is Ducasse's own brand of realism which, as we will show, succesfully resolves the problem at issue between his predecessors, the American New Realists and Critical Realists. Unfortunately Ducasse's major contribution is sometimes obscured by his detailed discussion of extraneous points and his shifting terminology. Our procedure in this chapter will be to give: (1) a detailed account of Ducasse's adverbial view of sensing, his dispositional analysis of properties, his critique of Broad and Moore, and his discussion of "the problem of objective reference"; (2) an interpretation and clarification of what he has done so the magnitude of his contribution can be seen; and (3) a criticism of the view held both by Ducasse and Roderick Chisholm that statements about sensing are *incorrigible*.

I

Ducasse's adverbial view of sensing and his dispositional theory of perception are reflected in the different ways he analyses 'I see the color red' and 'I see the apple'. Assume that I am concentrating on an apple and experience a completely specific red (specific with respect to brightness and saturation as well as hue) and express this experience by saying that "I see x shade of red." Such a statement is misleadingly similar to "I see the apple" and might suggest that a sensation of red or a red sense datum is somehow an object of sensing. In fact the analyses of the two sentences are quite different. As we shall see, the former is basic and simple while the latter is derivative and complex. The point of difference we want to notice at the moment is that the apple is the object of my perceiving and exists independently of it, while red is not the object of my sensing and does not exist independently of it. Experiencing a determinate red is a species or kind of sensing, and its whole *esse* consists in that sensing. Or, putting the point another way, sensing is an adverbial and not a substantive matter – "I see redly," not "I see this red color." When one dances a waltz, the waltzing is not a substantive but refers to a specific way or mode of dancing. So it is with sensing. When we sense a red color the red color is not a substantive but refers to a determinate way or mode of sensing. In the specific terminology of Ducasse, 'apple' is an adventitious or alien accusative of experiencing, while 'red' is a connate accusative of experiencing.[1] An alien accusative, as we shall see, may be something other than a perceptual object, but such objects are the most common examples of alien accusatives. A connate accusative is never an object of perception, though it is sometimes an object of introspection, or of recollection, or of a mental act of some other kind.[2]

Introspection has been held by various philosophers to be psychologically impossible, but Ducasse believes these contentions to be unwarranted. It has been argued that introspective analysis is impossible because analytical attention to a mental state automatically alters its nature. To attend to one's anger or to one's sadness is to lose the anger and sadness and replace it by curiosity. Moreover, the introspection of a mental state is impossible since at the moment one starts introspecting the state is past and what one is attending to then is only a memory of a previous state of consciousness. Ducasse was unimpressed. No doubt attention to one's anger or sadness dilutes the anger and sadness, but there is no point in exaggerating the facts of the case. It is paradoxical to claim that we cannot introspect our feelings at all since such introspection alters the feelings involved, for if one knows such attention alters feelings, it is only by introspective attention that one could discover this fact. The argument "tacitly presupposes the possibility of what it explicitly declares impossible . . ." [3] The argument that only past feelings or sensations can be attended to, Ducasse argues, is self-defeating in its own way: "Again, if what one is presently analyzing introspectively is only a memory of a mental state already past, that memory itself, at least, is *present*; and if it is possible to be analyzing it introspectively while it is present, no reason appears why this should not be equally possible when a present feeling, *e.g.*, hunger, instead of a present memory, is concerned." [4]

Ducasse's analysis of a perceptual alien accusative is quite complex. The overall structure and outcome of the analysis, however, are the main items of interest for the moment. 'I see the apple' is analyzed into a number of statements like 'The apple is red', 'the apple is round', and so on, and each such property statement is given a dispositional analysis. According to Ducasse, "such attributes of material things as 'being green', 'being fragrant', 'being noisy', etc. are properties of things in exactly the same essentially causal sense as are, for instance, 'being abrasive', or 'being corrosive', etc." [5] To say that an apple, then, has the *property* of being red is to say that.the apple, whether presently looked at or not, is such that under the conditions of observation that are standard for such an object, it would cause a sentient observer to see the color red. That is to say, the object is the cause, at least in part, of our sensing, in the adverbial way, redly. The qualification "in part" refers to Ducasse's mention of standard conditions. "The color we see always depends, not only on the thing looked at, but also on the conditions under which it is being observed . . ." [6]

Given his adverbial analysis of sensing and dispositional analysis of properties it follows for Ducasse that there is no paradox in saying that an apple presently unobserved is nevertheless red, since 'red' here has a dispositional sense. But there would be a paradox in saying that sensing redly had an existence independent of sensing, since 'sensing redly' has an occurrent, not a dispositional sense. "Where sense qualities are concerned, Berkeley is right; and all realists are wrong who claim it is possible that such qualities should, independently of their being sensed (or imagined), have any existence at all."[7]

II

Ducasse developed his adverbial view of sensing and his dispositional analysis of properties by way of arguing against phenomenalism in general and the sense-data theories of C. D. Broad and G. E. Moore in particular.

The trouble with phenomenalism is that it does not adequately account for the fact that what we sense depends upon the state of the observer and the conditions of observation as well as upon the nature of the object and physical stimulus. Ducasse stresses this fact in his dispositional analysis of perception. Thus how an object appears to a drunk or sober person will vary greatly, and some reference to those states involved (and in other cases to the conditions of observation involved) is required *before* one can construct a phenomenalistic vocabulary of appearances. Hence a phenomenalistic vocabulary presupposes the very thing it is trying to eliminate. Roderick Chisholm articulates this crucial point in the following way:

To translate or paraphrase a simple thing statement into a collection of appearance statements, or even to find a single appearance statement which is implied by the thing statement, we must find some appearance or appearances which can be uniquely correlated with the physical fact described by the thing statement. But we are not able to correlate any group of appearances with any particular physical fact unless we specify those appearances by reference to some *other* physical fact − by reference to some set of observation conditions and to the state of the particular person who is to sense the appearances. For it is the joint operation of the things we perceive and of the conditions under which we perceive them that determines the ways in which the things are going to appear to us. And this constitutes a difficulty in principle for the attempt to translate thing statements into appearance statements; whenever we seem to reach such a translation, we find that our translation still includes some set of thing statements which describe physical observation conditions and which have not been translated into statements about appearances.[8]

Ducasse argues that the sense-data theories of Broad and Moore lose the point they were originally invented to serve. Broad writes that sensa have some of the characteristics of physical objects; they are extended and have shapes, sizes, colors, temperatures, and so on (though they also have the characteristic of mental states in that they are private to each observer). However, this view of sensa entails that like physical objects they may appear to have properties which in fact they do not have and also not appear to have ones they in fact possess. But sensa were originally invoked to account for what it is we experience when objects appear to have properties they do not have and appear to exist when in fact they do not! Ducasse observes that "if the distinction between appearance and reality is made not only in the case of material things, but *also* in the case of 'sense-data' themselves, then the very same problems automatically reappear concerning sense-data, which sense-data were invoked to resolve concerning material things, but which sense-data have then been robbed of the power to resolve." [9] Ducasse himself accounts for the occurrence of illusions and hallucinations in terms of the variability of the state of the observer and the conditions of observation plus a statement concerning standard conditions and normal observers.

Ducasse believes that G. E. Moore's inability to abandon the sense-data view stems from his undue restriction of sensa to qualities. According to Moore one cannot intuit a determinate blue in a vacuum; there must be a patch, speck, line, or spot that *has* the quality blue. Hence there must be sense-data that have qualities somewhat similar to objects having properties. Ducasse argues that in this claim Moore overlooks the fact that what one *sees* comprises not only qualities, but also *extensities, shapes, quantities,* and *relations.* "These are *seen* just as literally as are qualities *seen*; and the 'good reason' which Moore rightly believes must exist, why the *esse* of seen qualities is *percipi,* is likewise the good reason why the *esse* of seen extensities, of seen shapes, of seen quantities, and of seen relations, is *percipi.*" [10]

The ultimate mistake Moore makes is that he simply tacitly assumes that the status of "presented objects" is intrinsic to sensations. The assumption is a mistake because they cannot be objects of awareness in the sense things are objects of awareness, and the way a sensation can be said to be the object of awareness is not one that endows it with substantive existence. [11] Sensations become objects of consciousness only when they are being introspected, that is, only when they are being attended to. (If 'introspection' is reserved for feelings, moods, etc. then 'inspection' may be used instead. Ducasse usually uses 'introspection' inclusively.) Attention to one's states of consciousness is what gives them the adventitious status, temporarily, of objects of consciousness. We have seen already how Ducasse rebuts the claim that it is impossible in principle to introspect states of consciousness.

III

Ducasse's critique of sense-data views, it is interesting to note, also entails the falsity of what might be called the "sense-data" analysis of *feelings*, a topic not discussed by Ducasse himself. According to this view, there is a nominative as well as an adverbial form of feeling words (just as the sense-data theorist believes that a *sense-datum* is the object of our *sensing*), and the latter always presupposes the former — e.g., '*P* painfully feels pain'. On this view, feeling words refer not only to a species of experiencing but also to an object of experience. Since pain is a datum of experience it makes sense to say that John Smith "owns" a pain datum, no one else can "have" it, and so on.[12]

There are various routes to this datum view of feelings, although advocates of it seem to prefer the ostensive definition route. They refer to facts like this: an ordinary person experiences pain painfully while a masochist experiences it pleasantly — hence we must distinguish between pain as a datum of experience and pain as a way of experiencing. There are several possible replies. First, one might deny that anyone ever finds pain pleasurable; pain is only a *means* in a variety of situations of producing subsequent experiences which are pleasurable. Second, if it is insisted that the masochist *does* experience the pain itself as pleasurable, the reply is that such a fact still would not warrant the datum interpretation of feeling. One cannot generate the distinction if he limits himself to the experience of an ordinary person; here there is *prima facie* no difference between saying "I am experiencing pain" and "I am experiencing painfully." To generate the distinction one needs the masochist. But such a case has a completely different analysis than the ordinary one. Experiencing painfully in the case of a masochist is a partial cause of his concurrent or subsequent pleasure, the rest of the cause being found in certain past events which the person himself has forgotten. It is in cases like this that it is true to say that others can know a great deal more about a person's feelings than that person himself. Since the case of the masochist can be given a causal interpretation and the case of the ordinary person needs no interpretation other than the adverbial one, the sort of comparison which generates the datum view disappears and thus the need for the view along with it.

IV

Ducasse discusses at great length what he calls the problem of objective
reference, which essentially is the problem of how the simple, psychic
connate accusatives of sensing are transformed into the complex, objective
alien accusatives of perception. In this context he uses the word "intuition"
as a synonym for the previously used expression "way of sensing." Ducasse
takes intuitions as primitive and shows, on the basis of referring to them,
"what it means to call a time, or a place, or an event, a relation, a substance,
etc., 'objective'." [13] He proceeds to discuss these items in the order given,
which he takes to be that of increasing ontological complexity. Ducasse's
strategy and way of arguing can be understood if we start with his discussion of place. The discussion of time is interesting, but there will be
enough detail without it. To simplify matters in his own discussion Ducasse
limits the concept of an objective place, event, or thing to what can be
known only through tactual and kinesthetic intuitions. At the end he
sketches the same analysis using visual intuitions and considers how the
tactual and visual elements become united to form full-blown notions of an
objective physical thing.

According to Ducasse, the intuition of objective place is an emergent
intuition growing out of a combination of pressure and kinesthetic intuitions. Suppose we have a pressure intuition which, since it has no name,
can be called to our attention – though in no way explicated by – the
expression "right-index-finger-tip pressure." Simultaneously with this
intuition we would also be experiencing a complex kinesthetic intuition
which again for lack of names for most tactual and kinesthetic intuitions we
can identify indirectly as a "right-arm kinesthetic complex." From these
two intuitions "there emerges an intuition of particular *place* as being at the
time 'occupied' by a pressure intuition of that specific sort." [14] If the
kinesthetic intuition remains constant and the pressure intuition varies, or
the reverse, then additional emergent intuitions of place occur. Further if
the pressure intuition persists while various alterations are occurring in the
kinesthetic complex, then the first place intuited after the original one is
said to be contiguous with it and what is intuited while these alterations are
in progress is said to be *motion* of the pressure intuition. Conceiving time in
terms of the "specious present" rather than as punctiform units, and
assuming that relations as well as places and qualities can be intuited,

Ducasse generates the intuition of three dimensional space as the result of intuiting various places as being "above," "below," "to the right," "to the left," "nearer than," and "farther than" the original place intuition. "Intuited space, which is the relation of each intuited place to every other, is in this manner discovered to be three-dimensional." [15] The concept of place thus has become objective in the sense that it is meaningful to refer to places not being intuited at the moment.

Turning to events as the next, more complex notion, Ducasse says that they become known as objective because among our pressure sensations there would be some which could not be traced to any proximate cause consisting in some other or previous intuition. (During this discussion one must keep in mind that on Ducasse's analysis of 'cause' a cause must only be an event but no other ontological restrictions are put on what the nature of C and E events must be.) Basically then a physical event means for us an event *"other than any of our intuitions, and having to these otherwise unexplained pressure intuitions the relation of cause to effect."*[16] 'Being pressed by something', then, refers to a physical event, and this event can be said to be perceived, though such perceptions, it is clear from the foregoing, have an inferential element. The inference, however, is implicit only, being "telescoped" and "unconscious." If 'inference' be restricted to discursive contexts then one simply needs another word for the interpretative element in all perceptions.

In discussing the perception of substances or physical things Ducasse distinguishes between their physico-psychical properties and their physico-physical properties. The former are the physical properties which are causal factors in the occurrence of intuitions; the latter are causal factors in the occurrence of other physical properties. Given the limitation to our sense modality imposed by Ducasse for the sake of simplicity in exposition, there is only one physico-psychical property that could be perceived, namely, tangibility. Perception of a "tangible place" would consist in *"unformulated belief that, at an objective place contiguous with a certain intuited place at which pressure is at the moment intuited by us, there is occurring throughout a certain period a physical event which is such as to cause in us a pressure intuition whenever during that period we intuit that certain place..."* [17] Such perception, whether veridical or not, of a "tangible objective place" would, under the assumed limitations, be the same thing as perception of *something tangible*, or perception of *tangible substance*. As in all perception, there is a crucial interpretational element; also such perception of psychico-psychical properties is a prerequisite for the perception of physico-physical properties. According to Ducasse, the perception of physico-physical properties can be "defined" as follows: "If a given sort of change A of physico-psychical property at one place is observed to be regularly attended by a certain sort of change B of physico-psychical property at another place, then what is being observed is a physico-physical property. That is, the first place is being perceived to have, through a given period, this property: it is such that occurrence of a change of kind A of property there causes a change of kind B of property at the other place." [18] The inferential element in perception has here become very large indeed.

Ducasse proceeds to a detailed analysis of physical objectivity in visual terms which is wholly isomorphic with the tactual-kinesthetic one. The difference between intuiting a color-shape and perceiving a colored physical thing is again the presence in the latter case of a causal element. Perceiving a physical substance having the *property* "being green" consists in (1) intuition of a quality green, and (2) the unformulated belief that immediately beyond the intuited place P occupied by the intuited green, there exists through a given time a non-intuited event which causes us to intuit green whenever during that time we intuit place P. "The green physical substance so perceived is thus simply a region of space (objective in the sense of *beyond* a certain intuited place) which, during a certain period, has the capacity to cause us to intuit the quality green." [19] In short, the *properties* of a physical substance are *always* dispositional in nature, while the substance itself is the *integrated set of dispositions* (or capacities) possessed by a region of space during a certain time. Ducasse does not analyze the nature of this integration in general but gives us a hint about how it operates in the case of tactual-kinesthetic and visual perceptions: "Perception of regular simultaneity of tactual perception of a substance, and of visual perception of contact between a part of our own body, and a substance, is what constitutes perception of 'sameness' of the tactually perceived substance and the visually perceived substance, and of 'sameness' of the place of each." [20]

To the objection that introspection reveals no psychic elements, events, or operations as he describes, Ducasse replies that his causal explanation and phenomenological irreducibility are perfectly compatible. Discrete intuitions and interpretations are causally involved in the experience of objective reference in the first place, but, once caused, the experience of space, objects, etc., as objective is phenomenologically irreducible into these causal elements.[21]

V

It is clear from the adverbial analysis of sensing, the dispositional analysis of properties, and the discussion of objective reference that Ducasse accepts some sort of epistemic realism. In our opinion it is a very sophisticated position and one that has been influential in recent epistemic discussion. Unfortunately the true nature of the position is often missed as a result of the prominence Ducasse gives to certain extraneous elements. In order to understand what Ducasse is about and to eliminate the distracting elements, it will be useful to place Ducasse's whole discussion in context and to interpret it as a successful resolution of the conflict between American New Realism and Critical Realism.[22] As we shall see, Ducasse frees the insight of each view from certain accompanying errors and combines them in a way that is more successful, we believe, than any other epistemic view.

New Realism was published in 1912 and was the joint effort of six American philosophers, E. B. Holt, Walter T. Marvin, William Pepperell Montague, Ralph Barton Perry, W. B. Pitkin and E. G. Spaulding. They defended the view that we are directly aware of physical objects and that physical objects have precisely the properties they appear to have. They completely rejected the idea that the only thing we are directly aware of are our own sensations, and that such sensations have to be interpreted as "messages" about the nature of physical objects which are in principle beyond our ken. They rejected the "messenger" hypothesis in both its forms. No impressions or sensations in a substantive sense exist at all, so there are neither "messages" that "resemble" the physical object nor messages that simply suggest the existence of physical objects.

The difficulties which proved fatal to new realism were the everpresent facts of illusion and hallucination. Unfortunately things do not always have the properties they appear to have, or appear precisely as they are. It is the train next to us that is moving; contrary to appearances our train is standing still. Also there are appearances which seem to be *of* an object but which in fact have no *object* of reference at all. There really isn't any elephant at all that has the property of being pink; but if appearances are identical with the object one ought to be able to ride the pink elephant just as well as the grey one.

Essays in Critical Realism was published in 1920 and was the joint effort of Durant Drake, A. O. Lovejoy, J. B. Pratt, A. K. Rogers, George Santayana, Roy Wood Sellars, and C. A. Strong. They defended the counterview that since we cannot be directly aware of physical objects (given the facts of illusion) we must be directly aware only of our own sensations, which, in turn, contain a "message" about the existence of physical objects. Not all the critical realists agreed about the nature of this message. Some of them seemed to hold, e.g., that the message "physical object – here, now" is contained in the specific characteristics of the appearance itself – hence the characteristics of red and round are attributed to the apple itself. However, such specific messages lead to trouble. Sometimes there are characteristics which can be ascribed to sensations which cannot be ascribed to objects. The appearance of a penny is elliptical but the penny itself is not. Hence the "message" of the appearance of *x* sometimes will be that the characteristics of the object are *unlike* those of its appearance. The "message" premise of critical realism, as a result of these considerations, became a very general one. The characteristics of an appearance are neither like nor unlike those of physical objects (the likeness claim being the fatal flaw of representative realism); but whatever characteristics the appearance may have, the appearance itself carries the message about the existence of a physical object in the vicinity, and the perception of objects consists in "reading" this message.

The difficulty which proved fatal to critical realism was the messenger premise. If the only thing we are directly aware of are our own sensations, or appearances in the sense-data, substantive sense, then we can never get beyond them and claim to know a physical object itself. The messenger premise puts the realist into a straight-jacket where skepticism about the possibility of external reference is the only result. And this skepticism results whether the claim is made that characteristics of the appearance resemble properties of the object or not. Skepticism follows in the resemblance case, since we have no way of knowing the properties of objects and comparing them with the characteristics of appearances which we do directly apprehend. Skepticism follows in the non-resemblance case, since the only "justification" that can be given for accepting the message about the existence of physical objects is "animal faith."

The genius of Ducasse is to fuse the insights of both realistic positions into a tenable whole and to avoid the pitfalls of each. He rejects the messenger premise of the critical realists. We are not directly aware of our own sensations since sensations are not objects of awareness at all; they are ways or modes of experiencing. Since there is no *messenger* in the case of perceptual knowledge, there are no *messages* that require interpretation in either of the two senses discussed by the critical realists. By avoiding the messenger premise through his adverbial view of sensing, Ducasse avoids the skeptical conclusions about the possibility of knowledge of physical objects to which that premise inevitably leads.

On the other hand, Ducasse rejects the view that physical objects have precisely the properties they appear to have. Such a claim is to confuse sensings or appearings with the dispositional properties of objects and to ignore the fact that how objects appear depends upon the state of the observer and the conditions of observation as well as the nature of the object. It is a recognition of this fact that makes it possible to account for illusory as well as veridical experiencing. However, it is also true that sensings and appearings are experienced always as *of* some object and in this way constitute a direct tie with the external world. Though it must not be supposed that Ducasse's realism is one involving a traditional concept of physical objects. For him, sensings and appearings are experienced always as *of* an object, but a physical object is defined as some place occupied by an integrated set of capacities for a certain period of time. It is not at all clear that this analysis of physical objects is an improvement over the substance interpretation which Ducasse was trying to avoid; but in any case the external and direct reference to the object is present however one analyzes the concept of physical objects. And the external reference is meaningfully present quite independently of whether future experience upholds or counts against the correctness of external reference in a given case. I directly experience the red as the appearing of an apple and subsequent experience bears it out, just as I directly experience the pink as the appearing of an elephant though subsequent sensings count against it.

This last point needs to be examined in some detail, since it is a complex notion and its complexity has often stood in the way of appreciating Ducasse's solution to the conflict between new and critical realists. Ducasse's discussion of this point, as we shall see, is clouded by virtue of being an unclear mixture of causal explanation and philosophical analysis.

In his discussion of "objective reference" Ducasse makes it quite clear that while sensing or appearing is always experienced as *of* an object, this experience of objective reference is only phenomenologically irreducible; it is not causally or epistemically basic. His long discussion of objective reference is an effort to show how originally distinct individual sensings are fused into the phenomenologically irreducible experience of being *of* an object. However, there are numerous difficulties with Ducasse's effort. In the first place, the psychological causal claims seem dubious in the light of current psychological opinion. Whatever the ultimate grounds of epistemic justification may be, Gestalt psychology has long thrown doubt on the assumption that a causal analysis of perception can be accomplished by finding a mechanism that pieces together atomistic, punctiform sensations into full-blown perceptions. Presumably the same point can be made when the atomistic elements are conceived adverbially as sensings or appearings rather than substantively as sensations or sense-data. Moreover, Ducasse's procedure and terminology in discussing this point is misleading in a fundamental way. Seeing how Ducasse "constructs" external reference out of "intuitions" plus the "inference" that they are caused by physical objects, a reader is often led to assume that Ducasse is doing precisely what classical British empiricists did. But we must not forget that for Ducasse the unfortunately substantive-sounding "intuitions" are still sensings or appearings and that "inference" in this case is telescoped, unconscious and wholly non-discursive. The terminology of "intuition" and "inference" is unfortunate since it tends to obscure the central point that Ducasse rejects the messenger premise and claims that sensings and appearings are always *of* an object.

Second, there is good psychological evidence that Ducasse is wrong in thinking that knowledge of physico-psychical dispositions is prior temporally, and logically, to knowledge of physico-physical dispositions. According to the Belgian psychologist A. Michotte the conception of causal connection arises first as a relation between physical objects themselves and not between objects and the self.[23] The idea of causality first arises from an awareness of things banging, bumping, and clashing among themselves. Only gradually does the child learn to isolate his own body for special attention, learn its prowess and various kinds of skill, and eventually arrive at an understanding of his own mental powers and their relations, both in perception and volition, with the outer world.

Finally, Ducasse never justifies the dubious premise which underlies his whole discussion of objective reference, namely, that the philosophical analysis of statements about objective reference (their meaning) consists in the elements of his psychological analysis. Throughout his discussion Ducasse refers "to what it means to call a time, or a place, or an event, a relation, a substance, etc. 'objective',"[24] and then proceeds to explicate the meanings of the expressions referred to by giving a psychological analysis of how they supposedly come to be understood or used in an objective sense. But clearly the *meaning* of saying "there is a cat on the roof," with its objective implications, does not consist in the psychological simples and the interpretation that Ducasse points to. It may be that Ducasse intended the psychological primitives to be taken as *epistemic* primitives – that is, as the court of final appeal in the *justification* of our belief about objectivity, which, of course, would be a legitimate and defensible claim. But in spite of the fact that Ducasse occasionally speaks of his primitive intuitions as the grounds for knowing that x is the case and refers to basic sensings as indubitable or incorrigible[25] – and hence a possible base for epistemic justification – there is no genuine effort on Ducasse's part to construct epistemic rules of evidence that, in conjunction with the primitives, would yield an epistemic justification of perceptual belief.

VI

For Ducasse what is expressed in sentences where the object is a connate accusative is *indubitable.* When I say "I am sensing bluely" or "I am feeling painfully" there is no way that I can be mistaken about the experience *being referred to.* If I am stuck in the finger by a pin and feel pain, Ducasse asks, what can I be mistaken about? I may be mistaken about what caused me to feel the pain; it was not a pin after all but a needle. But that mistake entails nothing whatever about my being mistaken about feeling painfully. It is also possible to be mistaken linguistically. A Frenchman unskilled in the use of the English language might express what he experienced by saying that he experienced a sharp tickle in his finger, but again he would not be mistaken in any sense about what the nature of his experiencing was. "For me to doubt the feeling [of pain] itself or the occurrence of it at the moment it is occurring – and similarly as regards the taste being tasted, the smell being smelled, etc., – is, I submit, quite impossible."[26] True, it is possible to doubt whether the pain I feel or the taste I taste has a given epistemic status – for example, sense-data as used by Broad and Moore. We can justly doubt, as we have seen, whether there are entities having the characters which are theoretically implied by this use of 'sense-data'. But Ducasse says, of course, that is not his sense, and, given his adverbial sense, he concludes: "I submit . . . it is simply absurd to speak of doubting *these* at the time they are being felt, tasted, smelled, etc. Any doubt present at that time is not of them but *about* them."[27]

Roderick Chisholm refers to a class of alien accusative sentences as "seem" or "appear" statements, and these statements, because they are epistemically basic, are construed to be indubitable or incorrigible. By "seem" or "appear" statements Chisholm does not mean epistemically qualifying assertions as "it seems or appears so-and-so, but I am not certain it is the case" but assertions about what is "self-presenting" as "the wine looks or appears red to me," whether it in fact is red or not. Again 'I seem to see a table' is an appear statement in the present sense, an avowal of immediate experience, a terminating judgment, and does not, in certain contexts, entail 'There is a table'. According to Chisholm,

> If for any such characteristic *F* [red, yellow, smooth, heavy, sweet, spicy, square, round, etc.] I can justify a claim to knowledge by saying of something that it *appears F* (by saying of the wine that it now *looks* red, or *tastes* sour, to me), where the verb is intended in the descriptive, phenomenological sense just indicated, then the *appearing* in question is self-presenting and my statement expresses what is directly evident . . . To the question, "What justification do I have for thinking I know, or for counting it as evident, that something now *looks* red to me, or *tastes* sour? " I could reply only by reiterating that something does now look red or taste sour.[28]

Chisholm calls these basic assertions self-justifying, though he thinks it would be just as correct to say that on this level the question of justification does not arise. In either way of speaking the same two facts are intended: (1) we can appeal to such statements in the process of justifying some other proposition which upon occasion may require it; and (2) the making of such a statement provides a "stopping place" in the dialectic of justification. These basic assertions are incorrigible, as they must be if they are to do the job required of them. Of statements like 'I am now appeared to in a way which is blue' we should say "that they are statements which cannot express any error or mistake." Or perhaps it should be said more technically "that the appear statements in question are statements with respect to which it would 'make no sense' to say that they can express any error or mistake."[29]

Ducasse and Chisholm may seem to be correct in calling their basic statements incorrigible since not going beyond the immediately present they run no risk of wrong predictions, but there are in the current literature compelling counter-examples to their claim. Suppose one is an avid birdwatcher and wants much to see a rufous-sided towhee. He sees a bird which *seems* or *appears* to him rufous colored and thinks he has seen the desired towhee. He takes a second look, however, and sees it isn't really rufous colored after all — just another sparrow. The crucial thing, however, is that a person may *remember* his previous sensing, or being appeared to, and conclude from that plus the present sensing that the *previous* sensing had not been rufous-colored sensing either. In the first case he mistook the way the sparrow *appeared* because he had a certain set of mind. This counter-example, of course, depends upon taking memory as reliable, and we shall argue later that memory must be given, along with adverbial sensings, ground floor space in our epistemic edifice. It will not follow of course that because memory can be said to be reliable it can be said that propositions depending upon it are incorrigible.

The experience of pain mentioned by Ducasse seems to be a difficult case for a counter-example. How is it possible to feel pain and not know that one feels pain? Statements about being in pain, if the person isn't lying and is using words correctly, certainly must be incorrigible. And yet consider the following interesting counter-example:

Even concerning pain, a more careful scrutiny will reveal possibilities of error. Imagine a somewhat hypochondriacal patient who knows himself to be hypochondriacal and who is aware that if the pressure of the doctor's fingers produces a pain in the abdomen that he then very likely has a serious illness. Such a patient might very well find it difficult to decide whether the pressure, uncomfortable as it is, is felt as pain or merely as a disagreeable sensation, especially if he knows that the symptom for the disease in question consists in a feeling, under pressure, of mild pain. The patient might, if excessively anxious about a possible disorder, confuse the pressure of the doctor's hand with pain and even jump as if in agony. But as the exploration continues and momentary distraction from the original anxiety occurs, it may become evident to the patient that no pain is felt; further, as he recalls the initial sensation, realizing that the present sensation is no different from the first one, it may become evident to him that no pain was felt initially.[30]

Again this counter-example depends upon the assumption that one's memory is reliable, but Ducasse and Chisholm are perfectly willing to grant that under certain conditions it is legitimate to accept what one remembers as reliable evidence of what was the case.

The crucial question to ask, and one usually left unasked in discussion about the corrigibility or incorrigibility of sensory statements, is why counter-examples like those given above are *possible* at all and why they appear to be effective. That they are possible (that is, that it makes *sense* to say that sensory statements are corrigible) follows from the fact that reports about present sensings or appearings are not self-contained the way Ducasse and Chisholm think they are. 'Rufous-colored' and 'pain' do not refer simply to how one is sensing or being appeared to at the moment but refer to instances of a kind of experiencing of which the present cases may or may not be genuine instances. One genuine instance no doubt is sufficient to provide the meaning of these concepts but no instance can be *known* as an instance of a kind unless there is a classing of it (implicit though it be) along with other instances previously experienced. Without such classification there would be no recognition of any sensing as an instance of a kind. Such knowledge requires the operation of a mnemonic apriori element: To say that I am seeing rufously or feeling painfully is to judge (though not explicitly) that the present sensings or appearings are like certain previous ones. Such implicit classification is the ground of the very possibility of our knowing what it is we are now experiencing. Without such comparison, involving both likeness and unlikeness, there would be no cognition, no effective intuitions of rufous-colored and pain as *sorts* of experiencing. Such comparison, moreover, is that which keeps a present experience from being self-contained. It adds a reference to other experiences, and in making such references one can be mistaken. Hence we have accounted for the possibility of the corrigibility of statements about "the given." And given the possibility of corrigibility on these grounds the plausibility and acceptability of the counter-examples become evident. The mnemonic element which usually functions adequately and thus gives sensing experience its usual validity is interfered with by other psychic elements which are by no means usual or standard. It is true that something in a given sensing remains incorrigible even on the present account, but that sense is not what is needed by Ducasse and Chisholm. It is true that I cannot be mistaken *that* I am sensing or being appeared to in a given case but from this fact it does not follow that I cannot be mistaken about *what* I am sensing or how I am being appeared to.

There are several points that need to be stressed to avoid misunderstanding. We are not denying the self-containedness of the given in the way that pragmatic epistemelogists insist upon. Indeed we believe they are mistaken and that Ducasse is quite correct in rejecting their claims. For the pragmatist 'x is hard' is analyzed in terms of a series of dispositional statements about what we would experience under specified conditions. 'X is hard' means 'if I push it across the surface of the desk, it will scratch the desk', and so on. Such an analysis denies the self-containedness of the given in a radical sense. It presents an elaborate definition-in-use of sensory concepts that theoretically can replace any specifically given concept of that sort. Using Ducasse's terminology we can say that this procedure confuses the meaning of sensory concepts, which receive their meaning denotatively, and the meaning of property terms, which receive their meaning by a set of dispositional statements. Our concept of the non-self-containedness of the given is much less radical. We are not denying that the meanings of sensory and affective concepts are denotatively given. We are claiming that any knowledge of a given sensing as an instance of a kind of sensing requires implicit reference to other cases of such sensings. This knowledge goes beyond any specific instance of a quality like 'red' or a relation like 'between,' say, but it does not go beyond the class of such instances.

NOTES

[1] C.J. Ducasse, "Introspection, Mental Acts, and Sensa," *Mind* 45 (1936) 181–92; "Moore's 'The Refutation of Idealism'," in *The Philosophy of G.E. Moore*, ed. by P.A. Schilpp (Evanston, Ill.: Northwestern University Press, 1942, pp. 225–51; *Nature, Mind, and Death* (La Salle, Ill.: Open Court, 1951), Chps. 12–17; "Minds, Matter and Bodies," in *Brain and Mind*, ed. by J.R. Smythies (New York: The Humanities Press, 1965), pp. 81–97; *Truth, Knowledge and Causation* (London: Routledge and Kegan Paul, 1968), Ch. 13. Cf. P.H. Hare and R. Koehl, "Moore and Ducasse on the Sense Data Issue," *Philosophy and Phenomenological Research* 28 (1968), 313–331.
[2] *Nature, Mind, and Death*, Chps. 13, 14.
[3] *Ibid.*, p. 296.
[4] *Ibid.*, p. 297.
[5] "On the Attributes of Material Things," *Journal of Philosophy* 31 (1934), 60. This reference to Ducasse's dispositional analysis of properties is usually the first one cited. However, this view is adumbrated in *Causation and the Types of Necessity* (Seattle: University of Washington Press, 1924), Ch. 10, and in "On Our Knowledge of Existents," *Proceedings of the 7th International Congress of Philosophy*, 1930.
[6] "On the Attributes of Material Things," p. 64.
[7] *Ibid.*, p. 72.
[8] Roderick Chisholm. "Appearances and Reality" in *Philosophy, The Princeton*

Studies [R.M. Chisholm, Herbert Feigl, W.K. Frankena, John Passmore, and Manley Thompson (Englewood Cliffs, New Jersey: Prentice-Hall, 1964)], pp. 326–27.

[9] "Minds, Matter and Bodies," p. 90.

[10] *Ibid.*, p. 91.

[11] *Ibid.*

[12] Cf. E.H. Madden, "Problems in the Philosophy of Mind," *Southern Journal of Philosophy* 4 (1966), esp. p. 36.

[13] *Nature, Mind, and Death*, p. 322. Cf. pp. 320, 335, 336, 337, 338 for references to Ducasse's conception of the problem of objective reference as being one of semantical analysis.

[14] *Ibid.*, p. 324.

[15] *Ibid.*, p. 326.

[16] *Ibid.*, p. 330.

[17] *Ibid.*, p. 334.

[18] *Ibid.*, p. 338.

[19] *Ibid.*, p. 346.

[20] *Ibid.*, p. 347.

[21] *Ibid.*, pp. 350–51.

[22] Cf. Roderick Chisholm, "The 'Myth of the Given'" and "Appearances and Reality" in *Philosophy, The Princeton Studies*, pp. 261–86, 312–44; and *Theory of Knowledge* (Englewood Cliffs, New Jersey: Prentice-Hall, 1966), Chps. 2, 4, 6; *Realism and the Background of Phenomenology* (New York: Free Press, 1960); and "Sellars' Critical Realism," *Philosophy and Phenomenological Research* 15 (1954–55), 33–47. Cf. Roy Wood Sellars, "A Statement of Critical Realism," *Revue Internationale de Philosophie* 1 (1938–39), 472–98; "The Meaning of True and False," *Philosophy and Phenomenological Research*, 5 (1944–45), 98–103; "Knowing and Knowledge," *ibid.*, 341–44; "Knowing Through Propositions," *ibid.*, 348–49; and C.J. Ducasse, "Some Comments on Professor Sellars' 'Knowing and Knowledge'," *ibid.*, 345–47.

[23] A. Michotte, *The Perception of Causality* (New York: Basic Books, 1963), esp. "Commentary" by T.R. Miles, pp. 373–415.

[24] *Nature, Mind, and Death*, p. 322. Cf. note 13.

[25] *Ibid.*, pp. 312–13.

[26] *Ibid.*

[27] *Ibid.*, p. 313.

[28] R. Chisholm, *Theory of Knowledge*, pp. 32–33.

[29] R. Chisholm, *Perceiving* (Ithaca: Cornell University Press, 1957), p. 65. Cf. *Philosophy, The Princeton Studies*, p. 274.

[30] Douglas Greenlee, "Unrestricted Fallibilism," *Transactions of the C.S. Peirce Society* 7 (1971), esp. pp. 82–86.

CHAPTER V

SUBSTANCE AND THE MIND-BODY RELATION

Ducasse analyzes the concept of substance, both physical and mental, very carefully, both because they are fundamental concepts and important in their own right and because they must be analyzed correctly before the mind-body relation can be understood clearly. Ducasse analyzes both mental and physical substance dispositionally and believes he avoids thereby the traditional puzzles of how it is possible for two such allegedly different substances to interact as they apparently do.

Our procedure in this chapter will be to state carefully Ducasse's analysis of physical substance, mental substance, and interactionism in that order and to criticize each analysis constructively immediately following its explication. The overall picture that will emerge is this: Ducasse's causal analysis of substance and his formulation and defense of interactionism are headed in exactly the right direction, and any analysis that turns out to be more adequate than his must incorporate his general orientation and some of the details of his carefully wrought views as well.

I

Ducasse's characterization of the concept of physical substance has two parts: the definition of 'substance' itself and the definition of 'X is an instance of substance S'.[1] As always he begins with commonsense examples, in the present case of what is to count as a physical substance. Examples of such substances would be chalk, lead, and copper, any piece of which is homogenous with the whole. Now the two questions can be phrased and contrasted in this way: "What does the concept of, say, copper mean?" and "What does it mean to say 'This is a piece of copper'?"

Ducasse's answer to the first question has several parts. First the concept of copper is analysed into that of a set of integrated properties consisting of malleability, ductility, conductivity, etc., where the 'etc.' refers to whatever other properties have been or may be discovered by the scientist or ordinary person in the past or in the future. Such an analysis, Ducasse says, constitutes the very *meaning* of 'substance', where again we have a *kind* of substance in mind: a substance in this sense *is* simply an integrated set of properties.

Ducasse in turn resolves the concept of property into the dispositional or causal concept of capacity. Properties of a substance such as malleability, fusibility, solubility, brittleness, abrasiveness, and so on are statable in, or translatable into, the form of causal laws or laws of co-existence, which are statements about the behavior, state, or action of the substance concerned in circumstances of specifiable kinds. For example, to say of the piece of paper not at the moment burning that it is combustible is to say that in circumstances of a certain kind, like the presence of oxygen but absence of a high wind, the application of fire to a sheet of paper regularly causes it to burn. Again, to say that carborundum is abrasive is to say that under the proper conditions rubbing it against certain other solids causes them to wear away, and to say that water is liquid is to say that under the proper conditions tipping its container regularly causes the water to flow. "More generally, to say that a substance S has a capacity P means that S is such that, in circumstances of kind K, an event of kind C, occurring in S or about S, regularly causes an event of kind E to occur in S or about S."[2] If the capacity of a substance analyses into a change in two of its own states it is an "internal" property, while if it analyses into a change in the states of two substances it is an "external" property. "It is an internal property of certain substances that if their temperature increases, their viscosity decreases." And it is an external property of a diamond and glass "that if a diamond's edge is drawn against glass, the glass gets scratched . . ."[3] The final definition of a substance, then, is that of an integrated set of capacities, where 'capacity' always has a causal explication. As we have seen from the beginning, the causal category is ontologically basic for Ducasse.

The causal analysis of the meaning of 'capacity' just given, Ducasse says, not only constitutes the definition of 'property' but also the meaning of a number of terms which are virtual synonyms of 'capacity', namely, 'ability', 'capability', 'power', 'faculty', and 'disposition'. He does not show the similarity in the usage of such terms but only asserts it. Then he observes that while 'disposition' is the fashionable term, 'capacity' is a better one to use, since 'disposition' has, in some contexts, the suggestion of *tendency* rather than capacity and, in other contexts, the suggestion of *episode* rather than capacity.

The concept of capacity is itself a complex one, and Ducasse distinguishes six formally distinct kinds or types of capacities — three being capacities "to do" and three of capacities "to undergo." The quoted terms designate the ontologically important distinctions between agent and patient and transitive and intransitive capacities. (i) There is the capacity for *activity* of some particular kind, as a ball, e.g., has the capacity of rolling, a twig of swaying, and a nose of twitching. (ii) There is the capacity *to be in a state* of some particular kind, as, e.g., liquid lead has the capacity of acquiring solidity. (iii) There is the capacity of a substance S to *affect* directly or indirectly a substance Z, where Z may be either the substance S or a distinct substance. This capacity is indicated by such terms as abrasiveness, corrosiveness, and toxicity. Insofar as a substance is exercising such a capacity its functional status at that time is that of *agent* — that is, of *operator on Z*. "Agency is thus essentially transitive; whereas activity, considered simply in itself (e.g., rolling, vibrating, waltzing, twitching, etc.) is intransitive. And what an agent, as such, 'does' is an *action*, i.e., an operation; and, as in the case of an enactor, an activity, i.e., a behavior."[4] When S is a purposive agent, then the instrument by which the effect is caused is an *act* and the effect intentionally caused a *deed.* (iv) There is the capacity for a substance Z to be affected directly or indirectly by a substance S; Z's capacity to be affected by S being more specifically either the capacity to be caused to undergo E, or to be prevented from undergoing it, or to have the undergoing of it facilitated or hindered by S's activity of kind C in the circumstances K. "In so far as the substant Z exercises a capacity it has for being affected by some substant S, it is functioning at the time as *patient*; it suffers, i.e., undergoes, a 'treatment' by S resulting from exercises by S of a capacity it has to affect Z. Examples of capacity of a substant to be affected by some substant, and more specifically to be directly operated on by it, would be abradability, corrodibility, intoxicability, vulnerability, irritability, etc."[5] (In later years Ducasse came to use the word "substant" instead of the more usual 'substance', since the latter term, he felt, was so suggestive of an underlying "stuff" that *has* properties or capacities that it could never be succesfully used to refer to the non-substantive sort of particular he has in mind.)

(v) There is the capacity for a substant S to *endure* changes, i.e., to continue generically the same notwithstanding the gain or loss of some particular capacities. An example would be the capacity of a knife to become dull and sharp again while continuing throughout to be the same knife. (vi) And there is, finally, the capacity of substant S *to change into something generically different*; an example being the capacity of water to be changed into uncombined oxygen and hydrogen and the capacity of a caterpillar to change into a butterfly.

To the second question, What does it mean to say 'This is a piece of copper' or 'This is an instance of an S of any kind', Ducasse replies that an instance of a given substance exists if the properties or capacities in terms of which the substance is defined "obtain somewhere." But to say that these capacities "obtain somewhere" does not mean that adjectives such as fusible, ductile, malleable, etc. which correspond to these capacities are predicable of that place itself. "They are predicable only of an instance, existing there, of the given kind of substance."[6] The kind of substance analyses exhaustively into a system of capacities but an instance does not. A place "is occupied by an instance of the defined kind of substance."[7]

This position seems to be commonsensical and unobjectionable. Ducasse seems to be saying that a piece of copper at a given place during a given time exhibits or has the integrated set of capacities ductile, malleable, and so on. But it is impossible for Ducasse to think about copper as anything distinct from its capacities, that which has and sometimes manifests these properties. So to conceive an instance of a substance is supposedly to add an unexperiencable dimension. To say that a piece of copper is something in addition to an integrated set of capacities is like saying a week is something in addition to the seven days which make it up. Hence Ducasse is driven, contrary to what we have just seen him say, to claim that existential statements about substance must be interpreted as statements about a given place during a given time having or possessing an integrated set of capacities. According to Ducasse, ". . . that a specified sort of thing exists, i.e. that it is present at a definite place and time, means nothing more or less than that, during that time, that region of space has the properties included in the definition of the sort of thing considered."[8] If we abstract from a given existing thing all its properties or capacities, we have left of the thing nothing describable but only something we can point to, namely a place in space during a time. "And just that, namely, empty space-time, is all that matter is apart from its properties. Such 'pure' matter, obviously, from the standpoint of observation, is nothing at all."[9]

II

Ducasse's analysis of 'physical substance', though extremely useful, does not seem to be wholly adequate. A causal analysis of capacity is a sound strategy, but the generic analysis of substance as an integrated set of capacities runs into trouble, and the existential analysis of 'this is an instance of S' equivocates between ascribing capacities to things or to regions of space-time.

One trouble in the generic analysis is that Ducasse has to assume an irreducible substantive in order to talk intelligibly about an integrated set of capacities. Ineliminable reference to a substantive or particular occurs already in Ducasse's definition of capacity. In defining this concept Ducasse writes that 'a substance has a capacity p' means 'S is such that, in circumstances of kind K, an event of kind C regularly causes an event of kind E to occur'. 'A piece of paper is combustible' means 'paper is such that, in circumstances where oxygen is present but a high wind absent, the application of fire to the paper regularly causes it to burn'. The crucial point is not that in defining a capacity Ducasse already refers to an S but rather that in referring to an "S such that" he is admitting a distinction between what S is and what S is able to do or undergo, a distinction which itself entails that an S cannot be analysed wholly in capacity terms. The paper does something under specifiable conditions, namely burns, because it is the sort of substance it is — that is, has certain characteristics which either in fact or in prospect explain why it acts the way it does under various specifiable conditions. And Ducasse needs precisely this distinction in order to make sense of the notion of *integrated* capacities he always uses but surprisingly never explicates. It is the structure of copper — in this case the atomic structure — that explains why a piece of copper acts and reacts the way it does under various conditions, or why it will act and react that way, or, in other words, why it is malleable, ductile, a good conductor of electricity, and so on. Hence it is what a substance is that not only explains what it does but also provides the framework in terms of which its capacities can be said to be integrated. The capacities labelled malleable, ductile, and good conductor are now seen not as unrelated, independent capacities but as interrelated and interdependent ones by virtue of their joint dependence upon the same explanatory characteristics of S.

Another difficulty is that Ducasse's claim that power, capacity, and dispositional statements are synonymous is, in fact, incompatible with his own analysis of *types* of capacities and his distinction within that framework of S's that are agents and S's that are patients in a given context. Only if we *distinguish* power and capacity statements can we make the agent-patient distinction among S's.

The different functions of power and capacity statements implicit in Ducasse's distinction among kinds of S's was adumbrated in Chapter One. The "sea" of air, the ocean of water, and the rolling boulders, we say, have the *power*, respectively, to raise water in a pump, crush the submarine, and flatten the houses when air is pumped out of the cylinder of the pump, the submarine dives too deeply, and the houses are in the path of the boulders. Power statements refer to what certain entities or particulars are able to do to other particulars brought into their sphere of action. Such particulars can be called active or powerful particulars or, as Ducasse calls them, agents. Conversely, a lump of sugar, a piece of copper, and a bridge with rotten timbers have the *capacity* or *disposition* to dissolve, flatten out, and collapse, respectively, when put into water, hit with a hammer, or subjected to the weight of an overloaded tractor passing over it. Capacity or disposition statements refer to what certain entities undergo as a result of being brought into the sphere of action of other particulars. Such particulars can be called passive or inert or, as Ducasse would call them, patients.

The difference between power and capacity statements is implicit not only in Ducasse's distinction between agents and patients but also in his distinction between transitive and intransitive capacities, the capacities "to do" and "to undergo." However, no particular is wholly active or passive, a point which Ducasse does not sufficiently emphasize; active and passive are simply different roles that every particular plays on different occasions – the landslide crushed the tractor that furrowed the earth – or to varying degrees on the same occasion – the chain saw cuts the tree which dulls the teeth of the saw.

Another difficulty is that Ducasse cannot explain natural kinds or account for the difference between counterfactual and accidental inference on his analysis of substance. The mark of a natural kind is that it supports counterfactual inference, while a nominal kind does not. The regular occurrence between C and E, in Ducasse's sense of C and E, that he offers is unable to do the job, for there are regularities that are lawful and those that are summative or accidental. It is surprising that Ducasse relies on the regularity view in this context, since, as we saw in Chapter One, he trenchantly criticizes the regularity view elsewhere in his work. However, if we continue to develop Ducasse's concepts of active and passive particulars along the lines indicated we will arrive at the desired goal of a concept of natural kinds and the ground of counterfactual inference.

Power and capacity statements are both promissory notes in the sense that they indicate the explanation of why S acts or reacts the way it does is to be found in some characteristics of S without specifying what these characters are. The explanation consists in showing how some character of S produces behavior x or y, in showing how what S does follows from what S is. It is the weight and pressure of the atmosphere and the water that enable them under proper conditions to raise water in a pump and crush the submarine, just as it is the weight and movement of the boulders that enable them to crush the houses in their path. It is the specification of the character of S − the identification of the causal model − that links it to x, and to y and z, that identifies S as a natural kind and allows one to say that given the structure of copper a piece of copper not now being struck by a hammer would flatten out were it so struck. It is the explanatory structure of S and not the regularity between the C and E events in Ducasse's sense that provides the necessary ground for counterfactual inference. To be sure, it is not impossible, at least in principle, to give causal explanations in turn of the characteristics of S which explain why S acts the way it does, but such additional analysis is not required for explanations given in terms of these characters to be valid and is in principle impossible when the concepts that form the framework for all the explanations of a given sort are reached.

As we indicated previously, the difficulty with Ducasse's analysis of 'X is an instance of substance S' or 'This is a piece of copper' is that it equivocates between ascribing capacities to things or to regions of space-time. The former is the commonsensical one Ducasse wants to espouse, but the latter is the one he is sometimes driven to since he cannot see what a thing can be except a set of integrated properties or capacities. Ducasse's problem can be resolved only by realizing that from the fact we know a thing through its properties it does not follow that a thing *is* a set of integrated properties. Appear statements constitute the epistemic base for justifying or amending perceive statements but they do not refer to a set of properties that constitute the being of the thing. As we have seen, the properties cannot be called integrated without reference to a thing. Moreover, our experiences,

whether veridical or illusory, are always *of* something and hence no one or
set of them can be identical with the thing they are of. This position is open
to Ducasse and it would end his equivocation by landing him securely in his
first alternative and ending the strange talk about regions of space-time
exhibiting sets of integrated capacities. This position would also finally
remove the one strangeness we saw in his epistemic realism. What do we
experience the appearings as directly of? — things, certainly, and not regions
of space-time. Interpreted this way, Ducasse's position becomes even more
clearly than before a perfect solution to the traditional arguments between
the New and Critical Realists. Given this interpretation Roy Wood Sellars no
doubt would have seen more clearly what Ducasse was trying to accomplish
in respect to this traditional controversy.

If more detail should be needed to make these views convincing, the
reader has only to go over very carefully all the arguments already
mentioned to show that *integrated* set of capacities implies that an S is not
identical with any set of capacities but requires that S have a nature (though
not an unchanging one) that explains why it is able to do and undergo
various things. Such an S is conceptually the same sort of thing arrived at on
ontological grounds as the S arrived at on the epistemic grounds just
mentioned.

III

In his analysis of mental substance Ducasse, as we shall see, follows the same
general course as that pursued in the case of physical substance.[10] He
attempts to answer first the generic question of what 'mental substance'
means and second the question of what it means to say of anything that it is
an instance of mental substance. The same clarity is present here as in the
former discussion until, as there, an effort is made to discover what an
instance of such a substance amounts to. Claims about the referent in the
present context turn out to be as ambivalent as in the previous one.

In addressing the question of what mental substance is, Ducasse
frequently uses the concept of a person without analysis, though he seems
implicitly to identify it with "a mind." In any case, whether mental substance or person, the concept is analyzed dispositionally, the same as was
the case with physical substance. To say that a person is irritable does not
mean he is at the moment experiencing the feeling called irritation but
rather that he is such a person that events of a certain kind which do not

cause irritable feelings in most people do cause such feelings in him. And so it is with all the other tastes, skills, gifts — intellectual, artistic, or other — and habits which a person possesses. "All of them analyze as capacities or dispositions, i.e., as abiding causal connections in him between any event of some particular kind and an event of some other particular kind, under circumstances of some particular kind."[11]

Again, Ducasse points out that while disposition is the favorite term the better term is capacity or power. 'Capacity' and 'power' are taken to be synonymous in this context also.

The capacities that together constitute the nature of a mind are of three comprehensive kinds: psycho-psychical, psycho-physical, and physico-psychical, depending upon whether, respectively, the cause-event and effect-event entering into the description of a given capacity are, both of them, psychical events, or the cause-event psychical and the effect-event physical, or the cause-event physical and the effect-event psychical.[12] (Thinking of his early poverty caused him to be anxious; knowing there was food inside and wanting it caused him to open the refrigerator; the light rays impinging on his retina caused him to see cerulean bluely.)

It must be kept in mind that the various capacities which together constitute a mind are not an aggregate of items but together constitute a *system*. Some dispositions are of a higher order than others in the sense that the former consist of capacities to acquire the latter. "An aptitude, as distinguished from, e.g., a skill, is a capacity to acquire a capacity." Moreover, "possession of certain capacities at a given time is in some cases dependent on possession of certain other capacities at that time."[13]

A mind, then, is an integrated set of capacities of the three kinds mentioned. But something has to have and exhibit capacities and what can this entity be, since Ducasse explicitly rejects the traditional Cartesian concept of substance? A mind *exists*, Ducasse says, not just because it can be characterized in terms of some set of integrated capacities of a generic sort but also because it has a *history* — during the course of time things *happen* to it which in part determine what it is at any given time. But what is "it" that exists? Granted that a mind is not a substance in the traditional sense, and that whatever it is it has a history, what substantive status does it have? Ducasse's search for a surrogate of 'substance', it seems, is inconclusive. Sometimes we are told that a mind is synonymous with the stream of consciousness and can be likened, as the Buddhist sage says, to a

rope where no strand (impression) is continuous but where various strands
are interwoven seriatim and overlapping. Thus though no strand (impression) is continuous, the rope (mind) is. Ducasse finds the analogy of a
musical composition even more useful. The notes are interwoven to produce
the continuous piece, though the notes, unlike the strands of hemp, are
intimately integrated into a whole, and hence the metaphor catches more
fully the phenomenal wholeness of the mind.[14] At other times Ducasse
suggests that the mind is an entity distinct from the set of integrated impressions and capacities.

> The foregoing account of what a mind is has revealed that a mind, and a physical
> substance such as sugar or a physical object such as a tree, ultimately analyze equally as
> complexes of systematically interrelated capacities. Had not the word "substance" so
> chequered a philosophical history, we could say that a mind is as truly a psychical
> substance as any material object is a physical substance. Let us, however, avoid the
> misunderstandings this might lead to, and say that a mind, no less than a tree or sugar,
> is a *substantive* — using this word as does W.E. Johnson for the kind of *entity* to which
> the part of speech called a "noun" corresponds.[15]

Unfortunately we are given no further notion of what the nature of these
non-linguistic referents are, whether the entity be mental of physical.

There is, finally, a distinction that Ducasse makes that applies to physical
and mental "substantives" alike — namely, the distinction between
fundamental and derivative entities. Fundamental physical entities are the
objects of inspection, and derivative physical entities are their imperceptible
constituents which we hypothesize to explain the behavior of fundamental
physical entities. Atomic and sub-atomic entities are excellent examples of
physical entities in the derivative sense. Ducasse, it must be added, takes a
realistic view of such entities and in no way counts them as only calcula-
tional devices. In the mental realm, the impressions or intuitions we can
directly introspect constitute the fundamental psychical entities, and
derivative psychical entities are those non-introspectible entities which must
sometimes be invoked to explain what we are aware of. "These would
comprise such items as the repressed wishes or impulses, the forgotten
emotional experiences, the complexes, censors, etc. which psychoanalysts
find themselves led to postulate as hidden constituents or activities of the
human mind, in order to account for some otherwise inexplicable psychological peculiarities of some persons."[16]

IV

Since Ducasse analyzes the concept of mental substance along lines similar to that of physical substance, it is not surprising that some of the previous criticisms apply in the present context also.

In the generic analysis Ducasse again has to assume an irreducible substantive in order to talk intelligibly about an integrated set of mental capacities, since the definition of a capacity is the same for both mental and physical substance. There is a basic reference to an "S such that" whether the S be a mental or physical substance. 'A person is irritable' means 'He is a person such that, circumstances which do not cause irritable feelings in most people do cause such feelings in him'. Again the crucial point is not simply that the concept of substance is referred to in the analysis of a mental capacity but rather that in referring to an "S such that" Ducasse is admitting a distinction between what a person is and what he is capable of doing and undergoing which is inadmissible in any analysis of the concept of substance wholly in terms of capacities. Again Ducasse needs this inadmissible distinction in order to make sense of 'mental substance' as *integrated* set of capacities, though the integrative ability of personality factors is no doubt significantly less than that of physical substance in the sense of physical objects or homogenous materials.[17]

Ducasse also runs into the same charge of self-inconsistency we saw before, since he claims that power and capacity statements about mental substance are synonymous and yet distinguishes in this context as before between capacities to do and to undergo and between the agent and patient roles of substances.

There is, however, a new dimension of difficulty in the present context, which was mentioned in another connection in Chapter II. On Ducasse's analysis of power statements in human agency 'P has the power to do Z' means that P is such that (has the character, personality, and so on, such that) together with some mental releasing event (perceiving x, wanting y, believing p, and so on) the nature of P causes P to do Z (and explains why P did Z). There are, however, two difficulties for Ducasse. As we have seen, on his own analysis of 'cause' only events and not substances are ever causes and hence events like believing x and wanting y should always count as the causes of Z, when Z is some human action. Believing that there is food in the refrigerator and wanting it causes P to open the door of the refrigerator. Consequently it is surprising to find Ducasse when defining the concepts of act and deed referring to the substance involved (the human agent) as the cause of Z. "When, however, an agent is a purposive agent, then the behavior through the instrumentality of which *he causes* [our italics] the effect he intends is termed specifically *an act*, and the effect intentionally caused by that act is termed specifically *a deed*."[18] It may be argued that Ducasse simply forgot himself for the moment, and this may well be true but nonetheless instructive for that. It illustrates that Ducasse finds it difficult when not directly analysing 'cause' to restrict its application to events but falls into using another perfectly good ordinary sense of the term, noted by Locke, wherein agents, whether physical or human, are referred to as causes since the power to bring about a result resides in them. And, as we have seen, on other occasions, it is perfectly legitimate to refer to both the agent and the releasing event as the cause of a given manifestation of the agent's power.

The second difficulty for Ducasse concerns deliberation. Some authors would object that the concept of cause is wholly inapplicable to human agents and hence that Ducasse is already mistaken in saying that believing there is food in the refrigerator and wanting it is the cause of P's opening the refrigerator. We have argued in Chapter III that certain influential arguments offered to establish this claim do not do so and that Ducasse is free as far as these arguments are concerned to continue to construe volitions as causes of actions. But the remaining question is whether Ducasse can analyse all "mental" dispositions plausibly in a dispositional-causal manner. 'P is irritable' fits Ducasse's causal analysis nicely, but 'P is deliberative' does not. There is a crucial difference between power statements when applied to physical agents and to human agents. In the former case the co-presence of the agent and the releasing event entails the necessity of Z's occurrence, while in the latter case the co-presence of an agent and a releasing event (wanting X, say) does not entail the necessary occurrence of Z. In this case P may "deliberately" choose not to exercise the power he possesses. Ducasse's effort to encompass the concept of deliberation within that of causality seems unconvincing: however we analyze deliberation it cannot be done in terms of Ducasse's motivational framework. Deliberation is not simply noticing that the reasons on one side motivate one more strongly than those on the other. Ducasse, in short, has not shown convincingly that all mental capacities can be given a dispositional, causal analysis.

Ducasse's analysis of 'X is an instance of substance S', where S is a mental substance, is again equivocal, though not of course in a manner identical with that in the physical context. Trying to avoid a Cartesian-like substance, and forgetting his own adverbial theory, he sometimes gives the stream of consciousness the status of substance. He tries to make this status clear by the rope and melody metaphors but with little success. There is nothing wrong in principle with metaphors, but the ones presented by Ducasse are not very helpful, suggesting, as they do, more disanalogies than analogies. Each strand of hemp that overlaps other strands is a substance or particular to begin with just as much as the length of rope; the melody is a series of events rather than a substance in either Ducasse's or the ordinary sense of 'event'; and so on. There is no point in going into detail, however, since Ducasse does not elaborate or press the metaphors and is himself disdainful of similar metaphorical procedures elsewhere as in the "double-aspect" interpretation of the mind-body relation.[19] Still feeling the need of a mental substantive, Ducasse says that it is the kind of entity to which the part of speech called a noun corresponds but, worrying still about Cartesian substances, he fails to say what sort of non-linguistic referent is being indicated by such nouns. If such referents are not substantives in the traditional sense but are not chains of phenomenal events either, what can they be?

It would seem that the best candidate for this role is a person; it is always a person and not a mental substance or a stream of consiousness to which we apply the attributes irritable, reflective, being appeared to redly now, and so on. Ducasse himself, as we have seen, usually refers to a "person," though he never analyzes the concept and tends to take it as synonymous with that of mental substance. Clearly, however, it is not synonymous in any intuitively clear way, and Ducasse's classification of mental capacities itself helps show why this is so. Psycho-physical and physico-psychical capacities clearly cannot be ascribed to a mental substance since they must be construed as a complex relationship, either causal in one of several of the senses already noted or completely conceptual, between mental events and bodily actions. In either case, anything which has the normal range of human powers must be embodied in order both to have them and to exercise them. Thus a person is not a mental substance but a psycho-somatic complex which cannot be referred to wholly independently by either mental or physical terms. Ducasse would be able to accept this view without violence to his general position, except that he would want to insist that psycho-psychical capacities can be said to exist independently of bodies.

This qualification would be important to him because it leaves something remaining that might possibly survive the body after death.[20] But for these psycho-psychical capacities that supposedly can exist without a body Ducasse is confronted again with the difficult problem of specifying what in their case the substance can possibly be of which they are predicated.

V

Turning to the question of the relation between mind and body, Ducasse notes that his analyses of 'cause', 'mental substance', and 'physical substance' contain nothing that would preclude interaction between minds and material objects, or between minds and bodies. The crucial question, he says, is to state precisely what it means to refer to a specific human body as "one's own."[21]

There are four criteria which indicate my ownership of the body I call my own. To begin with, it is the only physical object in which movements and other bodily changes are induced or inhibited directly by certain activities of my mind – e.g. blushing by my feeling embarrassed or indigestion by my worrying. The most important example, however, concerns volition: "I call mine the only body in which . . . my merely willing to raise an arm does, in normal circumstances, cause the arm to rise."[22] That the volition causes the movement of the arm is to be analysed in terms of the single-difference definition of 'cause' that we discussed in Chapter I. Moreover, "the experimental evidence that the volition causes the motion is of precisely the same form – Single Difference, and Regularity of Sequence – as for example the evidence I have that turning the switch of my lamp causes it to light, or that pressing a piano key causes the sound which follows."[23] There is no mystery about how a mental event can cause a physical event, since there is no ontological restriction on what a cause or effect can be except that they must be events. In this sense, Ducasse agrees with Hume that theoretically anything might cause anything.

A second criterion of which body is my own is that there is only one body physical stimulation of which in certain ways produces sensations of corresponding kinds. "For example, I might be perceiving half a dozen hands protruding from under a cloth and that a pin is being stuck in each in turn, and I would call a particular one of them mine if and only if the pricking of it caused me to feel pain."[24] All of the explications and qualifications that applied to the first criterion apply here also.

The third criterion is that there is only one body in which mutilations of the brain or neural connections directly cause alterations in my mental capacities. The destruction of certain cortical areas destroys, for a time at least, various linguistic and motor skills, while the severing of afferent or efferent nerves destroys the capacity to respond to the corresponding physical stimuli or to cause the corresponding bodily acts. The fourth criterion is that there is only one body, which we call our own, in which volitions to acquire habits or skills bring about more or less elaborate connections among brain neurons. To be sure, the acquisition of any skill depends upon recurrent practice, and the response may consist in automatic response to adventitious stimuli, the way, e.g., that one's mother tongue is learned. Ducasse's model would be, rather, the deliberate learning of some dead language.[25]

The upshot of the discussion about which body is our own is that mind-body interaction is *analytically true*. The traditional mind-body problem is, How are a mind and a physical object related, and how are a mind and its brain related? The traditional answers are versions of parallelism, epiphenomenalism, or interaction, or else the materialistic reduction of mind to matter or the idealistic reduction of matter to mind. Of these responses, interaction is not only true but analytically true — and the others necessarily false. The question How are a mind and its body related? resolves, after analysis of "What body is my own?," into "How is a mind related to that particular human body with which alone it immediately interacts? "

Thus, analysis of the meaning of the question makes evident the answer to the question; namely, that the mind-body relation, whose specific nature the question concerns, is that of *direct causal interaction*. That this is the basic relation between a mind and its body is thus true as a matter of conceptual analysis. That relation is therefore tacitly postulated in the very asking of the question. Indeed, it would be postulated equally in denial that a mind and its body are causally connected, since, once more, the expression "its body," which would figure in the denial as well as in the question, means "the body with which alone the mind concerned has direct causal connection." The denial therefore would be implicitly self-contradictory.[26]

The necessary falsity of parallelism, epiphenomenalism, materialism, and idealism, a result of the present discussion, fits well with conclusions Ducasse draws elsewhere on metaphilosophical grounds.[27] He conceives the function of philosophy to be that of finding non-arbitrary definitions of key philosophical terms like cause, capacity, etc. used in ordinary contexts. The definitions must be non-arbitrary in the sense that they fit the data — that is, explicate the meaning involved in a class of representative samples of usage. No philosophical analysis of the meaning of such a term can entail a change in the truth value of the sentences of ordinary discourse using those terms. If it does entail such a change then it is the philosophical analysis not the ordinary usage that must be rejected. Now ordinarily we say that a given person has the capacity to decide whether he will go to swim, the capacity to locate auditorially the direction from which a sound comes, the capacity to raise his arm, to raise a book, the capacity to perform arithmetical addition, to remember where he parked his car, the capacity to become a stenographer, an engineer, and so on. It will be noticed that a number of these capacities imply that a person causes effects in the physical world and the physical world in him, and hence parallelism, epiphenomenalism, materialism, and idealism must be neccessarily false, since they imply that all such ascriptions are false. They are all objectionable in further and distinct ways but they all agree in being wrong in principle. Why, then, have reputable philosophers been pushed into such extreme and strange positions? According to Ducasse it can only be understood as a legitimate reaction against the extremely weak and vulnerable formulations of the interaction thesis. Descartes, of course, is the main culprit. His analyses of the concepts of substance and cause make a mystery if not a miracle of interaction. Ducasse, then, intends to be understood as trying to provide an analysis of these terms, along with capacity and others, such that the inter-action hypothesis can be formulated in a plausible and non-mysterious way and hence the need for retreat into views that reject ordinary usage vitiated.

To say that a mind and its body interact is true but not specific enough. Ducasse spells out in detail the intimate way in which this interaction functions, of which the following is only a small sample. This part of Ducasse's consideration of the mind-body relation is extremely interesting and unfortunately usually neglected by commentators. The basic relation may be restated in terms of the agent-patient relation, the mind and body each playing both roles at different times and in different ways toward each other. In addition the brain is the *medium of causation* without which the mind would have no effect on the larger physical world and vice versa. However, the human brain is not merely a medium of causation but is an *integrative* medium "which more or less elaborately *processes the nerve currents* initiated by volitions or by stimulations of the sense organs."[28] After giving in detail the integrative processes involved in both automatic and voluntary responses, Ducasse concludes that these processes account for the fact "that destruction of certain brain areas may not destroy capacity for sensations or for muscular contractions, and yet may destroy certain perceptual or operatory skills related to them; and this in turn can alter profoundly in various ways the manifest personality."[29]

Finally the body has another and even more intimate relation with the mind for which it is difficult to find a suitable name but which might be captured by calling the body the physical *vehicle* of the mind.

The basic fact as regards the vehicular function is that the body is to a certain extent a self-contained little physical world. That is, some sensory stimulations originate within it, and some excitations of efferent nerve tracts result in proccesses that terminate within the body-motor or secretory processes that either do not affect the extra-somatic world at all or do so only indirectly. But these processes stimulate proprio-ceptive or introceptive nerve endings and thus cause certain sensations, which in turn may cause impulses, emotions, or other mental events, and these in turn further intra-somatic events. There is thus to some extent a circular relation between mind and body. In respect to it, the two constitute a closed circuit; whereas, in their relation to the extrasomatic world, they constitute an open circuit.[30]

Further implications of the vehicular function of the body is that it normally is the only part of the physical world that interacts *directly* with the mind and is the only one that, except during coma or deep sleep, does so constantly. Also the body functions as *material of physical self-expression* for the mind — such self-expression being either automatic as in the blush of embarrassment or purposive as in expressive dancing — and as *reflector* to the mind of such bodily effects as are caused by desires, volitions, feelings and other mental activities.

Were it not for this reflecting or, as we might say, mirroring activity of the body, we could not know, except through visual observation, whether, for instance, it is into our own pocket or into that of our neighbor that we are reaching, for we should have no kinesthetic perception of the position or movement of our hand.[31]

VI

It seems to us that Ducasse is quite right in some sense in contending that interaction is analytically true. The problem is to specify what interacts with what. The pricking of the pin causes (or, for us, causes in part) me to feel pain and my lifting causes a change in the position of the stone. These relations seem genuinely causal in nature whether the analysis of causality involved be Hume's, Ducasse's, or our own. The crucial question, however, is not only what the causal relation is between but also what the agent and patient involved are conceived to be. For Ducasse the causal relation is between a physical and mental event in the case of the pricking of the pin and pain, and between a mental and physical event in the case of lifting the stone. For Ducasse the agents and patients involved are mental and physical substances; a physical object is agent and a mental substance patient in the first case, while a mental substance is agent and a physical object patient in the second case. However, it seems clear from what was said in Section IV that mental substance is an inadequate concept of agent and patient (it does not qualify as a substantive in any clear sense at all) and must be replaced by the concept of a person. It is *you*, *I*, or *we* lifting that acts upon the stone and you, I, or we feeling painfully that is being acted upon by the pin. Mental substances do not lift stones or feel pain; people do. A person is not a mental substance or simply a stream of consciousness but an entity that has powers which must be embodied in order to exist and to be exercised. Interaction is analytically true in the sense that there are a number of causal contexts in which the agents and patients involved in acting upon each other, and in being acted upon, are people and physical things. Ducasse's examples of how we identify a body as our own exhibit several such cases, just as his analysis of "mental" capacities does. A person has the capacity to lift a book, to locate the direction from which a sound comes, and so on, and having these capacities implies that a person causes effects in the physical world and the physical world in him. (Note that our claim that interaction is analytically true does not include the case of volitions as causes of bodily movements. Ducasse, of course, does include this sort of case.) However, it should be pointed out that Ducasse does nothing special in his analysis of the question, "Which body is our own?," since the analyticity of interaction is already involved in Ducasse's previous classification and characterization of physico-psychical and psycho-physical capacities. Though the analyticity of interaction that we have distilled out of Ducasse's thought is present in both contexts, there is more analytical interaction in both cases than we are willing to accept. In both contexts Ducasse is committed to saying that interaction is analytically true in all cases of volition and bodily movements.

The analysis of the concept of a person is extremely complex, as we have learned from the large amount of literature concerned with it in the last decade. It is interesting to note that Ducasse's effort to describe the intimate relation between "body" and "mind" — by describing the former as the medium, vehicle, and so on of the latter — is an anticipation of the recent efforts to characterize the concept of a person as involving powers that require embodiment for their existence and exercise. It is, moreover, this concept of a person as embodied powers and capacities that is involved in the ordinary locutions which imply interaction, the truth of which assertions Ducasse is so concerned to mediate in his dispositional analysis. In ordinary discourse we say that a person has the power to lift a stone, jump two feet in the air, the capacity to see the color red and so on, and Ducasse is right in giving these power and capacity statements a causal analysis. However, the *meanings* of the terms in his analysans conflict with the *meanings* of the correlative ordinary terms. In ordinary parlance it is the *person* who does the lifting, jumping, and seeing, not mental substances or physical bodies. Ducasse's causal analysis mediates the truth values of the ordinary assertions but does not mediate the meanings of the terms involved in such assertions. Ducasse is very insistent on the mediation of truth values but explicitly rejects the idea that ordinary meanings have any use in philosophical analysis. He thinks the meanings of ordinary terms are vague and shot through with inconsistency. However, had he been more sensitive to ordinary meanings Ducasse himself might have come to see the philosophical importance of the concept of a person. We will not pursue this question of the relation between ordinary meanings and philosophical analysis in detail here, since we will return to the question in the last chapter devoted to Ducasse's meta-philosophy.

In the recent efforts to analyse the concept of a person some of the traditional mind-body controversies have re-emerged in a new context and several of the traditional positions have contemporary counterparts, the counterparts of course being isomorphic with the old views but not identical with them. Such is the case with the "identity theory" that has caused so much comment in recent years. In what follows we will state this view as simply and carefully as possible, show that it does not establish that there is nothing in the world except increasingly complex arrangements of physical constituents, that in fact it presupposes the concept of a person and hence does not undercut the concept of interaction that we have distilled from Ducasse's views.

The identity theorists are impressed by the fact that two different referring phrases can nevertheless have the identically same referent. They apply this fact to the mind-body problem by saying that statements about mental states and statements about brain states are different in meaning but nevertheless have the identically same brain state as referent. It is stated in defense of the theory that we know there is at least a close correlation between appearances and neurological events in the brain and that we ought not to multiply entities beyond necessity. The general conclusion of the theory is that only physical bodies and their properties, states, and processes can be said to exist and that adverbial appearings can be accommodated to the assumption that there is nothing in the world but increasingly complex arrangements of physical constituents.

As Roderick Chisholm has pointed out, even if the theory were true it would not "explain away" the process of being appeared to any more than it would "explain away" the correlated neurological process. "If we knew that the theory were true, then we would know something about certain neurological processes that no one knows now, namely, that they take place redly." [32] Moreover, the identity theory, even if true, would not show that there is nothing in the world except increasingly complex arrangements of physical constituents, since the concept of a person is presupposed in the theory. Jones is being appeared to redly and this is identified, according to the theory, with a neurological process in Jones' brain. However, what is directly evident to Jones is the fact that *he* is being appeared to redly. "The identity theory does not itself imply that Jones is identical with any physical body or with any property, state, or process of any physical body." [33]

We do not know the identity theory to be true, but is it even antecedently probable? There is some reason to suspect not. The identity theorist may be capitalizing on misleading metaphors. It seems clear to the identity theorist that common salt and sodium chloride, lightning and electrical discharge, etc. are simply different ways of referring to the same thing, or identical states of affairs. Hence, he concludes that since molar-micro physical states are identical, he has the right to assume, unless he is shown convincing evidence to the contrary, that mental states and brain states, as molar and micro, respectively, are identical. However, it appears that the supposedly clear-cut examples of common salt-sodium chloride, lightning-electrical discharge, and so on being identical are not as convincing as they appear at first sight. For in the molar half of all such supposed identities there appears to be an implicit reference to sensing, and hence to mental states. Hence the identity supposedly existing in molar-micro physical states cannot be used as a bridge to make plausible an identity between sensing and a process in the brain.

NOTES

[1] Cf. C.J. Ducasse, *Nature, Mind, and Death* (La Salle, Ill.: Open Court, 1951), Chapter 10; *A Critical Examination of the Belief in a Life After Death* (Springfield, Ill.: Charles C. Thomas, 1961), Chapter 4; *Truth, Knowledge and Causation* (London: Routledge and Kegan Paul, 1968), Chapter 7; and "Minds, Matter and Bodies" in *Brain and Mind*, ed. by J.R. Smythies (New York: Humanities Press, 1965), pp. 81–97.

[2] *Nature, Mind, and Death*, p. 165.

[3] *Ibid.*

[4] *Truth, Knowledge and Causation*, p. 65.

[5] *Ibid.*, p. 68.

[6] *Nature, Mind, and Death*, p. 167.

[7] *Ibid.*

[8] "On Our Knowledge of Existents," *Proceedings of the Seventh International Congress of Philosophy*, 1930, pp. 4–5.

[9] *Ibid.*, p. 4.

[10] Cf. *Nature, Mind, and Death*, Chapter 17; *A Critical Examination of the Belief in a Life after Death*, Chapter 6; *Truth, Knowledge and Causation*, Chapter 7; and "Minds, Matter and Bodies."

[11] *A Critical Examination of the Belief in a Life After Death*, p. 53.

[12] *Ibid.*, pp. 54–55.

[13] *Ibid.*, p. 55.

[14] *Nature, Mind, and Death*, pp. 409–10.

[15] *A Critical Examination of the Belief in a Life After Death*, p. 56.

[16] *Ibid.*, p. 49.

[17] Although in interesting correspondence with F.C. Dommeyer (October 13, 1963) Ducasse attempts a detailed explication of the notion of integration of capacities in terms of higher order capacities, he still has to make the assumption of an irreducible substantive:

The question you raise concerning the paper "Minds, Matter, and Bodies" of which I sent you a copy, as to what it means to say that a mind is a set of capacities "more or less well integrated", is a very proper one. I did not discuss it in the paper, partly because this would perhaps have made the paper too long, and partly because I assumed that the ordinary understanding of "integrated" would be good enough to make the main argument of the paper intelligible. Anyway, the question is important, and a clear answer to it has to be available.

That answer is, I think, constituted by what, in my article on "Hypnotism, Suggestion, and Suggestibility," I say in Section 3 concerning a person's "critical apparatus": The set of capacities which a mind comprises would be "well integrated" in proportion as it includes (a) the capacity mentioned there as constituting the second element of its "critical apparatus," namely, capacity to *bring to consciousness*, out of its stock of harbored ideas, those if any which are relevant to the acceptability or unacceptability to that mind of whatever may be the idea presented to it at the time; and (b) the capacity then to *discern* whether the idea presented is *supported by*, or at least consistent with, or perhaps on the contrary *clashes with*, such of its harbored relevant ideas as the now presented idea brings to consciousness — the term "ideas" being used throughout here to include not only *beliefs*, but also *attitudes* (i.e., tastes, distastes, affections, hostilities, interests, indifferences, etc.); and also *conations* (i.e., cravings, desires, intentions, purposes, or other impulses to action.)

To the extent that those two capacities (a) and (b) are a part of the nature of a given mind, and are stimulated to exercise by any idea presented to that mind for acceptance or rejection, to that extent *the whole of that mind*, not just some isolated part of it, is functioning in determining its acceptance or rejection of the presented idea. And just this, it seems to me, is what it means to say that that mind is *integrated*; that is, that it is a *system*, rather than only an *unorganized collection*, of capacities.

What is, I believe, probably only another way of putting ultimately the same thing is what I say in Sec. 7, "The Parts of Minds," and Sec. 8 "Molecular Minds," of Chapt. 17 (pp. 412–416) of *Nature, Mind, and Death*; where I point out that the *personality* of each of us consists of a plurality of "role-selves" (e.g., playboy, pater familias, citizen, bricklayer, churchgoer, etc.); his *individuality*, as distinguished from his *personality*, consisting of his native *aptitudes* (which Broad calls "supreme dispositions"); that is, his native capacities or incapacities to acquire various more determinate capacities.

These native aptitudes constitute the "actor," who is capable of playing not only the various roles comprised in the actual personality, but also the various other roles which it would be playing instead if, for instance, it had shortly after birth been taken to some country and family whose customs, beliefs, resources, and traditions were radically different from those of the social environment in which his now actual personality developed on the basis of the very same stock of basic native aptitudes.

A given personality is then an "integrated" one in proportion as its "conclusions" (whether cognitive, affective, or active) are the outcome of a "vote" of all its constituent role-selves; not the "conclusions" of only some particular one of those role-selves, "dissociated" from the others in the sense of being temporarily in exclusive control of "conclusions."

[18] *Truth, Knowledge and Causation*, p. 65.
[19] *A Critical Examination of the Belief in a Life After Death*, pp. 71–73.
[20] *Ibid.*, Chapter 13.
[21] *Nature, Mind, and Death*, Chapter 18; *A Critical Examination of the Belief in a Life After Death*, Chapters 7–13; *Truth, Knowledge and Causation*, Chapter 7; and "Minds, Matter and Bodies."
[22] *Nature, Mind, and Death*, p. 425.
[23] *Ibid.*
[24] *Ibid.*, p. 427.

[25] *Ibid.*, p. 429.

[26] *Ibid.*, pp. 429–30.

[27] Cf. *Truth, Knowledge and Causation*, Chapter 15.

[28] *Nature, Mind, and Death*, p. 437.

[29] *Ibid.*, p. 440.

[30] *Ibid.*, p. 441.

[31] *Ibid.*, p. 442.

[32] Roderick Chisholm, *Theory of Knowledge* (Englewood Cliffs, N.J.: Prentice-Hall, 1966), pp. 101–02.

[33] *Ibid.*, p. 102.

CHAPTER VI

PROPOSITIONS, TRUTH AND SIGNS

In the preceding chapters we have discussed Ducasse's most important contributions to metaphysics and epistemology. However, there are a number of other metaphysical and epistemological topics to which Ducasse gave considerable attention. The most significant of these additional topics — propositions, truth and signs — we shall consider briefly in this chapter.[1]

I

Ducasse makes a number of important distinctions in his discussion of propositions, and his definitions of key terms must be understood before his theory of propositions can be understood. His theory is limited to non-molecular propositions.

He defines a *proposition* as anything susceptible of being believed, disbelieved or doubted. *Belief, disbelief,* and *doubt* are never parts of propositions; they are rather psychological attitudes taken toward propositions, and they are attitudes which can be negative or positive and can have degrees.[2]

An *opinion* is a proposition *plus* some attitude toward it. An opinion consisting of a true proposition plus negative inclination to believe it, or a false proposition plus positive inclination to believe it, is *erroneous*. An opinion consisting of a true proposition plus positive inclination to believe it, or of a false proposition plus negative inclination to believe it, is *sound.* Erroneousness or soundness are "values" that opinions, not propositions simply, can have. Whenever an opinion is conscious, the constituents of the proposition which is the content of the opinion are apprehended by us (perceptually, conceptually, or imaginally). Our apprehending that proposition, however, is something distinct from the propostion itself which we are apprehending.

The discursive symbol of an opinion is a declarative *sentence.* The fact that a sentence symbolizes not only a proposition but also an epistemic attitude towards it has the consequence that the examples of "propositions" given in textbooks are usually examples of opinions, not of propositions. A proposition cannot be either affirmative or negative.

A true proposition does not correspond to but is identical with a *fact*. What corresponds, or fails to correspond, to a fact can be only an epistemic attitude or a sentence purporting to symbolize a fact.

A judgment is an opinion arrived at critically, that is, a consummation of an attempt to resolve a doubt. In the judgment which resolves the doubt, that which the doubt was about is the *subject* of the judgment, and that which was in doubt about it but is now affirmed or negated of it is the *predicate*. Since "subject" and "predicate" are thus each the name of a status in respect to an antecedent doubt, and not of a constituent of the proposition which is the content of the doubt and of the judgment, no proposition has subject or predicate; the same constituents of a proposition which functioned respectively as subject and as predicate in a given judgment might function instead respectively as predicate and subject in another judgment. The constituents of a proposition must in every case be capable of serving as subject and predicate in a judgment, and any pair of entities capable of being so used is a proposition.

The essential, irreducible constituents of a proposition are some *ubi* and some *quid* – some *locus* and some *quale*. Moreover, it is of the essence of a locus to be occupiable by some "What," and of the essence of a quale to be capable of presence somewhere. This means that any locus and any quale are automatically in the propositional relation to each other. To constitute a propositional pair they do not need any event external to both, such as somebody's affirmation or negation.

Care must be taken to distinguish between symbolization of an epistemic attitude and symbolization of a proposition. For example, in the sentence Napoleon was short 'was' formulates the attitude of belief, and 'Napoleon, short' formulates the proposition believed. And, if from the relational sentence John loves Mary we eliminate the symbol of the epistemic attitude, we have left 'John loving Mary' as symbol of the proposition believed.

II

There are a number of serious objections to such a theory of propositions. If any locus-quale pair is a proposition and any true proposition is a fact, then, as Ducasse says in a letter to Ushenko,[3] the elements of a proposition about leopards really bite. Many philosophers have objected to admitting a special realm of entities in addition to the physical realm and the mental realm; but Ducasse appears to be not merely proposing a third *additional* realm; he is proposing that strictly speaking the realm of propositions is the *only* realm, and the physical and mental realms are mere subdivisions of it. What else can there be in the world except locus-quale pairs? Anything normally called a physical event or a mental event would, in Ducasse's propositional ontology, have to be called strictly a true locus-quale pair (i.e. a true proposition) and the world would be exclusively populated with propositions. Of course, one may stipulate any definition of 'proposition' one wishes, but it seems that a definition which entails that the world is exclusively populated by propositions is seriously at odds with our ordinary ways of talking. As Everett Nelson comments, it is hard to believe "that a tooth-ache I may have is a proposition . . ." [4]

In addition to the problems created by the doctrine that a true proposition is a fact, there are the even more severe problems created by Ducasse's view of *false* propositions – he insists that false propositions, unlike epistemic attitudes toward them, are never mental.

The chief arguments philosophers have offered for the view that propositions are non-mental entities are familiar. Some of these arguments are: (1) the intentionality of consciousness entails that every mental act has an object, (2) the ability of different people (or the same person at different times) to think the same thing entails a single non-mental object of their thought, (3) the timelessness of truth and falsity entails timeless vehicles of truth and falsity, and (4) the ability to translate from one language to another entails a single set of objects which all languages talk about.

Many philosophers have been persuaded by these considerations to adopt a realistic theory of propositions, and so, in a way, it is not too surprising that Ducasse is also so persuaded. What is puzzling is that in other parts of his epistemology and metaphysics Ducasse emphatically rejects these arguments, yet when he comes to the consideration of the status of propositions he accepts them without question.

G. E. Moore relies on sensory illusion and the intentionality of consciousness to prove the existence of sense data, and Ducasse takes pains to show that Moore is wrong in thinking that sensory illusion and intentionality of consciousness entail the existence of sensa independent of sensing. Ducasse offers, as we have seen, a detailed account of internal or connate accusatives of sensing in which he points out that the introspective distinguishability of these accusatives does not entail existential independence.

It is strange that this adverbial approach he worked out so successfully elsewhere in his philosophy Ducasse did not use in his theory of propositions.[5] If Ducasse's theory of accusatives is applied to propositions, then some mental acts are to be considered as having both an external or alien accusative (i.e. a state of affairs or fact signified) and an internal or connate accusative (i.e. a proposition). In cases where the proposition is false the external accusative does not exist, but the intentional act still has the object it requires, namely, the proposition as internal object.

Fortunately, Ducasse's theory of propositions as objects existing independent of mind could be discarded and an adverbial theory put in its place without lessening in the least the value of many of the distinctions he makes in the course of his discussion of propositions. For example, the distinction between opinion and proposition as Ducasse works it out is valuable so long as it is understood that a particular epistemic attitude (e.g. a belief) is a species of the activity of opining, the connate accusative of which is a proposition. An opinion, then, is an opining plus its connate accusative, and the definitions Ducasse offers of 'sound', 'true', 'erroneous', and 'false' would still hold — though 'true' and 'false' would no longer apply to objects existing independent of mind.

III

Having developed his views on truth over a period of twenty years, Ducasse in his later work tries to combine his earlier and more recent insights to construct a workable theory of truth. However, interesting as Ducasse's various suggestions are, it is not clear that the resulting theory is an adequate one.

In his earlier papers Ducasse conceives of truth in terms of the outcome of test procedures. Such tests he describes in various ways. In 1925 he says that *"the truth of a proposition means the agreement, according to some definable test, between the notion and the object which the terms of the proposition stand for."* [6] About ten years later he makes the same basic point by saying: "To say that a given assertion *is true* thus means that *if* its subject and predicate should be compared by the procedure which defines what is meant by correspondence or sameness of its particular predicate and its subject, the outcome of the comparison *would be* as specified in the statement of the procedure. And the *criterion of the truth* of the given assertion consists in whether or not that outcome *is* as specified." [7] Having first spoken of truth in terms of correspondence between notion and object, and later spoken of correspondence between subject and predicate, he *still* later characterizes truth as correspondence between the "ultimate constituents" of a proposition, and these constituents internal to the proposition he takes to be a locus (or ubi) and a quale (or quid). [8] After twenty years he is still convinced that verifiability and correspondence are somehow part of the nature of truth and still convinced that truth is a causal capacity to bring about an outcome of agreement, but he is bothered by the fact that his earlier theory neither had a way of stopping an infinite regress of verificatory operations nor had a way of explaining just what this correspondence between ubi and quid is. Only a self-evidence theory of truth, he concludes, can both stop the regress and provide a meaning for correspondence between the constituents of a proposition. [9] He remains convinced that truth is to be understood dispositionally but concedes that the correspondence and verifiability he had earlier emphasized are only necessary conditions, not a sufficient condition, of truth. Self-evidence must be brought in at the last as the criterion and nature of truth.

IV

Ducasse endorses Descartes' method of showing that at least one proposition is known to be true. He next asks how we come to know this truth and finds that whatever may be the process by which we come to know it to be true, the last step of the process must consist of a change of some kind in our immediate consciousness. We cannot even know that it is true that the temperature of water is 180° unless our looking at the thermometer, together with various things we already know, cause a certain change in our consciousness. Consequently, only some state of consciousness can be the ultimate criterion of truth.

What is this final change of consciousness? Ducasse submits that the experience called belief is the ultimate criterion of truth, and the experience of disbelief is the ultimate criterion of falsity. In addition to proposing this *criterion* of truth, Decasse suggests a *definition* of truth (i.e. an account of the meaning of 'truth') based on the same idea: the truth of a proposition "consists in *ultimate* undisbelievability of the proposition; and falsity, in *ultimate* unbelievability of it." [10]

Since he recognizes that many persons believe some false propositions and disbelieve some true propositions, Ducasse stresses that propositions in these cases are only *initially* unbelievable or undisbelievable and not *ultimately* so, that is, at whatever time decisive evidence may be in and have been grasped. When there is only part of the decisive evidence, we can be certain only that the probability that the proposition is true is greater or less than on the even more limited evidence we had before. Though usually we must deal with comparative probabilities, the important point is that if we were not completely certain as to some things, we would not have even probabilities as to any other things.

Ducasse clarifies his self-evidence theory of truth by distinguishing different senses of 'evident'. He wishes to take 'self-evident' to be equivalent to 'being made evident not by something else'. Among those things made evident by things other than themselves, Ducasse distinguishes between what is *directly* evident (i.e. evidenced by an evidential item other than itself but not removed from itself) and what is *indirectly* evident (i.e. evidenced through an intermediary evidential chain). He emphasizes that something can be *perfectly* evident without being *self*-evident.

He gives as examples of propositions which are perfectly evident directly all propositions as to the apparent occurrence and apparent interrelations of appearances as such. Where appearances as such alone are concerned, he says, appearance constitues reality and reality consists in appearance. Such propositions are known to us "beyond all possibility of error." [11] The evidence or criterion of the truth of such propositions is that when we try to disbelieve such a proposition, we still believe it completely. That we so believe it is the sole and sufficient evidence of its truth, and it is *direct* evidence of it.

Having explained perfect and direct evidence, Ducasse goes on to distinguish it from self-evidence. The color of the type on a page appears different to us from the color of the blank paper between the letters, and the evidence which guarantees the truth of the proposition that the colors we see are different is simply that we believe the colors look different to us. This is perfect and direct evidence. But if we ask what evidence we have *that we believe* that the colors look different to us, the answer is that the occurrence of belief is its own evidence. Like light, which reveals not only other things but also itself, belief certifies not only the proposition here believed (as to the colors), but also the proposition as to its own occurrence at the time. This is the only case, Ducasse thinks, where truth *consists in* belief and belief *constitutes* truth, that is, this is the only case of *self-evidence* as opposed to direct and perfect evidence. Even in the case of disbelief, that it is true we disbelieve a given proposition is itself established solely by the fact that we *believe* that we disbelieve the given proposition. It is possible to be in doubt as to whether one believes something; but what is then certain is that one is in doubt about it, and this is certified by one's *belief* that one is in doubt.

The truth of a belief that we have a belief (or disbelief) is self-evident but a belief that the colors appear different is evidenced not by the occurrence of belief itself but by something other than belief itself, namely, the occurrence of appearances of color (perfect and direct evidence).

V

In answer to various critics, Ducasse elaborated this theory of truth. He was asked what he means by 'ultimate' when he speaks of ultimate disbelievability or undisbelievability, whose ultimate belief he has in mind, and how the belief is assumed to have been acquired.[12] Ducasse answers that he is referring only to persons whose degree of inclination to believe is such as the evidence they have rationally warrants, that is, persons who are, at least at the time in question, rational.[13] In this way Ducasse rules out those who are (temporarily or permanently) insane, hypnotized, careless, stupid, prejudiced, etc.

What is awkward about Ducasse's answer to these questions is that he appears to be covertly packing into his references to rationality and decisive evidence the various criteria of truth he has so carefully rejected. Normally when we speak of a person as believing rationally on the evidence, we imply that he has used such criteria as coherence, correspondence, and so on. In other words, the more Ducasse tries to strengthen his theory by excluding the untrustworthy, the less he has a theory which is distinctive and excludes criteria of truth other than undisbelievability.

It seems that Ducasse, though he thinks of his proposed criterion and definition of truth as giving the necessary and sufficient conditions of truth, is in fact giving undisbelievability as at most a *necessary* and never a *sufficient* condition of truth. If we encounter someone who tries but cannot disbelieve something, we do not accept what he says as true unless other conditions are satisfied, that is, unless we know that he used other criteria in addition to the criterion of undisbelievability. We may admit that we never take something as true unless there is someone for whom the proposition is undisbelievable, but of course that is an indication only that undisbelievability is a necessary condition, not that it is sufficient. A coherence theorist could as well argue that coherence is at least a necessary condition of truth. If undisbelievability is only a necessary condition of truth, then of course truth cannot be defined in terms of undisbelievability; truth cannot be said to "consist in" undisbelievability if undisbelievability is not both a necessary and sufficient condition of truth.

Perhaps Ducasse is led to define truth in terms of undisbelievability partly by a confusion of two very different senses of 'ultimate'. Because truth seems to have as a necessary condition an ultimate psychological event of belief, he may have come to suppose that truth has as its ultimate logical basis the experience of belief. However, it is clear that the temporal location of a psychological event relative to other psychological events is irrelevant to the logical role that event may play.

Ducasse's confidence in undisbelievability as a criterion of truth appears also to be partly derived from his analysis of self-evidence. As we have seen, in his analysis where there is self-evidence the occurrence of belief is its own evidence, and this "is the only case where truth *consists in* belief and belief *constitutes* truth." [14] To be sure, our believing *x* is *direct* evidence for our belief that we are believing *x*. In this case the evidence for a belief is the mere occurrence of a belief and not the occurrence of something other than belief, but the evidence is *not the occurrence of the particular belief in question, namely the belief that we are believing x.* Strictly speaking, this is not a case of "self-evidence" as Ducasse himself defines the term; it is rather a case where the direct evidence for one belief is the occurrence of another belief, and this sort of knowledge is no different from other cases in which we have direct evidence for beliefs about our own mental events; according to Ducasse's own conception of epistemic attitudes, after all, beliefs are merely a species of mental event.

According to Ducasse's definition of self-evidence, only propositions such as those expressed by the sentences "I believe that I am believing" or "I believe that I am thinking" are genuinely self-evident; in such cases a belief concerns solely its own occurrence and what is logically entailed by its own occurrence (the occurrence of believing entails the occurrence of thinking since believing is a species of thinking).

Ducasse's views on self-evidence and truth, unfortunately, involve another and more fundamental difficulty. If we grant that some beliefs are strictly self-evident and that other beliefs are directly evident, it is not clear what of fundamental epistemological significance follows from this. Cases of self-evidence and direct evidence are confined to beliefs about our own mental events and even if we disregard objections to the incorrigibility of introspective knowledge, we still must establish a deductive link between these beliefs about mental events and beliefs about the world. Descartes' arguments linking indubitable beliefs with beliefs about the world are, of course, not employed by Ducasse. Ducasse's argument appears to be much simpler: he supposes that since every manner of arriving at truths about the world must ultimately end in self-evident and directly evident beliefs about our mental events, all our empirical beliefs find their ultimate foundation in these self-evident and directly evident beliefs. However, as we have pointed out, from the fact that such beliefs are a *necessary* (and temporally ultimate) condition of all attainment of truth it does not follow that truth consists in self-evidence and undisbelievability or even that self-evidence and undisbelievability are alone an adequate criterion of truth. In short, Ducasse's self-evidence theory of truth, though it may provide an additional necessary condition of truth, fails to stop the regress of verificatory operations it was designed to stop and fails to give a meaning to 'correspondence' other than a purely psychical one.

VI

Signs and symbols Ducasse analyses in terms of "mental operations." Although he shares with behaviorists a causal theory in which signs are understood in terms of dispositions to respond, he differs from behaviorists in holding that a response need not be public. His theory of language can perhaps best be described as a phenomenological version of the stimulus-response theory.

Taking pains to examine Charles Morris' behavioristic semiotic, Ducasse argues that if this dispositional analysis is to have any plausibility it must construe "behavior" broadly enough to include images, ideas, feelings, desires, and attitudes such as belief and disbelief. He uses as an example awakening in the middle of the night and hearing the sort of sound ordinarily caused by raindrops on the roof; this sound, he says, is immediately for him a sign that it is raining. But, if he goes immediately back to sleep, what then is the mode of behavior appropriate to the presence of rain which the sound caused in him. He suggests that the "mode of behavior" can in this case have consisted only of the mental events called *thinking* of rain and *believing* that it was occurring.

A second important argument Ducasse uses against the behaviorists should be mentioned. No mode of behavior, he argues, can be said *simpliciter* to be appropriate to the presence of a sign or symbol, for the relation "appropriate to" is not dyadic but irreducibly tetradic: behavior can be said to be appropriate or inappropriate only for the attainment of purposes of a certain kind. Consequently, if we insist on defining 'sign' as a function of a person's perceptually observable behavior, the definition has to be this: something is a sign of something else for an interpreter to the degree that the presence of that sign, *conjointly* with purposes of a certain kind, *and* with belief by the interpreter that the circumstances are of a certain kind, *and* with belief that behavior of a certain kind in such circumstances would promote such purposes, causes the interpreter to behave in this manner. Such a definition, including as it does, purposes and beliefs, includes private as well as public variables. To this the behaviorist naturally replies that it is possible to give a behavioristic account of beliefs and purposes, and Ducasse's rejoinder (as we would expect from his theory of perception) is that the physical events in the behavior referred to by the behaviorist are definable only in terms of interpretation of (private) states of consciousness.

Although Ducasse, in opposition to the behaviorists, insists on the privacy of responses, he is as enthusiastic as the behaviorists in the rejection of an ideational theory according to which meanings are "ideas" somehow existing independently of a tetradic relation between (a) the *interpreter* (the complex of mental habits, dispositions, etc., of the person concerned), (b) the *context of interpretation* (the kinds of things whether subjective or objective, of which he is conscious at the time), (c) the *interpretand* (a change of some kind supervening in the context of interpretation and thus functioning as cause), and (d) the *interpretant* (a change of some other kind following it immediately and functioning as effect). While behaviorists avoid postulating such independently existing meanings by instead postulating minute neural and muscular changes, Ducasse wishes to avoid both the independently existing meanings of the ideationalists and the minute neural and muscular changes of the behaviorists.

Behaviorists have sought to avoid the difficulties of postulating minute neural and muscular changes by suggesting instead that a sign is a "preparatory-stimulus." A "preparatory-stimulus" is defined as something which causes a reaction in an organism but need not call out a response to *itself*, but only to some other stimulus. What they now postulate is a complicated set of dispositions to respond in observable ways under certain conditions. They might say, using Ducasse's example, that the meaning of the sound on the roof as a sign for him is a disposition to get up and close the window *if* the window is wide open, *if* it seems to be blowing hard, if . . ., if . . . On this analysis a meaning becomes an indefinitely long list of such dispositions to respond in observable ways, each with its list of "ifs." What is odd, of course, about this analysis is that we can know immediately the meaning of the sound heard on the roof without knowing anything at all about an elaborate set of dispositions to respond observably. Ducasse, however, without losing the advantages of a causal-dispositional model, can avoid this behavioristic difficulty. For him, when a sign and a private response are present conjointly with certain private beliefs and purposes, the sign's meaning is known independent of knowledge of observable responses that may occur in the future.

NOTES

[1] Our exposition of Ducasse's views on propositions and truth is based on articles he published over a twenty-year period: "A Liberalistic View of Truth," *Philosophical Review* 34 (1925), 580–98; "Verification, Verifiability, and Meaningfulness," *Journal of Philosophy* 33 (1936), 230–36; "Propositions, Opinions, Sentences, and Facts," *Journal of Philosophy* 37 (1940), 701–11; "Truth, Verifiability, and Propositions about the Future," *Philosophy of Science* 8 (1941) 329–37; "Is a Fact a True Proposition? – A Reply," *JP* 39 (1942), 132–36; "Propositions, Truth, and the Ultimate Criterion of Truth," *Philosophy and Phenomenological Research* 4 (1943–44), 317–40; "Facts, Truth, and Knowledge," *P&PR* 5 (1944–45), 320–32; "Some Comments on Professor Nagel's Latest Remarks," *ibid.*, 338–40; and "Some Comments on Professor Sellars' 'Knowing and Knowledge'," *ibid.*, 345–47. Almost none of the material in these articles was included in *Nature, Mind, and Death*, but the three most important articles were reprinted in *Truth, Knowledge and Causation*, and the latter volume will be cited when references are made to the reprinted articles.

Our discussion of Ducasse's views on signs is based on: Chapter 16 of *Nature, Mind and Death*; "Symbols, Signs and Signals," *Journal of Symbolic Logic* 4 (1939), 41–52; "Some Comments on C.W. Morris's 'Foundations of the Theory of Signs'," *Philosophy and Phenomenological Research* 3 (1942), 43–52; "Some Comments on Professor Wild's Criticisms of My Views on Semiosis," *P. & P.R.* 8 (1947), 234–38; and "Some Comments on Professor Wild's Preceding Remarks," *P. & P.R.* 8 (1947), 242–44. "Symbols, Signs, and Signals" is reprinted in *Truth, Knowledge and Causation*, pp. 73–89.

[2] Questions have been raised about Ducasse's exclusion of negatives from propositions. For a discussion of this issue see: Ronald E. Santoni, "Problems Regarding C.J. Ducasse's Analysis of a Proposition," *Southern Journal of Philosophy* 7 (1969), 257–60; Peter H. Hare, "Propositions and Adverbial Metaphysics," *ibid.*, 267f; and Santoni, "Ducasse, Hare, and 'Non-Assertorial Negatives'," *SJP* 9 (1971), 95–97.

[3] Letter to A.P. Ushenko, February 16, 1942. This letter is part of a lengthy correspondence between Ducasse and Ushenko concerning the nature of propositions.

[4] *Journal of Symbolic Logic* 7 (1942), 95.

[5] It is interesting that Roderick Chisholm once suggested to Ducasse that he adopt an adverbial theory of propositions. After several times in earlier letters (June 25, 1944; May 24, 1945; and June 25, 1945) expressing doubt that we need to suppose that there are propositions, Chisholm wrote Ducasse (November 29, 1951) that "[o]ne of your views, I believe might be formulated by saying that propositions are alien accusatives of believings. I think one could plausibly argue, applying Occam's razor, that propositions are merely *connate* accusatives of believings. Possibly you would regard this as an abuse of the technique [the technique of reducing allegedly alien accusatives to connate accusatives] – though I am inclined to feel that it may be applied to propositions quite as legitimately as to sense data . . ." Ducasse's reply to Chisholm (November 30, 1951) is interesting though somewhat inconclusive: "Your suggestion that propositions may be merely connate accusatives of believing is interesting, and, offhand, I do not see any particular reason why this could not be the case. The test would be whether any propositions 'exist' or 'subsist' which are not being believed, disbelieved, or doubted. Also is there such a thing as belief, disbelief, or doubt having no proposition as 'content' or 'object'. The instances of 'folie du doute', and of 'conviction' as a bare feeling or emotion (as in the mystic trance or the 'anaesthetic revelation'?) might be cases in point. As to existence or subsistence of propositions independently of their being believed, disbelieved or doubted, the first thing needed, of course, would be agreement as to what exactly a proposition is. If, as Baylis believes, a proposition is a particular kind of concept, then the answer would seem to be that they have no independent existence. If, on the other hand, in 'this table weighs 300 lbs.' the table which the words 'this table' denotes is, as I think, a literal constituent of the proposition that sentence formulates, then it would seem that at least some constituents of some propositions exist independently of their being believed, disbelieved, or doubted. As you say, it turns out to be a long story."

[6] *Truth, Knowledge and Causation*, p. 146.

[7] "Verification, Verifiability, and Meaningfulness," p. 231.

[8] *Truth, Knowledge and Causation*, p. 171; cf. p. 191.

[9] *Ibid.*, p. 172f.

[10] *Ibid.*, p. 173.

[11] *Ibid.*, p. 177.

[12] Ernest Nagel, "Truth and Knowledge of the Truth," *P&PR* 5 (1944–45), 53; and Charles A. Baylis, "Critical Comments on the 'Symposium on Meaning and Truth'," *ibid.*, p. 92.

[13] "Facts, Truth, and Knowledge," p. 326f.

[14] *Truth, Knowledge and Causation*, p. 178.

CHAPTER VII

ETHICS AND EDUCATION

Though C. J. Ducasse was a systematic philosopher who made significant contributions to almost all areas of philosophy, normative ethics is an apparent exception. He published much in meta-ethics, but there is little, if any, of his published work directed explicitly to the question what good *is*, or what one *ought* to do, whatever these evaluative terms might mean. Some philosophers have inferred from this fact, plus the nature of his "skeptical" meta-ethics, that he held no normative view of his own. But such an inference is mistaken. To think that Ducasse espoused no normative view is to miss one whole dimension of his systematic thought — one that knits together firmly certain of his views on education, art, and religion. The latter are not only individual areas interesting in their own right to Ducasse, but seen in certain ways they are part and parcel of his moral philosophy. The purpose of this chapter is to make clear the nature of his "progressive and universal hedonism" by examining carefully his published articles on education and, even more importantly, by drawing upon his unpublished notes on moral philosophy. Though a major point of this chapter is to fill in a gap in Ducasse's systematic philosophy, we will also offer criticisms of both his meta-ethics and progressive hedonism in the hope of throwing additional light on his ethical views as a whole. One particularly interesting point, as we shall see, is that Ducasse can rebut an objection to hedonism by applying his adverbial analysis of 'seeing this color' to 'experiencing this pleasure'. We will conclude with a discussion of other aspects of Ducasse's philosophy of education, including his concept of "wisdom."

I

Ducasse's meta-ethics, briefly, is that the job of the moral philosopher is the semantical one of looking at the contexts in which moral expressions are used, either individually or by a whole society, and forming precise and non-arbitrary definitions of the meanings of the moral terms that fit a specific usage context.[1] This semantical task has the value of showing if the meaning of 'right', say, in one usage is incompatible with the sense indicated in the bulk of usage in that context. If a person wishes to be consistent, then he must give up the unique usage or decide what case of usage is to assume the role of a paradigm case of what is to count as right.

The test of the adequacy of any definition that is proposed consists in the possibility of replacing the term defined by the proposed definition and then noticing whether the truth values of the original statements are changed. If they are, then the proposed definition is faulty; if not, it is acceptable. The proposed definition is adequate if the replacement "shall not result in making false any of the statements that were true, nor in making true any that were false, nor in altering the truth or the falsity of any other statement implying or implied by the given ones." [2] This test of adequacy "will be met automatically if a definition expresses a genuine equivalence, and will not be met unless it does." [3]

The result of semantical analysis is to discover the definitions of moral terms which are fundamental in the sense that they determine what is to count as moral in a given context of usage. But various contexts give rise to different ultimate standards, and none of the standards, or frameworks, can itself be established as the right one and the others wrong. The crucial point is that no ethical standard can itself be said to be right or wrong, since such standards provide mutually exclusive senses of these terms. "[T]he essence of [this] insight [is] that every ethical standard is equally tenable, each being exactly at a level of logical arbitrariness with each other." [4] The standards that determine what is right or wrong, just or unjust, are simply either factually used or not used by a given society, group, or person to distinguish as right or wrong things other than themselves.

Ducasse calls his view "ethical liberalism" and illustrates it by contrasting egoistic and universal hedonism, a contrast he takes to be fundamental in moral discourse. His view is that there is no way of proving the egoist to be immoral, any more than it is possible to prove the universal hedonist to be moral. Each constitutes a framework which determines the nature of what one ought to do. Nevertheless — and here is where his progressive hedonism enters the picture — theoretical, artistic, and religious education can contribute significantly to changes within both viewpoints and to a possible shift from egoism to altruism. Theoretical means-end knowledge contributes to both the egoist and altruist more efficient ways of bringing about the desired hedonistic consequences. It shows the former how better to maximize his satisfactions, just as it shows the latter how better to maximize overall good consequences. Also the education of taste, feeling, and emotion – that is, the widening of the scope of each – also makes it possible for the egoist to enlarge the range of his satisfactions, just as this sort of education, particularly through dramatic literature, opens one's eyes to new tastes, feelings, and emotions held by others and with which one can come to empathize. Such empathy is one crucial step in coming to care about others as well as oneself and thus a crucial step in moving from egoism to altruism. But the point is not that the egoist has been convinced by arguments that he is wrong, or, indeed, been shown to be wrong, but rather that the widening of horizons about what it is possible to enjoy and care about changed him into a person who *in fact* cares about others.

II

The nature of Ducasse's progressive and universal hedonism can be understood in detail only by making clear what he means by a "liberal education" and by drawing upon his unpublished notes on hedonism. We will do the first job in the present section and the second in the following one.

Having given a general meaning to the concept of education and classifying its special kinds, Ducasse turns to giving an answer to the question "Why educate? " He gives his most complete answer to this question in the process of describing what he considers to be an example of *good* education, namely, liberal education. In defending the merits of liberal education he explains what it is good *for.*

Liberal education is to be contrasted primarily with vocational education. Vocational (or technical) education is the development to a high degree of efficiency of those capacities which relate to the particular vocation an individual wishes to follow. Technical education, though it may include many of the courses included in a liberal education (e.g., sciences) fails to be liberal by virtue of the "narrowness of the outlook on life" which it brings about.[5] Unlike vocational education, liberal education is an education which endows students with "perspective." [6]

Since Ducasse wishes to define 'liberal education' in terms of perspective, the meaning of perspective must be explored in detail. The nature of perspective can be explained by describing its various "dimensions": discipline, history, context, philosophy, application, and thoroughness.

To give a student *disciplinal* perspective is to give him some personal experience of the disciplines other than the one in which he is concentrating.[7] For this purpose Ducasse distinguishes four disciplines: formal thought, empirical investigation, hypothesis, and appreciation. *Formal thinking* in logic or mathematics develops the capacity to "consider an argument purely on its merits, independently of such opinions or bias or wishes as one may happen to have concerning the matter at issue."[8] The discipline of *empirical investigation* develops the capacity to "question nature directly, and . . . to get from her, by means of observations and manipulations, which are inherently never more than approximately exact, answers whose probability and approximateness are quantitatively specifiable and capable of independent verification."[9] The third discipline, the discipline of *hypothesis* or *opinion*, develops an "awareness that although each of us has to act much of the time on the basis merely of the opinions he has, nevertheless opinions are one thing and knowledge is another; that opinions opposed to our own may happen to be true; that where opinions are concerned, openmindedness is in order; and that in any event we are likely to gain light from a candid examination of opinions divergent from our own . . . This discipline . . . is best obtained in the study of such subjects as political and economic theory, sociology, religion, or philosophy, where the hypotheses concern matters tied up, more closely than in the natural sciences, with our emotions, prejudices, tastes, or private interests."[10] Finally, the discipline of *appreciation* develops the "capacity to throw [oneself] open to the reception of the feelings, sensations, and emotional experiences which were embodied by the artist consciously in his works, or by nature unconsciously in her works."[11] Ducasse believes that a student who takes properly designed courses in each of these disciplines will develop disciplinal perspective.

In a liberal education there should be developed in addition to a disciplinal perspective what Ducasse calls "historical perspective." "For example, to have historical perspective in physics is to know the history of physics, or better, of science."[12]

The third kind of perspective Ducasse urges as a goal of liberal education is "contextual perspective." "To have contextual perspective on a given subject is to know something of the subjects materially contiguous with it — contiguous, that is, in the sense that no sharp line can be drawn between it and them at certain points."[13]

Fourth, philosophical perspective develops a capacity for scrutiny and criticism of evaluations. Fifth, applicational perspective is awareness of "the practical applications of a knowledge of [a] subject." [14] Finally, to have the perspective of thoroughness is to have experienced at first hand what "it means to know something thoroughly instead of only sketchily or super-ficially . . ." [15]

Having described the special forms of perspective, we must explain the more general nature of perspective and what it is good for, in Ducasse's opinion. Perhaps the best way of describing what Ducasse means by perspec-tive is to say that it is the ability to understand alternatives, to see and not reject out of hand or ignore the many points of view from which a matter may be observed, analysed or evaluated.

This awareness of alternatives is valuable because, Ducasse believes, it makes an individual free from his own impulses of the moment and enables him rationally to determine which of his impulses should be allowed to prevail. Perspective prevents any impulse from stifling the others and allows all impulses and desires the fullest possible expression in the long run.

In the background of Ducasse's discussion of the aims of liberal education we can discern his ethical views. Although he does not make explicit the link between his ethics and his concept of liberal education, the link is not difficult to find. Clearly Ducasse believes that an education which gives a person perspective and intellectual self-discipline thereby contributes to the likelihood that he will lead a life which is, on the whole, happy. Liberal education is, in other words, a means to a hedonistic end. And just as Ducasse insists that the kernel of truth in self-realizationism is the insight that we must deny ourselves certain pleasures in the present in order to develop new capacities which will make possible greater pleasures in the long run, so in education he opposes those who advocate only immediately enjoyable ("interesting," "stimulating") education and believes that the greater pleasures of intellectual adventure, aesthetic appreciation, and so on are only possible if an individual has sufficient self-discipline to learn things which are not pleasant to learn.

Not only is Ducasse's hedonism in education progressivist as his hedonism is elsewhere; it is also universalist. To develop perspective (especially in the humanities) is to develop an ability to grasp and empathize with the pains and pleasures of others who are in very different circumstances and have very different values. Someone who has acquired perspective through liberal education is someone who in his moral judgments can take into account all sentient beings affected by an action. Liberal education, in short, plays an essential role in equipping us to be moral.

III

The details of Ducasse's hedonism appear only in his unpublished notes. They are rich and diverse in nature, and we are able to give only a representative sample here. The sample will be large enough, however, to show where Ducasse fits into the spectrum of teleological moral philosophies and to exhibit his unique way of formulating counter arguments against criticism.

Ducasse rehearses his ethical liberalism in this context. It is no more possible to prove that one ought to care about the happiness of others than to prove that one ought to like the odor of a lemon. Unlike his published work, however, the notes concentrate on his variety of hedonism. As we shall see, the progressive and universal aspects tend eventually to merge.

The progressive aspect of his hedonism comes to the fore in Ducasse's discussion of perfectionism or self-realization ethics. He explains that he does not advocate a "purely empirical hedonism" in which "one's attempt to govern action is directed only by knowledge *already possessed* of its results for happiness or unhappiness, [since] one may be thereby robbing oneself of possible access to other and better sources of happiness." [16] Ducasse wishes to make his hedonism "progressive" in the sense "of developing *greater capacity* for happiness, capacity for appreciation of *new sources* of happiness, and attempt to make such new sources available." [17]

Progress to higher degrees and new sources of happiness, if there are such . . . requires a certain amount of *experimentation*, research, pioneering, or guidance from those who have done so. This may be a painful process (when mistakes are made). The renouncing of some *known* sources of happiness may be a prerequisite to the obtaining of *unknown* better ones, e.g., some renouncing of pleasure of self-indulgence is usually a condition of obtaining the joys of achievement (e.g., training table; hard and uninteresting study often prerequisite to achievement; thrift; etc.) . . .[18] That such development in the individual is *possible and should be striven for even at some* cost in terms of familiar sources of happiness is the true insight of *perfectionism.*[19]

The universalistic aspect of his hedonism is brought in when Ducasse discusses education and morality. He points out that we all at least sometimes take pleasure in giving pleasure to others. Furthermore, this ability to find pleasure in being responsible for pleasure in others is an ability which can be developed by education — particularly religious and aesthetic education. Religious education Ducasse conceives of as primarily concerned with developing the "heart," i.e., altruistic feelings, and is wholly independent of any special religious doctrine.[20] Aesthetic education develops the capacity to make the subtle discriminations of feeling necessary to tact. Dramatic literature develops our capacity for empathy. The humanities in general develop our sentiments.[21] In his notes Ducasse is quite explicit about the close connection between his concept of hedonism and a liberal education.

Ducasse believes that no hedonistic calculus is possible and presents his form of universal hedonism in terms of empathy and fellow-feeling and, to be consistent with his "liberalism," conditionally and descriptively. To know what we ought to do concerning others:

(a) we *imagine, as well as we can, the consequences* of each of the *alternative courses of action* open to us in a given case (in which we are in doubt as to what is right for us to do).

[and]

(b) In so far as we are *sympathetic*, we put ourselves in imagination in the places of the various persons that will be affected by those consequences, and imagine how *we* should like the lot our decision will involve for them.

[and]

(c) Then (having thus *identified ourselves with them by sympathy*) we simply *prefer* (i.e., judge as "happier") one of the sets of consequences to the others.

[and]

(d) We do this in the same *spontaneous* way, by the *same direct sort of preference*, as when the consequences of a decision affect only ourselves and we have thought them out, both pleasant and unpleasant. (Where *intensities* are judged equal, durations, and numerousness of affected existing persons (sympathized with), are decisive. Where intensities are not judged equal, no mathematical treatment is possible.)[22]

In discussing what he calls "the best conduct of one's life," Ducasse exhibits nicely how his concept of progressive hedonism, through enlargement of the self, actually merges with the concept of universalistic hedonism.

One lives most fully and happily in so far as one dedicates oneself to some "cause" or other that one regards as of greater objective importance than one's personal fate (i.e., than own comfort, advantage, wealth, fame, power, etc.)

These things, if possessed or sought, are then viewed only as *instruments in trust*, to be used only for the promotion of the "cause."

That to which one devotes (dedicates, consecrates, "sacrifices") oneself may be of many sorts: family, country, science, art, social reform, etc.[23] ...

Self-dedication to be a "noble," i.e., altruistic, ideal or aim is thus, no matter what the particular noble aim chosen may be, an organizing of one's life — of one's thoughts,

feelings, and activities – to the promotion of something good, helpful, beneficial, to
one's fellowmen . . .

Living one's life in such terms tends to resolve the conflict between duty and inclination, between impulses to self-preservation, self-gratification, self-aggrandizement, and
what society and/or one's altruistic interests expect or demand of us, or approves and
applauds. It does not destroy one's Self, but gives one a larger one. [24]

Ducasse defends his brand of hedonism against various criticisms, of which
the following is a small sample. This argument and counter-argument strand
constitutes a significant part of the notes and reflects the not unnoticed fact
that moral philosophers generally defend their positions by showing alternatives and criticisms to be faulty rather than by arguing directly for their
positions.

(a) "Question: Is altruism practicable for everybody? Are not many
persons so situated that they are forced to do evil things if they are to live at
all or to discharge their responsibilities to their families? E.g., a person
working for a crooked employer may have to do crooked things or starve.
Or again, in any field of competitive acquisition, putting one's competitors
at a disadvantage, or crippling them, or eliminating them, may be the condition of one's own survival and of one's fulfillment of one's personal obligations. Or again, the soldier in war.

"Answer: 1. It is almost always possible, *at the cost of some personal
sacrifice*, to act somewhat less crookedly, less cruelly, less harmfully than
the situation seems to demand of us. Every such sacrifice, even if small, is an
offering on the altar of the ideal of beneficence. It is a case of doing *as
much as we reasonably can*, even if not as much as we would wish to do, for
the fostering of a better state of human affairs . . . Such sacrifices are the
food which nourishes one's spiritual growth.

"[Answer] 2. Opportunities for beneficent action are indeed much greater
in some positions than in others: There are positions where action to foster
a given sort of altruistic aim is indeed wholly impossible.

"But *the more inclusive, comprehensive, the less specialized* is one's
altruistic aim, the more omnipresent become the opportunities of working
towards it in *some* way – if not in the way one would prefer, or in which
one is most expert, then in another. For even if you *cannot do the specific
sort of thing you had willed to contribute* to the good of mankind, the
possibility remains of *then willing to do what you can contribute instead to
it*.

"Thus the more inclusive, general, is your altruistic aim (e.g., helpfulness, beneficence, instead of e.g. helpfulness to *this* person, beneficence of *that* specific sort) the more numerous and various become your opportunities to work towards it; and the *less* becomes the chance of your being *wholly* frustrated."[25]

(b) A common objection to hedonism is that pleasure is not the only thing desired. Ducasse agrees that pleasure is not the only thing desired, and he points out that he is not defending *psychological* hedonism. He does not claim that desiring pleasure is the sole *cause* of action but rather that the *worth* of aims and of means is a matter of the pleasure and pain involved. Ethical hedonism, he says, is not a theory of causes or stimuli that actually induce actions but a theory of the moral worth of actions.

(c) It is sometimes argued (for different reasons, as we will see later) that there simply is no such thing as intrinsic value, i.e., value a thing has in itself.[26] If this objection were true, of course, hedonism would be an impossible doctrine, but Ducasse staunchly defends the existence of intrinsic value, saying that the denial of this view stems from a failure to recognize (1) that positive intrinsic value is *identical with pleasure*, and (2) that the accrual of subsequent disvalue does not vitiate the intrinsic value of an immediate result of an act — it simply over-rides it. Sometimes an act will produce a positive intrinsic value immediately, but cause in addition, more or less remotely, effects which cause occurrences of negative intrinsic value experience and thus "condemn" the initial experience by showing its eventual negative intrinsic value cost to be higher than the positive intrinsic value contribution of the initial experience. However, this remote cost in negative intrinsic value does not make the initial intrinsic value *unreal*, only costly. It is true that an act may be said, on the whole, to "lack value," but that is an elliptical way of saying that, considering all its effects, remote and immediate, the negative intrinsic values outweigh the positive intrinsic values. It is fallacious to attribute this over-all, net lack of positive intrinsic value to individual effects and to conclude that there can be no such thing as intrinsic value.

(d) An objection to universalistic hedonism which has long been popular is that it commits one to the view that the torture of one person would be right were it to save trifling annoyance to millions, the total of which displeasure is greater than the pain of the one tortured man. Ducasse's reply is that such comparison is in principle impossible since there is no hedonistic calculus to arrive at such comparative judgments. Although pleasure and pain are quantities, he says, not all quantities can be measured. Measurement of quantities is only possible when there is a fixed scale for comparison available, but there is no such scale in the case of the pleasures and pains of different persons. Therefore *"the hedonic calculus is a myth."* We cannot precisely calculate effects in any case; universalistic hedonism is merely a guide which is fallible and must deal with probabilities.[27]

IV

Almost every substantive issue in moral philosophy is raised by Ducasse's discussion, so it is not possible to criticize his views in detail here. We will limit ourselves to fundamental points and only a few of them. The ones discussed were chosen, among other reasons, because they help illuminate the nature of Ducasse's moral philosophy.

To begin with, the test of the adequacy of any definition of a moral term proposed by Ducasse is inadequate. To be acceptable, he says, any definition must preserve the truth values of the expressions in which they originally occur. However such a test would be so catholic as to be useless. It would scarcely rule out any moral philosophy. Epicureans, utilitarians, Kantians, and theological moralists all accept the same ordinary moral rules; they only disagree about the proper principle that justifies them. Nietzsche is one of the few moral philosophers who would be ruled out by this criterion. So at best the truth-falsity preservation criterion is a necessary condition of adequacy but not a sufficient one. And Ducasse never gives any justification why it is even a necessary condition. It is not clear why Nietzsche is *automatically* wrong in rejecting the moral rules ordinarily held.

Moreover, Ducasse encounters serious difficulty when he interprets moral principles or standards as providing the basic meanings of moral terms. He is no doubt right in saying that no standard can itself be shown to be right or wrong, or moral or immoral. But the truth of this view does not entail that acts and rules of behavior cannot be shown to be right or wrong. Quite to the contrary, they are so interpreted by tracing them back to some accepted standard or principle. Such standards provide the reasons why acts and rules are said to be right or wrong. Ducasse's difficulty is that in presenting standards as meaning analyses he unwittingly cuts himself off from interpreting them as reason-producing frames of justification. Let us examine this point in some detail.

The utilitarian view that one ought to contribute to general happiness, for example, can be interpreted as saying that 'ought' means 'contributing to general happiness'. In this case, the utilitarian claim is not itself a normative one but is a meta-ethical claim about the meaning of moral terms. On this interpretation, to the question "Ought I keep my promise?" it is meaningless to reply, "Yes, since keeping promises tends to contribute to the general welfare." Since 'x contributes to general welfare' and 'x ought to be done' are synonymous expressions, it is not possible to give·the former as a reason why we ought to do any given act. If I am asked for a reason for saying "John is Mildred's brother," I have not advanced the conversation any by replying "because John is Mildred's male sibling." However, since the utilitarian generally, like most of the advocates of other standards, *does* intend the claim, "Keeping promises tends to contribute to the general welfare" as a reason or justification for "I ought to keep my promise," it follows that he is using the phrase "one ought to contribute to the general welfare" not as a definition of 'ought' but as a statement of his commitment to general welfare as man's basic and final obligation, the one in terms of which all others are to be decided. In this case, the utilitarian claim is a normative one and not definitional in nature. Thus utilitarians in this sense are assuming that 'right' and 'ought' are intuitively meaningful in their own right, or perhaps altogether undefinable in nature. It should be clear, of course, that everything said about utilitarianism holds also for every other moral standard. The main point is that standards are generally interpreted as reason producing systems rather than definitional frameworks.

Ducasse's discussion of the relation between education and progressive, universal hedonism seems to us a superior piece of work. It is much more convincing than efforts to show that there are good reasons, even though not moral ones, which vindicate accepting a utilitarian standard. Still there are several qualifications one might want to make even though one is in the main sympathetic here. One might, for example, reject Ducasse's expressionist and emotivist view of art and hence reject the role Ducasse gives aesthetic education in the broadening of taste, tact, feeling, and emotion. However, it is likely that whatever analysis of the aesthetic response is given, aesthetic education will still play a crucial role in widening the individual's outlook — and that role is the point Ducasse is stressing in the present context.

Ducasse's concept of religious education, however, is quite unconvincing,

depending as it does, upon a strange and unjustified redefinition of the
ordinary meanings of 'religion' and 'religious.' According to Ducasse, the
dedication of self to general beneficence can be described as 'dedicating
one's life to the service of God', and the inducing and broadening of such
dedication can be denominated religious education. However, this stipulation of what is to count as "religion" and "religious" is strange indeed since
a beneficent naturalist on this view would be dedicating his life to the
service of God! Ducasse apparently realizes this difficulty for he writes,

That *mode of life* need not be described in terms of the idea of God if one does not
believe in such a being. Yet it may even then be said to be the essence of *a religious
life* . . .[28]

Unfortunately this redefinition of "religious" seems equally pointless. To
say that a naturalist who acts benevolently is thus leading a religious life is
simply to give "religious" an entirely new meaning when it has a perfectly
good one to begin with.

Ducasse's formulation of universal hedonism in terms of empathy has
various merits, not the least of which is that it avoids the untenable notion
of a hedonistic calculus. However, this formulation is not without certain
difficulties which will need to be discussed in detail in a full-blown examination of Ducasse's hedonism. One obvious difficulty is that while empathy is
useful in getting one to become sensitive to the feelings of other people in
the first place, it is not adequate as a standard of right and wrong. No one is
capable of feeling empathy for everyone, and yet if one is to become a
universal hedonist one is committed to producing *everyone's* pleasure whatever his own empathetic limitations may be.

Ducasse's rebuttal of criticisms is uneven, some of them being effective
while others clearly need shoring up. We shall say something briefly about
each rebuttal in turn.

(a) Ducasse's answer to the question "Is altruism practicable for everybody?" — and the more general question, "Is altruism practicable at all?" —
is very important because it introduces what amounts to a negative version
of utilitarianism. Unlike many moralists who are basically sanguine souls,
Ducasse realizes that continued existence is often incompatible with doing
what one believes to be right or just. We constantly have to compromise our
ideals in order to go on living. The question is how far one is willing to
compromise. The question is, are there any conditions under which one
would refuse to compromise, to choose not to go on living? The conditions

vary enormously from person to person. A Thomas More compromises only a bit; the prison guard in a Nazi camp who turns on the gas to avoid punishment himself has surrendered completely. What Ducasse is telling us here is this: never surrender and compromise as little as possible. And in your compromising let your moral standard be that of producing the minimum amount of painful results which, given the facts of life, it is possible to produce.

(b) Ducasse is clearly right in saying that his form of hedonism is a standard of worth and not a doctrine about the causes of action. His emphasis here might suggest to the reader that he believes a causal analysis of actions is always misplaced, that the explanation of 'He crossed the street to buy cigarettes' by 'His desire for cigarettes caused him to cross the street and buy them' is to commit a category mistake. However, this inference from his emphasis would be totally mistaken. Ducasse in fact, as we have seen in Chapter II, precisely formulated the classical doctrine that volitions, desires, and knowings are causes of actions and defended his view against ordinary language criticisms.

(c) In rebutting the criticism that there is no such thing as intrinsic value (and in numerous other places), Ducasse writes in a way that looks as if he conceived pleasure to be a complete mental episode which co-exists with other mental episodes in the same mind at the same time. Indeed, this view has usually been held by hedonists. However, it has often been pointed out that we cannot introspectively discover such mental episodes of pleasure. Ducasse, we should see, need not be committed to the view that pleasure is a separate mental event (e.g., a pleasure mental-event separate from the experiencing sweetly of a piece of candy). We need not suppose that Ducasse is committed to any "episodic" view of pleasure. There is no reason why he cannot adopt the adverbial view of sensing here that, as we have seen in Chapter III, he does elsewhere, and hold that pleasure is to be construed as an adverb modifying an experiencing, not as a separate mental event or episode. "We are experiencing sweetly, . . . ly, . . . ly, and pleasant-ly." A thing can be said to "have" intrinsic value insofar as it has the capacity to cause in a sentient being an experiencing so modulated, though that same experiencing may be modulated in a great many other ways at the same time. Although such an analysis of value would be dispositional, it would be quite different from the dispositional view advocated by Ryle in which the experience of pleasure (unlike that of pain) is considered translatable into a set of behavioral dispositions which do not involve states of consciousness. Ducasse by using his adverbial techniques can avoid both the episodic and behavior-dispositional views of pleasure. To have intrinsic value is to have a disposition to cause in a sentient being a certain modulation of consciousness called "pleasure," a modulation which co-exists in the same mind with other modulations.

(d) Ducasse's reply to this point is quite unconvincing. What is at issue here is the basic question of fairness in distribution of pleasures, but Ducasse in his reply does not tell us how 'fairness' can be explicated without going outside his hedonistic framework. He might have taken the tack that everyone stands to gain in happiness in the long run if the *rule* of fairness is respected, but he simply assures us that no calculus and hence no comparisons are possible. It is interesting to notice that he writes in his notes: "2. Why is 'equal distribution' *better*? In what sense?"[29] but that he does not offer an answer to the questions so nicely put.

V

Having seen how Ducasse's discussion of liberal education illuminates his normative ethics, we now turn to a consideration of that part of his philosophy of education intended to be independent of his ethics. However, the chief difficulty, as we shall see, in Ducasse's philosophy of education is that he does not always make good on his promise to keep normative ethics (the relevant aspect of which he calls "wisdom") separate from philosophy of education.

Unlike philosophy of education, which has the semantic task we have described, *wisdom*, for Ducasse, consists in knowledge of what in given circumstances would on the whole be the best thing for a person with given equipment to do. To make a wise decision a person must (a) inform himself of the relevant empirical facts as completely as possible, (b) take stock of the equipment available to him, (c) consider the positive and negative values which could be generated by each of the courses of action found possible in the case, and (d) judge himself which course of action would on the whole be best, that is, which would probably generate more positive value and/or less negative value for the persons it affected. Since this perception is bound to be somewhat different in persons with different values, the final judgment cannot be made by one person for another. "What another may do is only to *enlighten* his judgment by pointing out to him particular existing circumstances, or particular probable objective consequences of one or another possible choice, or particular kinds of value those choices or their consequences would have, of which the person . . . *was not aware.*" [30]

In the light of this contrast between philosophy and wisdom, we can now examine his definition of the philosophy of education, wholly a semantical concern. According to his definition, the philosophy of education "consists in *making clear* what diverse factors educational decisions must take into account if they are to be wise decisions." [31] He emphasizes that the clarification of what kinds of facts are relevant is entirely different from the process of trying to discover or establish those facts. The latter is no part of the philosophy of education. [32]

Yet sometimes Ducasse defines philosophy of education in terms of the questions it attempts to answer and some of these questions appear to require wisdom and not merely philosophy in their answers. One of the fundamental questions of philosophy of education listed by Ducasse is the question of what it means to educate and how educating is related to instructing, indoctrinating and training, and this question is clearly semantical; however, other problems of philosophy of education he mentions cannot be purely semantical: Why educate? What is the nature of this being called Man, who is to be educated? Clearly answers to the last two questions must include empirical (e.g. psychological) facts and value commitments. Although Ducasse frequently emphasizes the difference between philosophy and wisdom, he forgets himself on occasion and presents as *philosophy* of education what should properly be called wisdom in education. Needless to say, there is no harm in offering wisdom in education; we need only recognize that the *grounds* for wisdom must be different from the grounds for philosophy. We can establish the meaning of key terms used in educational disputes without having to appeal to particular value commitments or psychological theories, but this is not possible if we are trying to establish a particular educational theory as *wise*. It follows that one can accept Ducasse's explication of key educational concepts (his philosophy of education strictly so called) while rejecting some or all of what he thinks constitutes wisdom in education. And, indeed, Ducasse's wisdom in education has not been without its critics. Perhaps the most notable of these critics have been students at Brown, an institution on which Ducasse's views have had enormous influence.

In 1945 Ducasse was chairman of a committee that formulated the aims
of liberal education and set the undergraduate curriculum at Brown.
Although the students in their thorough 1968 report on education at Brown
acknowledge that "one of the strongest influences" on them was "the spirit
of the Ducasse Report, that is the quest for the understanding of the funda-
mentals of education and for the creation of structures coherently designed
to carry out explicit aims," [33] they question, for example, the role that
"perspective" plays in Ducasse's conception of a liberal education:

If prejudice and narrowness prevent men from "having a choice," from "being aware of
alternatives," from "possessing perspective," then the freeing of men from prejudices
and narrownesses seems to be a worthwhile aim. Yet numerous questions arise. What is
the definition of prejudice or narrowness? How can a student be made to realize the
prejudices and narrownesses that are part of his make-up? Do these have to be determined and measured, and can a structured attempt at this be made? How can they be
communicated to the student so that he will wish to change them and one will not slip
into other prejudices and narrownesses? Does realizing them really free men from
them? Is it assumed that experiencing a curriculum based on the tasks outlined for a
liberal education will solve these problems? If we can all agree what constitutes prejudice and narrowness, and can agree on structures to eliminate the prejudices and
narrownesses, then we might agree with this conception of liberal education, but so far
this has not been done. [34]

They are also doubtful of the wisdom of Ducasse's belief that a liberal
education should arouse the love of intellectual exploration:

Should this really be a goal for the university? Whenever one speaks of arousing a love
as an aim, there seems to be the assumption that the love for that activity is un-
questionably good for all people. In this case we are not sure that this is so. It has often
been expressed that a life of intellectual exploration is not the only, nor even the best
way for one to spend his life. Moreover, the objection might also be raised that should
the love turn to consuming passion, it would only result in another kind of narrowness.
We would agree with Ducasse that the love of intellectual exploration may, in some
cases, be a desirable attitude and that it will be developed as the result of interactions
between students and professors, but we do not feel that it should be an institutional
aim for all students. [35]

After posing a number of other questions, the students conclude:

The final problem in the statement of aims of the Ducasse report is that we do not
believe that it has worked. Whether this is because the aims could not be tied easily and
logically to the principles of procedure that it outlined or that have been outlined to
follow it, or whether the structures did not function properly, we do not know.
Whether it is because the statement of aims is twenty-two years old and is outdated we
do not know. [36]

Doubtless on some of these points the Ducasse Report could be convincingly defended, and probably on other points Ducasse would have wished

to modify his views in the light of additional experience and important social changes; nonetheless these criticisms by students illustrate the sort of challenge that can be made to Ducasse's conception of wisdom in education.

VI

Since, for Ducasse, the chief business of philosophy of education is to give an account of the meaning of 'education', we must next consider how he defines 'education' — whether that education be wise or unwise.

> Education is activity of one or another particular kind A, by a person T (teacher); activity A being motivated by T's desire to cause in a person P (pupil) – who may or may not be the same person as T – a response of kind R, which T believes will immediately or eventually result in acquisition by P of some capacity C which T desires P to acquire; activity A being shaped by T's belief (i) That the existing circumstances are of a certain kind S; and (ii) That, under circumstances of kind S, activity of kind A by T would more or less probably cause or contribute to cause directly or indirectly in P acquisition of the desiderated capacity C.[37]

Ducasse frames this definition broadly enough to include self-education but narrowly enough to limit teachers to persons. In his lectures in the philosophy of education, however, Ducasse offers a still more inclusive definition of education.

> Education of an individual is development in him of some capacity or capacities; this resulting from sometimes his responses to experiences adventitiously or factitiously caused in him by his environment; and sometimes from spontaneous expression by him of the impulses of his nature, together with the experiencing of the consequences of his expressions of those impulses . . . The foregoing definition is broad enough to include *automatic* as well as *purposive* education; education by the *extra-human* as well as by the *human* environment; *self-education* as well as *education by others*; the education of *evil* capacities as well as of *good* ones; education by *response* as well as education by *initiative*; and education in adult life, as well as education in infancy, childhood, and youth.[38]

Unlike more recent analytical philosophers of education who believe it pointless and even seriously misleading to seek *the* definition of a key term and suggest that such terms have many meanings connected only by family resemblances, Ducasse deliberately makes his definition as inclusive as possible so as to have a genus within which he can distinguish species.

Accordingly, having given the generic meaning of education, Ducasse distinguishes the various species of the genus. He has two different but compatible ways of distinguishing the species of education. Sometimes he subdivides education according to the *method* used to develop capacities and other times he subdivides in terms of the different *kinds of capacities* which can be developed.

In the subdivision according to method Ducasse distinguishes between instruction, training and indoctrination. Instruction is the process that incorporates *information* (knowledge about facts, relations, rules, laws) into the mind.[39] Training is "the process of imparting to someone the *skill* to perform some operation or set of operations whether mental or physical, and whether acquisition of the skill is or is not accompanied by understanding of the principles on which the operations depend." [40] Finally, indoctrination is carried on mainly by psychological suggestion. Instruction differs from indoctrination in that it involves submission of evidence as indoctrination does not, and indoctrination "psychologically *adapts* the child to — as distinguished from only *informing him about* — the social context in which he lives." [41]

Ducasse's subdivision in terms of the kinds of capacities to be developed is based on a conception of the nature of man, a conception which he says is of the same general type as Plato's. Man's nature consists of a complex of capacities: (1) intellectual, (2) physical, (3) volitional, (4) social, (5) aesthetic, (6) moral, and (7) religious.

Intellectual education consists in giving the student surface knowledge of all areas and knowledge in depth of one area. But at least as important a part of intellectual education is the development of "the power of objective and careful observation and of precise and logically ordered formulation of what has been observed, and of any ideas one may have about it . . . the power of rigorous inference; practical grasp of the nature of experimental procedure; the habit of verification; the ability to read understandingly and critically; and development of the intellectual independence and initiative which consists so largely in the capacity to think of questions not before raised about matters already familiar." [42]

Since a man's body is a man's most useful domestic animal, *physical* education, Ducasse thinks, should do "for the body what the intelligent owner of a valuable horse would do for the horse." [43] Physical education establishes "physical habits conducive to health and to fitness of the body to do its work, and development of the versatility that renders the body quickly adaptable to the specialized physical tasks or situations which life may thrust upon it . . . [P]hysical education does not mean asceticism, but only restraint of bodily cravings or impulses within the limits compatible with health and bodily efficiency." [44]

Volitional education or education of the *will* consists in the "development of the capacity to make oneself do the things which one has the ability to do and desires to do. It is education in the overcoming of inertia, sloth, and procrastination; in perseverence, in firmness of purpose, in courage under difficulties, and in readiness to take pains and to take care." [45]

Social education or education in *social dexterity* consists in the development of "the ability to deal effectively with other human beings *as they are*, in the variety of relations one may have with them — the ability to make contact with them easily, to enlist their good will and cooperation, and to avoid antagonizing them." [46]

Aesthetic education Ducasse has discussed at length on many occasions because he thinks that it is a kind of education that is seriously neglected. Aesthetic education has two parts: the development of sensory discrimination and the development of emotional discrimination. To develop fine discrimination in sense impressions direct contact with the works of painters, sculptors, and musicians is necessary. Reading discourses on the technique or history of art, contrary to popular belief, does not develop such discrimination; such reading develops only the ability to *talk* about art. The development of emotional discrimination Ducasse interprets broadly to include the development of discrimination of moods, attitudes, longings, impulses, dispositions, aspirations, inclinations, aversions, all of which are felt but not intellectually analysed. [47] Such education of the feelings can be achieved through novels, poems, dramas, biographies. "The reader can project himself in imagination and, losing for the time being his own identity, he can gain vicariously many experiences which he could neither obtain nor afford in his objective life. Moreover, although the situations depicted in those literary works are lived through by the reader only in imagination, nevertheless the feelings, sentiments, moods, or attitudes thereby generated in him are not imaginary but quite real for the time being, and may constitute emotional insights genuinely novel to him." [48] Again Ducasse emphasizes that the reading of books or listening to lectures *about* the arts (in this case the literary arts) will not so educate the feelings.

Moral education is the development of the capacity to act out of duty with a sense of justice. *Religious* education or "education of the heart," as Ducasse conceives it, is distinct from moral education in that it develops a capacity to act not out of a sense of obligation or justice but out of free altruistic feeling for one's fellow man. The religiously educated man finds his greatest happiness in bringing happiness to others. Religious education does not mean instruction in religious texts or beliefs except where such instruction serves as a means to the cultivation of altruistic impulses.

VII

In addition to whatever faults the genus-species style of philosophical analysis may have in general, it should be noted that Ducasse's use of it in education has the fault that it does not preserve his fundamental distinction between philosophy of education and wisdom in education. Although his distinctions between instruction, training and indoctrination are based primarily on analysis of language facts, his account, described above, of the species of education according to the different capacities of man is plainly based largely on his empirical beliefs about the psychological make-up of human beings and his normative views on which of the myriad of human capacities *should* be developed to form "the complete man." Consequently, the former is philosophy of education strictly so called, while the latter is wisdom or would-be wisdom in education.

NOTES

[1] C.J. Ducasse, *Philosophy as a Science* (New York: Oskar Piest, 1941); *Nature, Mind and Death* (LaSalle, Ill.: Open Court Publishing Company, 1951), pp. 3–87; *Truth, Knowledge and Causation* (London: Routledge and Kegan Paul, 1968), pp. 238–55; "Liberalism in Ethics," *International Journal of Ethics* 35 (1925), 238–50.
[2] *Truth, Knowledge and Causation*, p. 244.
[3] *Ibid.*, p. 244.
[4] "Liberalism in Ethics," p. 248.
[5] C.J. Ducasse, *The Relation of Philosophy to General Education*, mimeographed, 1932, p. 6.
[6] C.J. Ducasse, "A 'Terminal' Course in Philosophy," *Journal of Higher Education* 24 (1953), 405.
[7] C.J. Ducasse, "Liberal Education and the College Curriculum," *Journal of Higher Education* 15 (1944), 4.
[8] *Ibid.*, p. 5.
[9] *Ibid.*
[10] *Ibid.*, pp. 5–6.
[11] *Ibid.*, p. 6.

[12] *Ibid.*, p. 7.
[13] *Ibid.*
[14] *Ibid.*, p. 9.
[15] *Ibid.*, p. 10.
[16] "Morality," Lecture Notes, p. 35. The italics in the notes are apparently not for emphasis and may have functioned perhaps as "eye-catchers" for Professor Ducasse as he lectured.
[17] *Ibid.*, p. 32.
[18] *Ibid.*, p. 35.
[19] *Ibid.*, p. 36.
[20] C.J. Ducasse, "What Can Philosophy Contribute to Educational Theory?" *Harvard Educational Review* 28 (1958), 294–96.
[21] C.J. Ducasse, *Art, The Critics, and You* (New York: Hafner Publishing Company, 1948), pp. 131–50.
[22] "Morality," Lecture Notes, pp. 34–35.
[23] *Ibid.*, p. 39.
[24] *Ibid.*, p. 41.
[25] *Ibid.*, p. 42.
[26] Cf. C.J. Ducasse, "Intrinsic Value," *Philosophy and Phenomenological Research* 28 (1968), 410–12.
[27] "Morality," Lecture Notes, p. 34. Cf. C.J. Ducasse, *The Philosophy of Art* (New York: Dover Publications, 1966; originally published in 1929), p. 195 fn.
[28] "Morality," Lecture Notes, p. 42.
[29] "Morality," Lecture Notes, p. 34.
[30] "On the Function and Nature of the Philosophy of Education," *Harvard Educational Review* 26 (1956), 111.
[31] *Ibid.*, p. 109.
[32] *Ibid.*, p. 105.
[33] Ira Magaziner *et al.*, "Draft of a Working Paper for Education at Brown University," mimeographed, 1968, p. 92.
[34] *Ibid.*, p. 89.
[35] *Ibid.*, pp. 89–90.
[36] *Ibid.*, p. 91.
[37] "On the Function and Nature of the Philosophy of Education," p. 108.
[38] "What Education is, in the most inclusive sense," Section 1, Chapter 4, Lecture Notes for Philosophy of Education course (Philos. 54 or 154) given in 1952 and for some years before and after, pp. 4.1,5.
[39] "What Can Philosophy Contribute to Educational Theory," p. 287.
[40] *Ibid.*
[41] *Ibid.*, pp. 287–88.
[42] *Ibid.*, p. 291.
[43] *Ibid.*, p. 292.
[44] *Ibid.*
[45] *Ibid.*, p. 293.
[46] *Ibid.*, p. 292.
[47] "Are the Humanities Worth Their Keep? ", *American Scholar* 6 (1937), 461.
[48] "What Can Philosophy Contribute to Educational Theory?" p. 293.

CHAPTER VIII

AESTHETICS

Although Ducasse's work on the problems of metaphysics and epistemology undoubtedly has more fundamental significance, his aesthetics has had far more popular appeal. *The Philosophy of Art* has been a standard work ever since its original publication in 1929,[1] and the reprinting of an essay by Ducasse in John Hospers' recent *Artistic Expression*[2] is an indication of Ducasse's secure standing in the field.

The large audience Ducasse's aesthetics has had for many years has been rightly attracted to two aspects of his work: (1) his emotionalist view of the work of art, the aesthetic attitude, and the aesthetic object, and (2) his relativistic view of the standards of artistic criticism. In this chapter we shall discuss, in turn, these aspects of his philosophy of art, indicating how most of the major criticisms of his views can be succesfully rebutted. We shall also indicate how an awareness of the relations between his aesthetics and other parts of his philosophy usually strengthens the case for his aesthetics but sometimes shows that modifications are called for.

I

For Ducasse,[3] art is not a quality of things but an activity of man, and, contrary to popular belief, the activity of art is not aimed at the creation of beauty. There is no essential connection between beauty and art; each can exist without the other.

There are many ugly objects which are undeniably works of art. In speaking of ugly art it is not art which gives a pleasing (i.e. beautiful) representation of an ugly or painful subject which Ducasse is referring to. Ugly art he takes to be art in the aesthetic contemplation of which we get displeasure. Naturally such art is not much noticed or purchased, for most buyers of art want beauty. Beauty is thus almost a condition of the social visibility of a work of art, but it is not a condition of the existence of one. Ugly art, though easily overlooked, nevertheless exists in great quantities.

There are also many beautiful objects, both products of human effort and products of nature, which are not works of art. Someone who blows on a window pane in winter causing beautiful crystals to be formed cannot be considered an artist, and a beautiful flower is not a work of art.

Although every artist appears to derive pleasure from whatever success he has in his activity, this pleasure is not to be confused with the experience of beauty. The pleasure of success has no special connection with art. Neither is the skill exhibited in a work of art something which is necessarily beautiful to the spectator. If the spectator already happens to value the object, he may find additional pleasure in the contemplation of the skill which he supposes was required to produce it. But if he finds the object unpleasant, he will probably feel indignation at the misuse of skill.

Art, instead of being an activity aimed at the creation of beauty, is an activity aimed at objective self-expression. The artist's aim is to give adequate embodiment in words, lines, colors, or what not, to some particular and probably nameless feeling or emotion that possessed him. This objectification of the artist's feeling must be conscious or critically controlled to distinguish it from such expressive activities as yawning. To say that expression of feeling is objective is to say that something has been created such that in contemplation that thing yields back the feeling of which it was the attempted expression. Such objective self-expression usually requires trials and errors. Every trial at the moment it occurs is itself blind as to whether or not it has achieved objectivity of expression. Consciousness of this has to be gained by contemplation of the product of the trial, and critical judgment of it, i.e. judgment either that it does, or does not, truly mirror back the inner state to which it was intended to give expression. Although the mirroring-back of feeling is not itself an end, it is proof of the success of an attempt at objective expression.

A question may be raised concerning the supposition that the feeling ultimately expressed can be precisely the same as the feeling originally intended for expression. According to Ducasse, the qualitative identity of the feeling does not change, but there is a gain in the clarity with which we experience it. The clarification of feeling through expression in art is like the clarification of meaning. One starts with "feeling something" just as one starts with "having something to say" or "being ready to formulate something," and this feeling or meaning, as the case may be, becomes clarified without losing its identity. Although there is pleasurable exaltation in the act of creative expression, the clarity comes, not from this act, but from the contemplation of its results; in such contemplation we apprehend clearly what it was we were attempting to express. This clearness as to what we felt itself contributes a new fact, as a result of which new feelings may occur to us which otherwise would not. Usually the feeling which the work of art finally comes to embody is born in the artists only gradually, its growth being dependent on the process of its own objectification. Ducasse's emotionalist theory of art thus takes full account of the influence of medium in the development of feeling.

In the trial-and-error artistic process, the artist is free to correct the self that is expressed instead of correcting the product of the attempted objectification. When confronted clearly with the objectification of a self, he may wish to disown that self in favor of a corrected self. Self-exhibition to oneself makes possible self-editing.

Contrary to Tolstoi, Ducasse does not believe that the *transmission* of feeling to others is part of the pure art-impulse. For Ducasse, language is not *essentially* communicative, though of course it can be used as an instrument of communication or cooperation. Language is merely the intentional, external expression of an inner psychical state. Accordingly, art is the language of feeling without being essentially communicative; objective self-expression need not be accompanied by successful communication. However, just as one may buy fancy pajamas simply became one likes them, and yet display them if occasion suggests, so may the artist have created his work solely because he felt inwardly compelled to do so, and yet eventually show it to others when an occasion arises that encourages self-display. That products of art are capable of communicating feeling and are at times so used does not mean that they occurred as a result of the intention to do so.

The art impulse must be distinguished from the practical impulse as well as from the impulse to communicate. Art as such is never born except of the pure art impulse, although other impulses may provide a stage on which to perform that the art impulse could not itself have afforded. An author, for example, may be moved to write by his need to make a living. This need, however, leaves the writer free in many respects. Art is possible when the imposed limitations are not so cramping as to preclude all initiative; and it actually begins only when the limitations are not only understood and accepted, but are perceived as definite and positive opportunities for free self-expression.

Unfortunately, Ducasse's definition of a work of art as critically controlled, objective expression of feeling is easily misunderstood. Since it is intentionalistic Ducasse's proposed definition may be thought to possess the familiar difficulties associated with the appeal to the artist's intentions in aesthetics and art criticism. It will be asked how we can know what the artist's intention was in many cases. If we use an intentionalistic definition of art and are not in a position to know the artist's intention, it will be asked why we are not forced to the absurd conclusion that we do not know whether many magnificent paintings are works of art.

These and other familiar difficulties with intentionalistic definition are avoided by virtue of Ducasse's crucial distinction between a work of art and an aesthetic object. To know whether an object is a work of art we must know what sort of process brought it into being, but to know something to be an aesthetic object no knowledge of how it came into existence is necessary. An aesthetic object is simply the content of attention in aesthetic contemplation. Within the aesthetic attitude, anything can become an aesthetic object, whether it be the product of natural forces, of the human practical impulse or of the art-impulse. The origin of an aesthetic object is irrelevant to its contemplation. We can with complete consistency judge something to be a genuine work of art (i.e. the objectification of the feeling of the artist) and at the same time judge that when that work of art is aesthetically contemplated the aesthetic object is unsatisfactory by our standards of criticism. We can equally consistently judge an object to be an extremely inadequate expression of the feeling of the artist (i.e. not a work of art) and at the same time judge the object when aesthetically contemplated to be an entirely satisfactory aesthetic object. Much misunderstanding of Ducasse can be avoided if this distinction between his intentionalistic definition of a work of art and his attitudinal definition of an aesthetic object is kept in mind.

Is Ducasse's theory able to meet the familiar criticisms of expressionist theories of art? One question frequently asked is whether the autobiographical reports of artists support the view that artists are trying to objectify feelings which possess them. Does the writer of a tragedy have tragic emotions while he is expressing tragic emotions in his writings? Could he even write competently if he experienced such emotions while writing? Feelings of some kind accompany almost any human activity whether it be sweeping the floor, arguing with one's neighbors or working on a mathematical proof, but is the artistic process especially emotional? Mediocre artists often suffer agonies of creation, while many superb artists are no more emotional while engaged in artistic expression than they are in any kind of work requiring concentration.

In his recent work in aesthetics Ducasse has suggested how his theory can meet this familiar objection to the expressionist theory. The artist expressing sadness, he says, "need not at all — and preferably should not — himself *be* sad at the time . . ." [4] The role of *feeling images* (as distinct from feelings themselves) in artistic expression must be understood. A work of art, in Ducasse's recent formulation, is intended to evoke, not feelings, but *feeling images*, and the artist himself need have only feeling images to create something which will evoke feeling images. To say that an artist objectively expresses feelings is to say that he has certain images and creates something the contemplation of which yields back the feeling images he had while creating it. An artist, in other words, can objectively express a feeling of which he has an image but which he does not experience as such. [5]

A second question often asked by critics of the expressionist theory is what can it possibly mean to put emotion into a work by a process of catharsis. They find puzzling the notion of the transfer of feeling from the mind of the artist to the work of art as if a feeling were like paint being transferred from a brush to a canvas. Feelings, these critics insist, cannot be ejected out of the mind and made to reside in artistic materials.

Ducasse's conception of artistic expression, it should be noted, does not entail such mysterious catharsis and transfer. Ducasse believes that materials such as colors and sounds *naturally* evoke feeling images in those contemplating them aesthetically. Since the materials have this capacity to evoke feeling images without anything being put into them by artists, the artist's job is not to eject feeling in catharsis but to select, combine and organize materials which already evoke feeling images.

A question may also be raised regarding the relation between this definition of art and Ducasse's definitions of other key terms in philosophical discourse. As we shall see in our final chapter, in his discussion of 'real', Ducasse defends the legitimacy of the various definitions that have been given in the history of ontology, yet in aesthetics many definitions of fine art have been offered which Ducasse wishes flatly to reject. He rejects, for example, Tolstoi's view that communication of feeling is an essential part of art. He argues that there can be genuine art when there is no possibility or desire of communication. Indeed, Ducasse has made it amply clear that there is an important sense of 'art' according to which art is independent of the possibility of communication. The question is not whether this is an important sense of the term, it is whether this is the *only* legitimate sense.

Furthermore, in the field of philosophy of religion where narrow, monotheistic definitions abound, Ducasse proposes a functional and extremely inclusive definition of religion, but, strangely, he considers such definitional inclusiveness inappropriate in aesthetics. Although willing to consider humanism a religion, he is unwilling to consider either critically controlled transmission of feeling or the critical control of feeling aimed at beauty to be pure art.

Without question, there is much value in the demonstration that there is a sense of 'art' according to which art is independent of such traditional associations as with communication and with beauty. However, once the legitimacy of that sense has been established it seems as illegitimate to restrict the meaning of 'art' to that sense as it would be to restrict the meaning of 'religion' to the varieties of monotheism.

Perhaps a definition of fine art comparable to Ducasse's definition of religion would be: any artifact primarily intended for aesthetic consideration.[6] Such a definition would be compatible with Ducasse's unrestrictive view of definition without committing him to the view, popular with some aestheticians, that no set of necessary and sufficient conditions (i.e. no true definition) of art can be given.

II

In speaking of art as the objective expression of feeling, Ducasse explains that objectivity of expression consists in the reflecting back in *contemplation* of the feelings of which the work was the attempted expression. An understanding of the nature of this contemplation (i.e. the taking of the aesthetic attitude) is crucial not only to the understanding of his definition of art but also to the understanding of his entire aesthetics.

Aesthetic contemplation, according to Ducasse, is an attitude of directed but contentless receptiveness, a "listening" or "looking" with our capacity for feeling, a throwing of oneself open to the feeling import of an object. It should be noticed that there is no special emotion present in the aesthetic attitude. The aesthetic attitude consists in a certain kind of receptivity, but the receptivity to feelings is not itself a feeling any more than a particular focus of a camera is itself a special photograph.

Attention, though presupposed by aesthetic contemplation, must be distinguished from it. We direct our attention *to* the qualities (e.g. colors, sounds) and design relationships of an object, but we so direct our attention *for* the feeling import of those qualities to which we make ourselves receptive. Ducasse's expression theory does not entail ignoring the qualities of the object in the interest of indulgence in the feelings it may arouse. On the contrary, he insists that only if there is painstaking attention to such qualities are we in a position to receive all the feeling import of the object. If we are "listening" for the feeling import of the qualities of an object and those qualities are badly blurred or unnoticed because our attention is not sharply focused, we will be unable to find that feeling import regardless of how receptive to it we may be. Ducasse agrees with those who say that aesthetic contemplation is sustained, discriminating, concentrated attention to the qualities and formal relationships of an object; he disagrees only when it is contended that contemplation consists *only* in such attention; such attention when present in aesthetic contemplation is *for* the feeling import of those qualities just as attention *to* words on a page is *for* their meanings.

In speaking of receptivity to feeling import (i.e. "ecpathy"), Ducasse is not postulating a special, aesthetic sense, a sixth sense, any more than he postulates a sixth sense in speaking of being open to the meanings of words (in "lectical" contemplation). To be receptive to the feeling import of the qualities of an object is not to have a sixth sense but instead to let those qualities arouse feeling images in the contemplator and to shut out all other effects which those qualities might have on his mind. Sustained, discriminating attention to the qualities of an object can have various effects on our consciousness; such attention may move us to action; it may bring meaning to mind; it may encourage us to compare and classify the qualities; and so on. Aesthetic contemplation is present insofar as we can be receptive to feeling images aroused by such attention to qualities and can prevent such attention from having other effects on our mind. Such selective reception presupposing complete attention to qualities can hardly be called a new sense.

Also it should be borne in mind that the feeling images which we have in aesthetic contemplation are not themselves attended to. Far from advocating an emotional revery or debauch in which we attend to our own feelings, Ducasse points out that to attend to one's aesthetic feelings or feeling images is, in fact, to cease having those feelings since the feelings can be had only by attending closely to the qualities of the object. An ordinary emotion like anger is usually felt as *in us*, and as sensualists finding sense pleasure in, for example, tasting wine we focus our attention on our sensations as such, but all aesthetic feelings are apprehended not as in us but as emotional qualities of the object toward which our attention is directed; in aesthetic contemplation our *attention* is on, say, the sounds of a piece of music, while our *interest* is in the feeling images which they arouse in consciousness. Furthermore, *having* but not attending to such feeling images is an end-in-itself for one engaged in aesthetic contemplation.

It may appear that in an expression theory of art like Ducasse's with its constant reference to feelings there is the assumption that aesthetic contemplation is characterized by extraordinary emotional intensity. However, Ducasse's claim that aesthetic contemplation consists in the selective reception of feeling images does not imply that aesthetic experience is accompanied by any more emotional intensity than other kinds of experience which require concentrated attention. Since it is only feeling *images*, and not feelings themselves, which are received, they may be received in great numbers without emotional intensity out of the ordinary. Analogously, in reading we understand the beliefs expressed without actually adopting those beliefs; if we could not do so, reading the morning newspaper would be a traumatic experience indeed.

It may also appear that in an emotionalist theory of art aesthetic contemplation is shamefully easy since all we do is let our feelings go and we need not pay close attention to the complex of qualities and formal relationships in the object. Yet, on the contrary, it is probably much more difficult to develop the ability to notice subtle differences between feeling images than to develop, for example, the ability to recognize pitch. There is nothing especially easy about noticing the difference between the feeling image aroused by one shade of red and the feeling image aroused by a slightly different shade. Each shade of color, bit of line, tone or design pattern has its individual feeling-tang or emotional taste. Human feelings are endlessly various, though only a very few, such as love, fear and anger have been named. The vast majority of these feelings are of lower intensity than the so-called passions, do not last as long and do not recur as often; but they are no less real for their lower intensity and frequency. Although our practical interests encourage us to ignore these subtle differences of feeling, aesthetic contemplation demands that these emotional subtleties be noticed.

Probably Ducasse's conception of the aesthetic attitude is not as different from other conceptions as it seems. Other aestheticians have said that aesthetic contemplation is nothing more than sustained, concentrated attention to an object in which there is no ulterior purpose and the attention is an end in itself. Such a *negative* characterization of the aesthetic attitude Ducasse agrees with. Indeed, he wishes to make the negative characterization even more thorough than it usually is; he wishes carefully to exclude from the aesthetic attitude any *cognitive* ulterior interest; care must be taken to avoid confusing concentrated attention with only a cognitive ulterior purpose with concentrated attention in which such a cognitive purpose is excluded along with other ulterior interests. If we attend to an object with no practical interest but with an interest in classifying it, comparing it, or using it to satisfy a perhaps unformulated curiosity, we are not attending to it with an aesthetic attitude, but rather with a cognitive attitude. A completely thorough negative characterization will exclude such a cognitive, ulterior purpose as well as other purposes. However, once this cognitive ulterior purpose has been eliminated, what remains in contemplation? To give Ducasse's *positive* characterization of the aesthetic attitude is nothing more than to describe what remains after all ulterior purposes, including the cognitive, have been excluded. Ducasse, in other words, accepts the most thorough exclusion of ulterior purposes, and claims that what remains should not be bare attention without interest, but instead attention with the only interest that can be entirely internal to the attention, namely, an interest in the object's feeling import. Similarly, Ducasse accepts the doctrine of psychical distance but says that it amounts to no more than the *absence* of practical relations between ourselves and the object and does not go on to indicate that the positive character of the aesthetic attitude consists in receptivity to feeling import.[7]

Finally, the difference between the aesthetic attitude and empathy should be noted, since in an emotionalist theory of art there is a temptation to confuse them. To be receptive to the feeling import of an object is not to empathize with it. Empathy, Ducasse says, is the non-discursive, intuitive process by which we perceive or imagine conscious doings and undergoings in others; in empathy we perceive or imagine these doings and undergoings with the same immediacy as that with which we intuit our own doings and undergoings. But to perceive or imagine the action of others is one thing and

to contemplate such action aesthetically is another. Aesthetic contemplation and empathy can exist independently of one another. There can be
aesthetic contemplation of colors, tastes, odors, shapes, and lines without
empathy; and empathy can be used to predict the future movements of a
dangerous man without aesthetic contemplation of his action.

Although empathy and aesthetic contemplation are distinct, there is an
important connection between them: aesthetic contemplation presupposes
empathy where the object of aesthetic contemplation is human action since
empathy is precisely the process by which that sort of action is put before
aesthetic contemplation. We cannot aesthetically contemplate human action
without first perceiving the conscious doings and undergoings of the agents
involved. However, we must not allow this important connection between
empathy and aesthetic contemplation to mislead us into an identification of
the two.

III

An aesthetic object is defined by Ducasse as any content of contemplative
attention, whether the object attended to is a work of art or a natural
object. The aesthetic object and the physical object need not be the same.
When we speak of contemplating a line, for example, we mean the perceptual or phenomenal line, and not the line as physics regards it. Furthermore, an aesthetic object usually consists of much more than the content of
sense observation; much of the content of attention is not sensuous but
imaginal and *conceptual.*

Emotionalist theories of art are often thought to underestimate or ignore
entirely the role of meaning in aesthetic experience. However, Ducasse has
repeatedly insisted that meanings are often crucial parts of the content of
aesthetic contemplation. When the object of aesthetic contemplation
contains meanings, we are not gaining an understanding of those meanings
but are contemplating aesthetically something which we have already understood. Aesthetic contemplation always has as its objects things presented to
it by the senses, by empathy, or by the understanding; aesthetic contemplation is an activity which presupposes, but is over and above, such presentation. Ducasse would be the first to agree that, for example, the words of a
novel have meaning import; it may take many hours of laborious interpretation to discover that meaning import; but such meaning import becomes
part of the *aesthetic* import only when those meanings are contemplated for

their feeling import *after* the interpretation of meaning has been finished. More complicated works of art must be seen, heard or read many times before their meaning import has been grasped and aesthetic contemplation can legitimately begin.

Nor does Ducasse exclude thoughts from the content of aesthetic contemplation. Most of the feelings with which drama deals, for example, can be expressed only in an object consisting of some scheme of human relationship, and human relationships can be presented to consciousness only by being thought or meant through perceptual facts. Aesthetic contemplation of such human relationships is an activity which presupposes representation in thought, but is an activity over and above such representation.

Not only does Ducasse have a place for meanings in the content of aesthetic contemplation, he also has a place for symbolization. Great care must be taken, however, to understand the very special sense in which Ducasse speaks of symbolization. The aesthetic object, he says, is the natural, immediate, and unique symbol of an aesthetic feeling. The symbolizing of aesthetic feelings by aesthetic objects is not ultimately arbitrary and conventional, as in the *logical* symbolizing of meanings by words. One can make a given word mean what one pleases by simply laying down a definition or stipulation, but one cannot make a given object the aesthetic symbol of any feeling one pleases. The import of aesthetic feeling which a given aesthetic object has for a given person at a given time is a bare matter of psychological fact. Such facts are not immutable but they cannot be changed simply by laying down a stipulation. The changes that occur in the feeling-import of an aesthetic object for a person are psychological effects of experiences of various sorts. Associations, of course, affect the feeling experienced, and are variable, but associations are *internal* to the aesthetic object; when the associations of some entity change, the aesthetic object (consisting as it does of the entity and its associations) itself has changed.

Since in aesthetic symbolization arbitrary stipulation plays no role, in the language of feeling there is nothing corresponding to a definition in the language of meaning; in the language of feeling no symbol is ever completely interchangeable with any other.

For Ducasse to speak of art as a language in which symbolization is without convention and stipulation may seem odd. If we are to understand how Ducasse can explain aesthetic objects in terms of a language of feeling, we must first understand Ducasse's distinctive conception of language.

Language, he says, is an intentional, external expression of an inner psychical state. It should be noted that, for Ducasse, communication is not an essential part of language. Since convention and stipulation are primarily aids to communication, not to expression, it is not so strange that Ducasse speaks of art as a language without conventions. For Ducasse to say that an aesthetic object naturally and uniquely symbolizes certain feelings is to say that an aesthetic object arouses certain feeling images and not others, and that it came to arouse those feeling images not from stipulation but from physical and psychological causes, and finally that no other aesthetic object can arouse precisely the same feeling images. To speak of art in general as a language of feeling is to indicate that we have an indefinitely large vocabulary of possible aesthetic objects with which to express the particular feelings we may wish to express.

It may appear odd to insist that an aesthetic object always symbolizes certain feelings and no others in the face of the well-known fact that different people react to a work of art differently, and the same person may react differently at different times. First, it should be noticed that Ducasse says that the aesthetic object, not the work of art or natural object, symbolizes feeling uniquely. The aesthetic object, it will be recalled, is simply the content of aesthetic contemplation, and *internal* to that content are associations of all kinds. If two people have different feeling images when they gaze at the same painting (the same work of art) or at the same mountain range (the same natural object), they may, because of associations, be contemplating quite different aesthetic objects, aesthetic objects which consequently symbolize different feelings. The same person may find different symbolization of feeling at different times in the same work of art or natural object; his emotional nature, understanding, or information may significantly change between acts of contemplation, leading to a new aesthetic object and different feeling images.

While the variability of feeling import is seldom denied, many are concerned about the implications of such variability for the objectivity of aesthetic experience. A single, identifiable, permanent object with stable qualities is demanded. Feeling qualities, it is insisted, must belong to such an object if we are not to be lost in a subjectivism in which an aesthetic object can be identified with anything experienced by almost anyone under almost any conditions.

Ducasse is well aware of these epistemological and metaphysical questions.

Indeed, as we have seen in earlier chapters, he has devoted no small part of his philosophical writing to this and related issues. In formidable detail he has argued for a "non-messenger" form of realism though he of course cannot repeat all those arguments in discussing issues in aesthetics.

In his realism in aesthetics, Ducasse holds that music, for example, cannot be said to be vigorous and forceful *in itself*; it can be vigorous and forceful only in the sense in which quinine can be said to be bitter even when nobody is tasting it; 'bitter' being not the name of a taste-sensation but of a *capacity* – the capacity to cause the particular taste-sensation named "bitter taste" whenever the quinine is put on the tongue of a normal human being. Music which is not heard is vigorous and forceful only in the sense that it has the capacity to cause feeling images of vigor and forcefulness in a human being if and when he hears it and his interest is aesthetic, and not practical or inquisitive.

To some this appears tantamount to saying that music is unreal, a mere happening in the mind. However, as we have seen, Ducasse has worked out a theory of objective reference and consequently sees no reason why the distinction between the objective and the subjective cannot be preserved within a realistic framework. Ducasse is not denying the crucial difference between using a work of art to engage in revery and directing sustained, discriminating attention to the qualities of the object. He is merely insisting that that distinction can be preserved without saying that some perception is perception of qualities the object has in itself; the distinction can be made in terms of the different kinds of dispositions or capacities, the different ways in which attention can be directed, and the different interests one can have in such attention. Ducasse insists as adamantly as anyone that while one is engaged in aesthetic contemplation the feelings are apprehended *as qualities of the object*, not as processes in the contemplator; if feelings stop being apprehended as qualities of the object, aesthetic contemplation has stopped and non-aesthetic activity has begun. There is a difference between, for example, evoking terror and expressing it. A snake may evoke terror without expressing it. This fact is not in dispute. The question is what is the status of the object when we are not actually engaged in aesthetic con-templation but are instead explaining such contemplation and its object. When explaining aesthetic contemplation, Ducasse says, we are fully aware of the fact that the feeling is experienced by the subject. From such an explanatory standpoint there is nothing mysterious about a dispositional account of the aesthetic object. Confusions occur only when those engaged in aesthetic contemplation are mistakenly asked to adopt simultaneously an explanatory standpoint which is psychologically incompatible with the activity of aesthetic contemplation. Ducasse never asks that these two standpoints be taken simultaneously. He considers both standpoints essential — one is essential to the actual engagement in aesthetic contemplation and the other is essential to the attempt to understand the status of the object of such contemplation.

Moreover, it may be objected that Ducasse's emotionalist view of the aesthetic object does not do justice to the considerable merits of the formalist theory of art. To explain the aesthetic object entirely in terms of feeling seems to ignore the purely formal aesthetic values the object may have.

To be sure, Ducasse's vehement and witty attacks on the excesses of formalism give the impression that he ignores the merits of formalism. However, Ducasse's invective was designed merely to counteract the fashion of extreme formalism in aesthetic criticism at the time he was writing. If the more technical discussions in which he is not concerned with counteracting fashion are carefully read, it is clear that Ducasse appreciates the truths of formalism and incorporates those truths into his emotionalism. Repeatedly Ducasse insists that he does not wish to exclude from aesthetic experience formal relationships such as those between lines or sounds nor does he wish to exclude color qualities. According to Ducasse, each and every formal relationship, sound or color has a distinctive feeling import. He often speaks, for example, of the feeling of a shade of blue. Everything which the formalist includes in the aesthetic object Ducasse also includes but includes as something attended to for its feeling import. The only formalism to which Ducasse objects is that formalism which insists that such "surface" qualities *independent of their feeling import* can be considered part of the aesthetic object.

Although some may think it strange to suppose that mere formal relationships or colors independent of their associations with life situations can express feelings, Ducasse argues that such feeling import is simply overlooked because most of us are not in the habit of taking the aesthetic attitude toward formal relationships and colors and also because these millions of distinct feelings lack names (only feelings of great practical importance acquire names).

Does such a doctrine interpret feeling so broadly as to make the emotionalist theory vacuous? Many aestheticians have supposed that there is no way of avoiding the crucial difference between surface qualities and expressive qualities, and to say, as Ducasse does, that all surface qualities involve feeling is merely to obscure the distinction by using the term feeling loosely.

However, Ducasse is able to preserve the distinction between "surface" and "expressiveness" within his emotionalist theory by distinguishing different *sources* of feeling import. For example, there is an important difference between the feeling import of a certain shade of blue and the feeling import of weeping on stage, but the difference is one of source; if we are not engaged in aesthetic contemplation and are instead *explaining* aesthetic experience, we notice that the feeling image evoked by the shade of blue exists independent of any associations whereas the feeling images evoked by the weeping are caused by associations. The difference is not between feeling and something other than feeling but between different sources of experiences that are equally genuine feeling images.

IV

The most widely known part of Ducasse's aesthetics in his attack on art criticism in which he advises consumers of art to refuse to let themselves be awed or bluffed by the impressive but aesthetically irrelevant learning of the so-called authorities. In certain respects one can legitimately say a work is good or bad without knowing anything about its date, its author, history, or technique. Ducasse denies that there is a fundamental difference in this respect between judgment of the aroma of a cigar and judgment of the merits of music, painting or literature. In order to judge a cigar's aroma one does not need to know where the tobacco was cured, and similarly in the judgment of art, Ducasse thinks, the technical information provided by critics is usually irrelevant and merely a disguised attempt to intimidate the public into adopting the likes and dislikes of the critic.

Nevertheless Ducasse readily admits that scholarly investigation of art has a justification. Minute historical studies are genuine manifestations of the scientific spirit and are self-justifying to those who carry them on and to others curious about such facts. Such studies have considerable intrinsic value to all those who love knowledge for its own sake. Ducasse is merely pointing out that, for the most part, such scholarly knowledge is useless for the purposes of both enjoyment and evaluation of art.

In a literary work, for example, historical information has importance for appreciation or evaluation only to the extent that such information is needed to enable us to understand the statements we encounter in it — to the extent needed to understand allusions, archaic words, the nature of the customs and beliefs of the place and time the book is about, and so on. But unfortunately scholarly critics often are carried away by their expertise and become convinced that every scrap of historical and scientific information they may find is somehow relevant to appreciation and evaluation. To be capable of aesthetic appreciation is one thing; to be able to discuss a work's history and technique is another. Neither capacity entails the other. Aesthetic sensitivity, Ducasse says, grows from firsthand acquaintance with a variety of works of art, not from lectures and readings in history and technique. Contrary to popular belief, technical information instead of increasing the capacity for aesthetic appreciation often tends to inhibit and displace that capacity. The story writer who reads a story is conscious less of the story than of the literary devices; the archeologist who digs up statues may be less capable of responding to the statues aesthetically than one of the laborers hired to do the digging.

It is true that in appreciation and evaluation we need to know *in practice* how to recognize whether, for example, a poem is a sonnet or a piece of music is a sonata, but we do not, as many scholars imply, need to know *discursively* what a sonnet or sonata is, that is, we need not be capable of listing all the defining characters of sonnets and sonatas.

Moreover, it should be kept in mind that the fact that a given work of art is considered good of its kind by scholars does not bear on the aesthetic evaluation of the work because something (e.g. a perfect forgery) can be good of its kind without being good.

Having clarified the difference between scholarly investigation and aesthetic evaluation, Ducasse discusses the nature and basis of such evaluations. In evaluation the critic is determining whether a given work possesses this or that property which the critic regards as a good or bad one for a work of that kind to possess. Such properties constitute the critic's standard of criticism. The difference between judgments made by a trained critic and those made by an unsophisticated consumer of art is that the critic traces his evaluation to specific features that make it for him predominantly pleasing or displeasing, whereas the amateur is pleased or displeased without knowing which are the features that cause his pleasure or displeasure.

Unfortunately, the critic's ability to trace the causes of his pleasure or displeasure is often confused with an ability to prove or present evidence for his judgment. The critic, in fact, has no more evidence for his judgment than the unsophisticated consumer; this becomes obvious when the critic is asked why he thinks a work of art should have or not have that property. Every attempt by the critic to justify such a standard of criticism must, Ducasse says, end in questionbegging epithets. There is in the end nothing the critic can say, except that that property interests *him*; there is no such thing as *objective* goodness or badness of taste.

Instead of there being one objective standard of criticism there are an indefinite number of relative standards. Ducasse discusses several such standards without suggesting that his list is exhaustive. Among the standards by which a work of art or aesthetic object may be judged are: (1) the success of the attempt at self-expression, (2) signability of the work of art by its creator (i.e. the creator's willingness to *own* the feeling objectified), (3) signability of the work of art by its beholder, (4) capacity to transmit the artist's feelings to others, (5) beauty, and (6) capacity to do moral good. There is no need for us to explain here the special features of each of these standards. The chief point being made by Ducasse is simply that none of these well known standards or any others can be objectively defended or criticized.[8]

There are of course a formidable number of objections to such a relativistic view of aesthetic judgment, and Ducasse has taken pains to meet these objections.

First, it may be supposed that Ducasse is defending nihilism and anarchy in art criticism. It may seem that Ducasse is encouraging people to judge a work by, for example, how hard it makes them laugh instead of by more relevant standards; he may seem to be encouraging aesthetic irresponsibility. However, Ducasse is actually not encouraging carelessness and irresponsibility. Although he holds that one's standard of criticism cannot be defended against other standards, he recognizes that a given person with given tastes should judge carefully in accordance with those tastes; he should know what he likes. If someone bases his judgment of a design of a new house on his first reaction after seeing the drawings, he will probably be unhappy with the house after it is built; he needs to examine carefully his aesthetic pleasures in the past and to make rough inductive generalizations; he needs to know the principles which govern his own tastes so that he can predict (assuming his tastes do not change) what he will like in the future and thus avoid disappointment. The relativity of standards does not imply that an individual, who wishes to get all the aesthetic pleasure he can, does not have to know rules and theories concerning what a painting or other work of art must or must not be if it is to give him (with his peculiar tastes) aesthetic pleasure. Ducasse is not saying that those who are irresponsible in their aesthetic judgment are no worse off than connoisseurs. The latter have a capacity to find pleasure and avoid disappointment that the former lack, but the value of this capacity *presupposes* a particular standard of criticism and does not constitute proof of such a standard.

A second objection to aesthetic relativism is that it overlooks the objective standard of *sensitivity*. Ducasse recognizes that some persons are objectively more sensitive in the sense that they are able to get pleasure or displeasure from differences in an object that, to other persons, make no difference. It should be borne in mind, however, that such sensitivity, while it makes possible aesthetic pleasures which others cannot experience, also makes possible displeasure which others cannot experience. More important, it must be borne in mind that sensitivity may with equally good reason be described as progress or perversion, depending on whether we think the pleasures experienced aesthetically good or bad. Although sensitivity makes possible aesthetic pleasures and displeasures denied to others, it does not objectively prove that what is made available is aesthetically good or bad.

A third objection to aesthetic relativism is that, although some standards suggested by critics may be grossly inadequate, there are a number of standards which appear to withstand skepticism remarkably well. Unity, complexity and intensity are sometimes proposed as such standards. Ducasse would have no objection to calling these "objective reasons" so long as it is made clear that they only become evaluative *if we assume* that we get pleasure from contemplating objects which have these traits. He recognizes that such an assumption is based on an empirical generalization (about what people find pleasure in contemplating) which is, by and large, correct. Such traits can indeed be of some use in *predicting* what a large number of people will consider beautiful, but predicting what people will experience is one thing and proving that they *ought* to have such an experience under those conditions or that such an experience under those conditions is *aesthetically good* is another thing. No consensus or "test of time" constitutes objective evidence of aesthetic value.

A fourth and very popular objection to aesthetic relativism is that it cannot make sense of the obvious fact that we often say "that's a good painting, but I don't like it." Ducasse has little difficulty giving a satisfactory explanation of this way of speaking. Everyone recognizes that certain traits (e.g. unity, complexity and intensity) are associated with favorable judgments by connoisseurs. By observation and empirical generalization of the "experts'" responses under a variety of conditions a consumer of art can often make a guess as to what the response of the experts would be to this particular work of art.

Sometimes the traits correlated with the favorable judgments of connoisseurs seem much less aesthetically relevant than unity, complexity and intensity. After seeing a new painting by a famous contemporary artist, an unsophisticated consumer of art may say "I know it's good, but to me it seems a messy bore" because he knows that *any* painting signed by that artist will inevitably be considered good by many critics and command an enormous price.

In other and more interesting cases the consumer of art may say that a work of art is good though he does not like it not on the basis of empirical generalizations about the responses of connoisseurs but on the basis of generalizations about *his own responses.* He knows that he ordinarily responds favorably to novels with all the traits of this novel but he cannot in this case because, for example, this novel has as its hero a fanatic Christian Scientist and he cannot abide Christian Scientists; his father happens to have been a Christian Scientist who bullied his mother into not going to a doctor and, as a consequence, his mother died prematurely.

Finally, it may be objected that it is absurd to suppose that art critics serve no function at all in aesthetic appreciation and evaluation and to suppose that the untutored would be in a better position to appreciate and evaluate art if they were only unencumbered with the irrelevant and distracting scholarship imposed on them by critics.

This objection misses the mark because Ducasse never denies that in important respects critical scholarship is an aid to appreciation and evaluation. He points out repeatedly that critics specialized in a certain kind of art can be invaluable as *guides* who give directions for perceiving, narrow down the field of possible orientation, and help us in the discrimination of details.

The critic's technical knowledge of what traits are usually associated with favorable aesthetic response make him able to help the consumer of art especially if the critic has a fairly accurate idea of what the tastes of the person to whom he is speaking are. The critic in his proper role is, Ducasse thinks, like a guide to a foreign city who points things out on the basis of his knowledge of the city and what he guesses are the tastes of the visitor.

The critic-guide often can also guess that if the untutored consumer of art has certain features regularly pointed out to him as he, for example, reads novel after novel, he may gradually come to respond to these features in a way he did not at first.

Yet this useful ability to predict aesthetic response or predict what may gradually become the response is, Ducasse insists, an ability totally different from the ability to prove that the consumer *should* respond to those features or that those features are aesthetically good.

This may appear to be an extremely anti-intellectual assessment of the function of art criticism. Admittedly, Ducasse's remarks are occasionally quite anti-intellectual. He sometimes suggests that technical knowledge of art is not only irrelevant to appreciation and evaluation but acts as an insurmountable barrier to appreciation. These statements, however, should be understood in their context. Ducasse is trying to counteract the illegitimate pretensions of the critics and in doing so he sometimes overstates his case. Ducasse does not mean that no one with technical knowledge of art can properly respond to a work. The point he is making is simply that too often in the past technical recognition of traits in a work has been confused with aesthetic experience. The connoisseur often gets so much genuine satisfaction from developing and displaying his technical knowledge that he comes to think that *any* use of that knowledge constitutes aesthetic experience; he forgets that it is aesthetic experience only if he takes the aesthetic attitude toward the objects about which he has such impressive technical knowledge. The fact that his technical knowledge may lead, if and when the aesthetic attitude is taken, to more satisfying aesthetic experience than if he had aesthetically contemplated the work without such knowledge does not show that technical awareness is the same as aesthetic experience. Ducasse has no objection to the connoisseur's appreciation of technical virtuosity in art so long as that technical appreciation is recognized as not being *aesthetic* appreciation. Furthermore, the critic's ability to juggle technical terms in talk about art is not a reliable indication of his capacity for artistic appreciation. One critic may be mediocre in juggling jargon yet have extraordinary aesthetic sensitivity, and another critic may be able to talk circles around his rivals and yet be amazingly insensitive to subtle differences in aesthetic experience.

Ducasse is not fundamentally anti-intellectual in his attack on critics; he wants only to curb the tendency of the critic to assume that he has a monopoly on aesthetic sensitivity and judgment, a monopoly so complete that he can sometimes issue a verdict and learned justification of that verdict without ever having aesthetically contemplated the particular work of art he has judged, a monopoly which frightens the ordinary consumer of art away from any attempt to appreciate art for himself and makes him accept the critic's verdict without seeing for himself.

Ducasse seems to give an eminently fair estimate of the role of technical knowledge in aesthetic appreciation; it is only the tyranny of intellectualism in art appreciation to which Ducasse objects, and if we are familiar with the history of art criticism, the vehemence of his objection to this tyranny seems not without justification.

NOTES

[1] C.J. Ducasse, *The Philosophy of Art* (New York: Dial Press, 1929). Reprinted in 1966 by Dover Publications.

[2] New York: Appleton-Century-Crofts, 1971.

[3] In addition to *The Philosophy of Art*, the more important of Ducasse's numerous publications in aesthetics are: *Art, the Critics, and You* (New York: Oskar Piest, 1944); "Aesthetics and the Aesthetic Activities," *Journal of Aesthetics and Art Criticism* 5 (1947), 165–76; "The Sources of the Emotional Import of an Aesthetic Object," *Philosophy and Phenomenological Research* 21 (1961), 556–57; "Art and the Language of the Emotions," *JAAC* 33 (1964–65), 109–112; and "Taste, Meaning and Reality in Art," in S. Hook (ed.), *Art and Philosophy: A Symposium* (New York: New York University Press, 1966), pp. 181–93. Our exposition of Ducasse's aesthetics in this chapter will be based on these publications.

[4] "Art and the Language of the Emotions," p. 110.

[5] For a discussion of objections that might be made to use of the notion of feeling image in an expression theory of art see Peter H. Hare, "Feeling Imaging and Expression Theory," *Journal of Aesthetics and Art Criticism* 30 (1972), 346–49.

[6] It is interesting that in his 1947 paper, "Aesthetics and the Aesthetic Activities," while he is concentrating his attention on other matters, Ducasse in passing happens to offer precisely the inclusive definition we have suggested: "And *aesthetic art*, we may say, is art – that is skilled creation – in so far as its products are intended for contemplation rather than for use as implements or as stimuli to curiosity." (p. 167)

However, in his 1964 paper, "Art and Language of the Emotions," he returns to his earlier definition.

[7] One of the most familiar objections to the expression theory is that numerous instances can be cited of genuine aesthetic experience in which no emotions are felt. Emotion-arousal, so the objection goes, is at best incidental to aesthetic experience and at worst incompatible with it. For a discussion of this objection see Peter H. Hare, "Feeling Imaging and Expression Theory," pp. 345–46.

[8] There is an important respect, however, in which Ducasse's discussion of the standards of criticism appears to be strangely unrelativistic. He says quite emphatically that, although there are many equally legitimate standards that can be used in evaluating works of art and aesthetic objects, evaluation in terms of beauty and ugliness is the only kind of *aesthetic* evaluation, that is, evaluation of a work in terms of the pleasure or displeasure caused by the work in a beholder who contemplates it aesthetically is the only genuinely aesthetic evaluation of it. It is not clear how Ducasse can defend this exclusiveness of aesthetic evaluation. To be sure, beauty is the most commonly used standard, but Ducasse has himself said that appeals to consensus are worthless in art criticism. Suppose, for example, someone finds a work of art which seems to him when he contemplates it aesthetically to be either ugly or to be neither beautiful nor ugly and yet he considers it to have great aesthetic merit. Perhaps it has a capacity to cause in him *intense* but not pleasant feeling, and he believes this capacity to cause intensity of feeling to be equivalent to aesthetic value. How can Ducasse dispute this as an aesthetic standard without abandoning his relativism? Or to give another example, someone might say that a work of art is to be evaluated according to its capacity, when aesthetically contemplated, for communicating feeling. It seems that the only limitation on aesthetic evaluation compatible with relativism is that the object being evaluated be the content of aesthetic contemplation. For someone to evaluate a painting in terms of, for example, its combustibility without contemplating it aesthetically (i.e. with the aesthetic attitude) is not to evaluate it aesthetically, but so long as the object evaluated is the content of aesthetic contemplation the object can be evaluated aesthetically in terms of any sort of effects that object may have. There is no relativistic way of limiting aesthetic evaluation to a consideration of the *pleasure* or *displeasure* which the content of aesthetic contemplation may cause.

CHAPTER IX

ETHICS OF BELIEF

No better introduction to Ducasse's views on religion can be found than his lively correspondence with Dickinson S. Miller on the ethics of belief in which both men used William James' work as a point of departure. Accordingly, in this chapter, we shall reproduce and comment on this correspondence between old friends, and in the next chapter Ducasse's ethics of belief will be placed in the context of his philosophy of religion as a whole.

I

In American philosophy few papers have generated as much discussion as William James' essay "The Will to Believe." James is America's most provocative philosopher, and this is one of his most controversial papers. According to R. B. Perry, "the most important of the discussions stimulated by *The Will to Believe* was that in which the leader was Dickinson S. Miller, one of the closest of James's personal friends, and on other issues a powerful ally." [1]

After reading the title essay of *The Will to Believe* as separately published in 1896, Miller engaged in extensive correspondence with James. In one of these letters James, with his customary charm, refers to Miller as his "most penetrating critic and intimate enemy." [2] The ideas Miller developed in this correspondence he brought together in an 1899 paper published in *Ethics*. [3] So critical was this paper that, we learn from the Ducasse-Miller correspondence, it "strained [their] friendship." [4]

Although Miller said that "there has been no human being of whom I should like so much to be a disciple as William James," [5] he continued to develop his criticism of the Jamesian doctrine of the Will to Believe for more than half a century. That Miller's interest in this topic never lessened is evident in his publication of another criticism[6] of the doctrine in 1942 and also in his lengthy correspondence with Ducasse in the 1940's and 1950's, when Miller was in his seventies and eighties. This correspondence was started when Miller sent Ducasse an offprint of his 1942 article. In reply

Ducasse said that he agreed with almost all of Miller's criticisms of James, but that there was one significant point left untouched.[7] Miller, as we shall see, unwilling as ever to yield ground on this topic, replied that even that remaining point must fall before his critical assault.[8]

A few years later Ducasse sent Miller the typescript of *A Philosophical Scrutiny of Religion*, inviting him to write a foreword. Although Miller expressed great admiration for the scholarship of the book, he declined because he said he would feel conscience bound to criticize both Ducasse's defense of the Right to Believe and his favorable appraisal of the results of psychical research.[9] Ducasse's insistence that he shared Miller's reservations about the Will to Believe[10] led to further correspondence in which they continued to clarify their respective positions.

II

Ducasse initiated the correspondence with the following:

January 18, 1943

Dr. Dickinson S. Miller
95 Pinckney St.
Boston, Mass.

Dear Professor Miller,

Thank you for the reprint of your paper on James' "Right to Believe." I had intended to read it when I saw it in the *Philosophical Review*, but was diverted from my purpose by some one or other of the numerous things demanding immediate attention when one is teaching.

Permit me to say that your discussion seems to me admirably sound, penetrating, and clear throughout — much more so than any other that has come to my notice. This is what I expected, for in the days, about 1908, when I began to study philosophy, my teacher, Savery, often had occasion to point to the keenness of various articles from your pen.

The one important and sound point in James' essay — which, however, has nothing to do with volition to believe, or with a right to will to believe — seems to me to be that there are options which are "forced" not only in the sense that there are only two alternatives, Yes and No, but in the sense that the situation is one in which we cannot suspend decision between Yes and No (as Descartes mistakenly asserted was always possible), because to refuse to decide is then automatically to be deciding; *and* that there are cases of this sort in which evidence as to the probability of truth of a decision on one side or the other is either wholly lacking to us or is equally balanced. To illustrate this to my students, I usually ask them to suppose themselves on a street car going down a hill when suddenly the brakes fail. There are then two possible things for a passenger to do: to jump off, or to stay on. But he does not know which of the two is more likely to save him from injury, and he cannot put off deciding which to do until he has consulted the records of other accidents. In such a case decision is and has to be non-rational in the sense of being instinctive, impulsive, temperamental, instead of based on in your words "a rational gauging of the exigency." It might be denied that there ever is a case where we have an exact balance of evidence pro and contra, or no evidence at all pro and contra. But if it is true (as I think it is) that there are such cases, then I do not see how it can be denied that in those cases the decision has to be – not indeed irrational, but – non-rational in the sense just stated.

This is, I think, the one sound point in James' essay; but of course it affords no basis whatever for choice one way rather than the other; for claiming, for instance, as I think James was temperamentally disposed to do, that the instinct of affirmation is sounder, wiser, more likely to pick on the truth, than the instinct of negation. It means only that there are cases in human affairs where decision has to be pure gamble.

But although pure gamble is, by definition, non-rational in the sense that the alternative one chooses to bet on is not known to be more probably true than the other; yet pure gamble may be rational in another sense, viz., that, irrespective of whether one loses or wins one's bet, some immediate reward is known to be attached to *the act itself of betting* on a given side, whereas no such reward, or a lesser one, is attached to the act of betting on the other side.

Let us suppose, for instance, that a person – perhaps as a result of childhood suggestions – finds himself believing that there is a God, and that, after careful scrutiny, he comes to the conclusion (a) that the conception of God which he holds is free from internal inconsistencies; (b) that there is no empirical evidence either for or against the existence of the sort of God he believes in; and (c) that his belief in that God is to him a source of comfort, courage and strength, and an inspiration to beneficence, in his daily living; and, so far as he can see, has no bad consequences. Let us suppose, further, that this person knows that although beliefs cannot be relinquished or acquired by the mere volition, yet there are various psychological devices, to which one can, if one wills, have recourse, which in many cases are effective in inducing or destroying beliefs not based on a preponderance of evidence.

Then the question is: Ought such a person in such a case to try, through the use of these psychological devices, to destroy the belief he has in his God? Or ought he, by means of them, try to strengthen it? So far as I can see, the latter would be the rational thing to do; but it would be rational, not in the sense that there is a preponderance of evidence for the truth of the proposition he believes and that his belief of it is determined by this, but in the sense that although he has no evidence for or against the truth of that proposition, belief itself of that proposition has the effect of making him a happier, more courageous, more beneficent person than would disbelief of it.

I wonder whether this is not perhaps the, as it seems to me, sound idea which, in spite of all confusions and errors in James' essay, people somehow get out of it, and which vindicates something that might be not inaptly described as (in cases of the kind supposed) a right to believe.

Sincerely yours,
[C. J. Ducasse]

To this Miller replied:

20 January, 1943
Dear Professor Ducasse:

... As to the street-car, yes, there surely might be a case where one would see no data for a conclusion and would go solely by impulse. It would seem however possible, as you describe the case, to think in a flash of how the land lies at the foot of the hill, just what are the chances of a smash-up, and to make a hasty comparison of the danger of jumping off at once. Our most rational effort of the moment might not be rational in the eyes of careful subsequent reflection but it would be none the less our best effort of reason.

Your final question as to the legitimacy of choosing to strengthen a religious belief for which there is no evidence happens to be identical with one I have been putting to myself since the article appeared. My best answer is this. Choices are right or wrong according as they produce or tend to produce good ar harm, satisfactory life or the reverse, for all those concerned. Now the great deficiency of our morals, it seems to me, lies in the absence of any emphasis on the conscience of the mind, on the duty of being as intelligent as we can. It is a central duty because unintelligence bears more fruit of misery, wretchedness, and frustration than any other human weakness or sin. From the point of view of life at large it seems of primary importance to think with our best intelligence and clearest realism on every subject. And particularly in religion the ill consequences of baseless faith are enormous. I could not therefore think that such a faith would be an inspiration to genuine beneficence in daily living; not as much beneficence as clear-sighted intelligence on the subject would bring ...

Yours very truly,
Dickinson S. Miller

In this exchange Miller's reaction to Ducasse's presentation of the Right to Believe is similar to the reaction to James which he expressed in 1899 and again in 1942. In horror, Miller had said in 1899 that " 'The Will to Believe' is the will to deceive — to deceive one's self; and the deception, which begins at home, may be expected in due course to pass on to others." [11] It is not surprising to find Ducasse as puzzled by this reaction as James had been. Ducasse, like James, had taken pains to stress that he was speaking only about situations in which there is no preponderance of evidence. He is not recommending that anyone fail to attend to evidence. To be sure, if he were asking that we ignore evidence, Ducasse could understand the charge that we are being asked to deceive ourselves and to abandon our intelligence.

There seem to be two possible grounds for Miller's prophecy of doom. First, he may fear that if we acquire or strengthen belief by the "psychological devices" Ducasse mentions, our belief will be of a dogmatic sort which will discourage further inquiry and prevent us from recognizing a preponderance of counterevidence should it appear in the future. This fear, however, appears to be unjustified because the belief which James and Ducasse are speaking of has no special immunity to criticism in the future should new evidence appear. Miller, like W. K. Clifford, wishes at all costs to avoid error and thinks that any belief not supported by a preponderance of evidence is an open invitation to error. James and Ducasse, however, have never suggested that we invite error by failure to attend to evidence. They understand intelligence to be attendance to whatever evidence can be found; intelligence for them, however, is not something which paralyzes persons when there is no preponderance of evidence.

Not only do James and Ducasse insist on the duty to attend to the evidence, but they also limit the Right to Believe to the situations in which an option is "living," "forced," and "momentous." Miller's worry is unjustified both because the number of situations in which the Right to Believe applies is small and because even in those cases constant attention to new evidence minimizes risk of serious error.

The second possible ground for Miller's prophecy of doom appears to be his anticipation of the spreading of the Right to Believe into areas in which there is a preponderance of counterevidence or in which the option is neither "forced" nor "momentous." Belief without a preponderance of supporting evidence is, for Miller, a malignancy which will spread throughout our whole body of beliefs. This fear appears to be greatly exaggerated if we once understand that James and Ducasse insist on the duty to attend to evidence. In fact, James expressed fear of the opposite sort of spreading. He feared that this skeptical condemnation of belief where there is no preponderance of evidence might spread to areas where there is a supporting preponderance in the form of a probability. If we accept Miller's views, we may eventually find ourselves and others insisting on near certainty and unwilling to act on probabilities. One kind of spreading is as dangerous as the other.

However, although on most occasions Ducasse asks only for tolerance of those who *happen* to believe without a preponderance of evidence, on some occasions he argues that a rational man will do what he can to *induce* a belief in himself by placing himself in a favorable psychological environment and by acting as he would if he had certain beliefs which in fact he does not have but wishes he had.[12] Ducasse has described in detail the techniques of suggestion and hypnosis that can be used to induce beliefs.[13]

This proposal that we use suggestion and related techniques to induce beneficial beliefs is permissible within his ethics of belief because he is not advocating the inducement of a belief where there is a preponderance of evidence against its truth; he is limiting the legitimate use of suggestion to circumstances in which there is little evidence either for or against, or to circumstances in which the evidence is evenly balanced. Nevertheless, Ducasse would have done well, when speaking of suggestion and hypnosis, to realize that at least *some* of the uses of these techniques seriously erode both our ability to attend to new evidence and our ability to distinguish between trivial and momentous and between avoidable and forced options. When there is no preponderance of evidence, a person may in some cases use powerful techniques of suggestion which virtually preclude recognition of the relevance of any *future* preponderance of counterevidence. Although, on the one hand, philosophers are mistaken who suppose that belief without adequate evidence *almost invariably* impairs our ability to attend to evidence, on the other hand, philosophers are equally mistaken who suppose that it is *impossible* or *highly unlikely* that belief induced when evidence is inadequate will seriously impair the ability to attend to future evidence. All such generalizations about the benefits and dangers of suggestion and hypnosis are questionable.

III

In his book, *A Philosophical Scrutiny of Religion*, which appeared about ten years after this exchange of letters, Ducasse used almost exactly the same example of a "living," "forced," and "momentous" option.[14] The only difference was caused by the passing of the streetcar from the New England scene, and it became an automobile which one must decide whether to jump out of. He went on to say that for many persons religious belief is "genuine in the very sense specified, and . . . cannot be decided by them rationally for lack of the knowledge which would be necessary for this. *For such persons,* then, and, *in the absence of possession by them of such knowledge, wishful decision* as to whether to believe or not believe any particular such religious doctrine *is not merely legitimate but unavoidable.*"[15] Ducasse makes it clear that this Right to Believe is not merely something to which the uneducated and unsophisticated can resort.

No matter how intelligent, educated, vigorous, powerful and resourceful a man may be, there is always some limit to what he can do to safeguard his values. Hurricanes,

earthquakes . . . threaten at times . . . either himself or the things or persons he holds
most dear, in spite of his best efforts to safeguard them.[16]

Such a man, Ducasse claims, is justified in accepting an "hypothesis which,
if true, would offer a way, more or less probably effective, of safeguarding
those values, or if not, of anesthetizing himself more or less to their loss."[17]
In short, for Ducasse a "fool's paradise" is preferable to a "fool's hell."[18]
Again Ducasse is insisting that we have a Right to Believe anything which we
think will be a "source of comfort, courage, and strength, and an inspiration
to beneficence" *provided that* it is not in conflict with our duty to attend to
evidence, and it cannot be in conflict with that duty if there is no preponderance of evidence. Intelligent and well-educated men are equally justified in
taking advantage of this right because there are always areas in which no
investigators have been able to establish a preponderance of evidence.

However, when Ducasse sent the typescript of the book to Miller and
invited him to write a foreword, Miller, while deeply pleased, was no happier
with Ducasse's remarks in the book than he had been about what he had
said in the letter some nine years before.

186 Marlborough Street
Boston, 16   10 Sept. '52.

Dear Professor Ducasse:

. . . My difference of conviction as to will to believe happens to be profound, bound up
with the principle that ethics calls upon us to be as intelligent as we can for the sake
of results in life. I wrote two long articles against W. to B. the first being during James's
life, and it strained our friendship . . .

Yours cordially,
D. S. Miller

In his reply Ducasse tries to explain that the Right to Believe, as he
conceives it, is in no way incompatible with being "as intelligent as we can."

September 11, 1952

Dear Dr. Miller:

. . . As to the "will-to-believe," it seems to me that I agree heartily with what you say
about it. I don't have any use for any *will* to believe. I hold that one ought indeed to
be as intelligent as possible, and always to abide by such evidence as one has or can get.
Only, there are cases where one has none and can get none, or where the probabilities
are equal pro and contra, and yet where one cannot put off choosing because putting it
off is equivalent to choosing a particular one of the alternatives. In such cases, the
choice – or, if one cannot properly call it "choice," then the "behavior" or "action"
or "belief" – cannot, *ex hypothesi*, be based on the greater probability, but has to be a
psychological instead of a logical matter. Whether James meant more than this by his

unfortunate expression "will to believe," I am not sure. But, to me, his pointing out that situations of this peculiar kind sometimes occur is the real contribution of his essay . . .

Cordially yours,
C. J. Ducasse

Miller in his next letter is more passionate than ever in his rejection of the view that it is ever justifiable to believe anything without adequate evidence.

186 Marlborough St.
Boston 16
[no date]

Dear Professor Ducasse:

. . . I am flatly and insuperably debarred from doing what I want to do, namely acting upon your suggestion that I should write a Forward [sic], — which is, I think, the highest philosophical honour I have ever received. And this because I *couldn't* honestly write it; some of the chief points of Tendency in the book (I have given you frankly my estimate of its scholarship, breadth, intellectual grasp and style of exposition) are in conflict with convictions as deeply rooted and (critics might say) fanatically held as any in my life . . . I hold that a religion should be true and verifiable, and that indulging a belief — not doing everything to dispel it in one's own mind — which is unsupported by evidence is in deadly enmity with human progress. I hold that none of James's arguments are sound — e.g. that suspension of judgment is practically equivalent to disbelief. Above all, I do not accept the view that theism (for example) is a subject in which one has no evidence and can get none; I believe that there is decisive evidence against one conclusion and in favour of another. I am persuaded that human progress is bound up with the will to believe the evidence — and the will (it often requires a good deal) to suspend judgment where there is none . . .

Yours cordially
Dickinson S. Miller

Once again Miller expresses his conviction that the Right to Believe is incompatible with the intelligence necessary for human progress; he fails to recognize that intelligence, as we have pointed out, does not demand suspension of belief but demands only attention to evidence. Miller argues for the absolute prohibition of belief without supporting evidence on the grounds that if any such belief is permitted it will spread and the ability to suspend judgment will be destroyed; the prohibition must be maintained at any cost.

Miller's fears are similar to the fears of those who urge an absolute prohibition of lying on the grounds that if a few lies are permitted they will lead to more and more lies until it is impossible to trust anyone. However, it is clear that there are special circumstances in which lying is justified. Few wish to condemn someone for using a lie to save a human life, and few expect that lying under such special circumstances will spread to ordinary circumstances. Similarly, it seems unreasonable to suppose that belief without supporting evidence in the special circumstances of "living," "forced," and "momentous" options will spread and destroy the ability to suspend judgment in ordinary circumstances.

Miller also challenges in this letter the notion that the Right to Believe argument applies to theism. He does not believe that, as far as theism is concerned, the evidence is in balance. It may well be that he thinks the evidence is in favor of theism, or conceivably against it; but in either case, on Ducasse's view, then, the Right to Believe argument does not apply. Ducasse himself, for that matter, does not believe that his argument applies to theism. He is quite convinced, as we shall see in the next chapter, that the evidence of gratuitous evil shows conclusively that theism is false. Ducasse, however, does have certain nontheistic beliefs for which he does not have adequate evidence, which he would like to believe, and which therefore he insists he has the right to believe.

IV

Ducasse in his next letter takes a somewhat different tack.

September 24, 1952

Dear Dr. Miller:

... It seems to me that you do not give sufficient weight to the fact that the regimen of strict reason, which is suitable and practicable for you, and pretty well for me too, is not so for the vast masses of mankind that have neither the intelligence, nor the education, nor the time to think things out, and yet have to act from moment to moment. For suspense of judgment — or I should rather say of opinion, since I would define "judgment" as opinion based on the weighing of evidence — furnishes no basis for decisions, and yet the inaction which such suspense motivates has consequences just the same; and these (as my example of the car running down hill, I believe, definitely shows) sometimes are the same as would be those of deciding in favor of one of the alternatives. Of course, you might say that although, in this example, the person concerned is confronted by a "forced" and "genuine" option, yet there are none such in religious matters. I am not sure that is so even for me; but I think that for many persons, being what, *psychologically*, they are at the moment — irrational, uninformed, and yet equipped with some beliefs which *they* rank as definite and certain knowledge — there are in religious matters some options that are "forced" and also "genuine" in the other two respects. True, these options would not be "genuine" for you or for me. But the persons I have in view are not you or me; they just don't have, and cannot get at the time or at all, the intellectual equipment possession of which makes those options not genuine. And yet they are alive (after a fashion!) and (*qua* human beings rather than mere animals) they have to have *some* set of beliefs by which to act. But here I go again! So I'll quit before this becomes another book.

As ever, cordially,
C. J. Ducasse

In order to avoid the complicated question of whether for the most intelligent and educated persons there is a preponderance of evidence and a "genuine" option in religious matters, Ducasse in this letter limits himself to the more modest claim that the Right to Believe should at least apply to "the vast masses of mankind" who are neither so intelligent nor so well educated. He asks Miller whether he wishes educated persons to try to persuade the less educated to suffer the serious consequences which suspension of judgment may have for them.

186 Marlborough St.
Boston 16   26 Sept. '52

Dear Professor Ducasse:

. . . I decidedly would not disturb the faith of anyone to whom it gave consolation and moral motive, if he was not . . . of a rational type; such disturbance would upset, do harm, cause unhappiness to no good end. Few people are rational helmsmen of their minds.

But I would not *advocate* the indulgence of any belief without sufficient reason.

I would not in a particular case disturb beliefs ready-formed, but would not advocate forming such beliefs . . .

Moral life, i.e. life guarding and increasing happy life, does not depend on unevidenced doubtful beliefs, though to an unenlightened person it may be promoted by them.

Cannot agree that suspension of opinion (taken with whole situation) furnishes no basis for decision. The decision to investigate, the decision to wait and see, the decision to *try* an action though ignorant of how it will turn out, are possible. Etc. We may *try* because attractive, not on any probability – and without belief . . .

Ever cordially yours,
Dickinson S. Miller

In great haste –

Miller concedes that we should not disturb the unsupported beliefs of those not "of a rational type." He appears to make this concession on the civil libertarian grounds that we should allow someone to perform whatever immoral act (that is, a belief without evidence) he wishes so long as the act does not adversely affect the welfare of others.

Miller asks only of James and Ducasse that they "not *advocate* the indulgence of any belief without sufficient reason." But it is doubtful that James and Ducasse ever intended such advocacy. On the contrary, their concern is to persuade Clifford, Miller and others to stop advocating suspension of judgment as a duty. They would agree that advocating belief without evidence as a duty is unjustified, but they insist that advocating suspension of judgment as a duty where there is no preponderance of evidence is equally unjustified. The doctrine of the Right to Believe is an attempt to discredit both duties and to uphold only the duty to attend to the evidence.[19] This doctrine does not discredit Miller's wish to himself suspend belief in cases where there is no preponderance of evidence. The Right to Believe is a defense of belief where there is a "genuine" option and no preponderance of evidence, but it is also a defense of the right to suspend judgment under those circumstances. James and Ducasse may personally prefer a more affirmative attitude but they do not wish to argue that Miller is abandoning his duty by suspending judgment. The Right to Believe is the right, in circumstances where there is a genuine option and no preponderance of evidence, to take any attitude our "passional nature" dictates. James and Ducasse are not disturbed by the fact that Miller's passional nature dictates suspension of judgment; they are disturbed only by his attempt to impose his inclinations on everyone else; they are disturbed by his attempt to show that it is everyone's *duty* to suspend judgment under those circumstances regardless of what his passional nature may demand.

Consequently, Ducasse can agree with much of what Miller says in this letter (the last which deals with the ethics of belief) without altering in the least the Right to Believe. Ducasse can agree that "[m]oral life . . . does not depend on unevidence, doubtful beliefs" and can agree that suspension of judgment for some people can furnish a basis for decision. He can agree on these points because he never intended to *exclude* suspension of belief as one of the attitudes which the passional natures of some people require and have every right to take. He intended only to include as equally legitimate (that is, equally compatible with the duty to attend to evidence) the attitudes of those with different passional natures.

NOTES

[1]   *The Thought and Character of William James* (Boston: Little, Brown, and Company,

1936), Vol. II, p. 240. Dickinson S. Miller (1868–1963) was a student of William James. James was instrumental in getting him an appointment at Bryn Mawr College in 1893, the year after Miller's graduation from Harvard. Miller left Bryn Mawr in 1898 to teach at Harvard and later at Columbia. He received a D.D. at Berkeley (California) Divinity School and in 1911 started to teach apologetics at the General Theological Seminary in New York City. Later he occasionally served as a Unitarian minister in the Boston area. Miller's was an extremely penetrating and constructively critical mind. His article provocatively entitled "Free Will as Involving Determinism and Inconceivable Without It" (1934), published, for obscure reasons, under the name of R.E. Hobart, has become a *locus classicus* of the free-will controversy. Cf. Herbert Feigl, *The Encyclopedia of Philosophy*, ed. by Paul Edwards (New York: The Macmillan Company and The Free Press, 1967), Vol. V, pp. 323–24.
2 *The Letters of William James* (Boston: The Atlantic Monthly Press, 1920), Vol. II, p. 48. In another letter about the Will to Believe, James calls Miller "illustrious friend and joy of my liver," *Letters*, Vol. II, p. 84.
3 Dickinson Miller, " 'The Will to Believe' and The Duty to Doubt," *International Journal of Ethics* 9 (1898–99), 169–95.
4 Letter of Miller to Ducasse, September 10, 1952.
5 Dickinson Miller, "James's Doctrine of 'The Right to Believe'," *Philosophical Review* 51 (1942), 552.
6 *Ibid.*, pp. 541–58.
7 Letter of Ducasse to Miller, January 18, 1943.
8 Letter of Miller to Ducasse, January 20, 1943.
9 Letter of Miller to Ducasse, September 10, 1952.
10 Letter of Ducasse to Miller, September 11, 1952.
11 " 'The Will to Believe' and The Duty to Doubt," p. 173.
12 C.J. Ducasse, *A Philosophical Scrutiny of Religion* (New York: The Ronald Press Company, 1953), pp. 160–61.
13 C.J. Ducasse, "Hypnotism, Suggestion, and Suggestibility," *International Journal of Parapsychology* 5 (1963), 5–20.
14 *A Philosophical Scrutiny of Religion*, pp. 163–64.
15 *Ibid.*, p. 165.
16 *Ibid.*, p. 166.
17 *Ibid.*
18 *Ibid.*, pp. 166–167.
19 See E.H. Madden, *Chauncey Wright and The Foundations of Pragmatism* (Seattle: University of Washington Press, 1963), pp. 43–50.

CHAPTER X

PHILOSOPHY OF RELIGION

I

Although some of Ducasse's discussions of religion *taken individually* are misleading and appear incompatible with other discussions, we believe that, if all his publications on the subject are taken into account, a consistent (if not altogether plausible) position emerges.

Dickinson Miller, as we have seen, is disturbed by what he thinks is Ducasse's advocacy of reckless belief without adequate evidence, and we have tried to show that most of Miller's worries are without foundation. But, if we are satisfied that Ducasse's ethics of belief is largely reasonable, what are we to make of later publications[1] in which he apparently abandons all talk about evidence and considers religious assertions to be cognitively meaningless? If religious belief is cognitively meaningless and Raphael Demos is correct in thinking that religious belief, for Ducasse, is just "a beautiful feeling," [2] what point can there be in worry about evidence for or against it? Surely evidence is irrelevant to a feeling that can be neither true nor false.

To see that Ducasse is not inconsistent, it is important that a short and little noticed paper "What has Science Done to Religion?" published in 1959 outside the philosophical journals be carefully considered.[3] In this later paper, following his exchange with Demos, it is apparent that his earlier charge of cognitive meaninglessness was intended only as part of his long-standing insistence that science should cut away the nonsense and illegitimate knowledge claims traditionally considered essential to religion in order to leave intact the cognitively meaningful overbeliefs that are genuinely essential to religion — overbeliefs that can legitimately perform the social and personal functions that Ducasse believes religion, and only religion, can perform. "[W]hat modern science has done," Ducasse says, "has been to clean out and dispose of some of the myths that had no religious functions, and that only served to anaesthetize unsatisfied scientific curiousity." What disturbs Ducasse is that scientifically inclined philosophers have, in their enthusiasm, gone on "to throw out the baby with the bath water." "This is understandable," he thinks, "because the water was pretty dark, as well as viscous! " [4] Consequently, his strenuous objections to the dark and viscous nonsense presented by Demos and others in no way indicates that Ducasse has abandoned his ethics of belief, according to which there are meaningful overbeliefs (i.e. the "baby") that can perform the functions of religion and that we have an epistemic right to hold.

Having shown that his later charge of cognitive meaninglessness is compatible with his earlier discussions of the ethics of belief, let us now give an account of the fundamental orientation of Ducasse's philosophy of religion, indicating in what respects we find his views inadequate, and, in the following sections, a detailed statement and critique of these views.

Ducasse is deeply interested in presenting a philosophy of religion that is fair to Eastern religion and free of the monotheistic bias so common in Western philosophy. The first step in the construction of a philosophy of religion free of such bias, he thinks, is the formulation of a neutral definition of religion. Since widely varied beliefs called religious have nothing substantive in common Ducasse suggests that such a neutral definition can be made only in terms of social and personal functions performed in common by various religious beliefs. Having defined 'religion' in terms of common functions, Ducasse asks which set of religious beliefs we have an epistemic right to adopt. His ethics of belief leads him to the unusual and controversial conclusion that, while we do not have an epistemic right to believe in monotheism, we do have a right to use certain non-Western beliefs to perform the functions of religion. Although his affirmation of the right to adopt non-Western beliefs and his denial of that right to monotheism is certainly a healthy challenge to monotheistic assumptions, Ducasse has not, we shall argue, been entirely fair to monotheism. Many of the arguments for the existence of a monotheistic God which he subjects to devastating criticism are no longer taken seriously by theists themselves; furthermore, he has not taken account of the many modifications of monotheism introduced by twentieth-century philosophers of religion to meet familiar objections. In his admirable desire to avoid monotheistic bias, Ducasse has gone so far as to develop an *Eastern* bias which leads him to overlook the more sophisticated forms of monotheism and to accept uncritically non-Western beliefs. The problems of non-Western religions may be very different from those of monotheism, but Ducasse has not shown that they are any less severe.

But not only has Ducasse failed to show that we have an epistemic right to hold these non-Western beliefs; he has also failed to show that, once these beliefs have been separated, as Ducasse thinks they must be, from the nonsense with which they are usually associated, they will still be able to perform what Ducasse takes to be the social and personal functions of religious belief.

II

Having throughout his career held that "all theoretical problems of philosophy are essentially semantical,"[5] Ducasse begins his attempt to arrive at a neutral definition of religion with an investigation of the different ways in which the word religion is used. His purpose in this empirical survey is to discover a meaning which all uses of the word, both Eastern and Western, share without falling into the error of arriving at a definition so broad as to include unwittingly moral experience and other aspects of culture.

The upshot of Ducasse's investigation is that no definition of religion in terms of either a set of beliefs or a set of practices is satisfactory; only a functional definition can be made neither too exclusive nor too inclusive a specification of the meaning of the term religion. A religion can be defined, he says, as any set of beliefs and practices which performs the following social and personal functions: (1) "provide[s] motivation for just or altruistic (and therefore socially beneficial) conduct, in those cases where the interests of the individual conflict with those of the group and where the forms of social pressure we have mentioned [legal, etc.] fail to provide such motivation, whether because they are not strong enough or because they cannot be brought to bear"[6] ; and (2) "bring[s] to the fervent devotee calm in time of danger, endurance in time of adversity, courage in time of despair, self-respect and dignity in time of obloquy or frustration . . . But the personal function of religious faith is not limited to times of adversity. Whereas in worldly misfortune it operates as a tonic, it works on the contrary as a sedative in times of worldly good fortune. It then gives the religious man a measure of humility on occasions of pride, and of prudence in times of success; and a sense of responsibility in the exercise of power."[7]

Although Ducasse's desire to do justice to such nontheistic religions as humanism and Buddhism is admirable, it is doubtful that his functional definition succeeds in giving necessary and sufficient conditions for something counting as an example of religion. Beliefs and practices directed toward, for example, a national government may perform the personal and social functions Ducasse describes, yet such beliefs and practices would be flatly rejected as an example of genuine religion by many.

Ducasse, in fact, exhibits here as elsewhere remarkable confidence in philosophy's ability to find a set of necessary and sufficient conditions for each key term involved in any philosophical discussion. This confidence is not shared by many contemporary philosophers who advocate a definitional skepticism in which it is supposed that we can offer a philosophical analysis of a term without being able to offer a formal definition of it.

III

To perform their functions the dogmas of religion, Ducasse says, need not all be true but only firmly believed to be true.[8] If religion can, and (so Ducasse thinks) only religion can, perform these valuable functions, and if they can be performed without establishing the truth of religious belief, then Ducasse asks, as we have seen in the previous chapter, why everyone does not have the right to benefit from these valuable functions even though he cannot establish the truth of religious belief.

However, although Ducasse thinks that the functional effectiveness of religious belief is independent of its truth, he urges us to recognize that some kinds of religious belief are in serious conflict with the facts and hence cannot be salvaged by the Right to Believe doctrine. He argues that the existence of a traditional monotheistic God who is all-good and all-powerful is incompatible with the amount and distribution of evil in the world. Taking up each of the traditional solutions of the problem of evil in turn, he concludes that each is unsuccesful.[9] The cosmological, teleological, and ontological proofs of the existence of a monotheistic God are likewise demolished.[10]

Unfortunately, in his eagerness to avoid monotheistic bias Ducasse ignores the fact that many twentieth-century monotheistic theologians and philosophers no longer put much stock in the traditional rational arguments and often do not pretend to defend the existence of a monotheistic God conceived traditionally as omni-this and omni-that.

Neo-orthodox theologians like Karl Barth and Paul Tillich shun rational theology all together. Rational theology, for Barth, is sinful because it puts human reason above revelation. Tillich rejects such theology on existential grounds; however metaphysical or empirical one's concept of God may be, it is really based, he says, on an immediate experience of ultimate value and being of which one can become intuitively aware. Thus commitment determines a "theological circle" which cannot be penetrated by "foreign" criticisms. This existential theological circle has been transformed by some writers into a linguistic theological circle. Intelligibility takes many and varied forms, the argument goes, but there is no norm for intelligibility "in general." Criteria of logic arise in the contexts of "ways of living" or "modes of social life" and only make sense in their respective frameworks. Science, for example, is one such mode of life and religion is another, and each has criteria of intelligibility peculiar to itself. Given the fact that the language-game of religion is played, it is argued, there simply is no way in which it can be logically inappropriate or improper to engage in it. It cannot be criticized from the outside; indeed, it cannot even be understood from the outside.[11]

A genuinely unbiased treatment of monotheism would have to consider, as Ducasse does not, these attempts to *evade* the problems of monotheism. As it happens, this evasion fails because the very concept of theological circle encounters serious difficulty. If the claims implicit in it were true, it would make the use of any particular frame of reference wholly arbitrary; but certainly it is possible to discuss the consistency, adequacy, and genuineness of different frames and hence arrive at good reasons for accepting some and rejecting those incompatible with the ones accepted. It is true that all systematic arguments and justifications of particular judgments must occur within a frame of reference, but it is also true that good reasons can be given why one framework should be adopted or rejected. As involved and subtle as this sort of indirect argument is, to deny the possibility of it is to land in skepticism, not monotheism.

Our point is that Ducasse does not make these observations about monotheism because, in his eagerness to avoid monotheistic bias, he limits his attention to old-fashioned monotheists. Yet he cannot hope to persuade monotheistic philosophers to be fair to non-Western beliefs if the account he gives of Western monotheism is seriously inadequate.

Another way in which twentieth-century monotheists have attempted to deal with traditional difficulties pointed out by Ducasse, and to deal with the problem of evil in particular, is to modify the metaphysical concepts of theism in the direction of a temporal and/or pantheistic concept of God.

The trouble with traditional monotheistic efforts to solve the problem of evil, these monotheists believe, is that they depend upon false metaphysics; they depend upon the traditional notions that God is unlimited in power, is outside of and not included in the universe, created the universe *ex nihilo*, is Pure Form and non-temporal in nature, and determined at the moment of creation the whole string of subsequent events. Deny one or more of these assumptions and the problem of evil is solved, or disappears. If God is limited in power, evil occurs in spite of him; if God is not outside the universe, then evil is not something external to him to be eliminated but is a crucial part of God's own nature; and so on.

While these metaphysicians reject various monotheistic assumptions they are careful to retain others. They want to retain, among others, the notions that God is in some sense conscious, is a relevant object of worship, insures that good will eventually prevail, and is essentially compatible with the truths of the Judaeo-Christian religious (as distinct from theological) tradition. In short, these quasitheists wish to produce a conception of God that has all the worshipability of the traditional monotheistic God without the traits that create the problem of evil.

We believe that it can be shown that each of these efforts to modify monotheism to solve the problem of evil fails, partly for reasons indigenous to a particular view, partly for reasons indigenous to the type of quasitheism involved, and partly for reasons that seem to apply generally to all views.[12] But the point again is that Ducasse in his eagerness to avoid monotheistic bias fails to take account of sophisticated modifications of monotheism and *prematurely* pronounces monotheism's problem of evil unsolved.

IV

Unlike most critics of monotheism, Ducasse does not embrace naturalism or humanism. "Earnest atheism," he says, "is a species of faith not of knowledge – a negative instead of an affirmative faith."[13] Although humanists have the Right to Believe in humanism if they find it psychologically helpful, Ducasse has "little patience with those Humanists for whom the word 'Supernaturalism' is a red rag to a bull because they are so intoxicated with the remarkable achievements of the natural sciences that they tacitly assume the universe can have no other dimensions than those already discovered by those sciences."[14] Instead of suggesting naturalism or humanism as a substitute for monotheism, Ducasse makes a case for Eastern beliefs which combine polytheism with belief in transmigration and a Quaker-like ethic. Although his personal sympathy with this sort of alternative is almost completely suppressed in his published work in the interest of critical objectivity, his attraction to this sort of religious option is made very clear in his unpublished correspondence.

I may say that I have been religious myself for many years and it has not interfered with my philosophical thinking; for my religious beliefs are substantially those of Hinayana Buddhism. I have sometimes described myself as a Buddhist Quaker.[15] Of the various great religions, Buddhism, in its original form as nearly as it is known, is more congenial to me than any of the others, because of its absence of theological curliques and because of its simplicity and psychological sanity, and its teaching of self-reliance.[16]

If I were to go in for any theism, it would be polytheism, of a kind where, as in Buddhism, the gods, like the bugs, the snakes, etc., are just part of the population of the universe. (Indeed, the Buddha's teachings were intended by him for the guidance not only of men, but of the gods too.)[17]

I think it quite possible that, in the universe, there may exist personal beings whose wisdom and power transcend, in various degrees, those attributes as found in man; and perhaps in so high a degree in the case of some of those beings as to warrant description of them by the adjective 'divine.' But if this possibility should happen to be the reality, I should expect many such beings rather than a single one. That is, polytheism would then seem to me much more probable than monotheism. So far as I am able to discern, there is not much, if any, evidence that the universe is 'governed' by purposive extrahuman persons, whether gods or devils or both, but I do not think the possibility is excluded. If there is such government, however, it seems to me that the empirical evidence as to the nature of the governing agency would then be overwhelmingly in favor of the conclusion that it is something more or less like our own blessed U.S. Congress – that is, composed of beings who, even if transcending man in power, and intelligence, are all of them finite in these respects, and also in respect of moral goodness or evilness . . .[18]

Polytheism and transmigration are closely linked for Ducasse, transmigration being that process by which beings (better or worse, stronger or weaker) become distributed in the various levels. And this Buddhist, polytheistic form of reincarnation had evidently commended itself to Ducasse since before he began his philosophical studies at the University of Washington.[19]

As we have pointed out, Ducasse thinks that his ethics of belief permits him to adopt this form of Buddhism, though it does not permit the adoption of monotheism. Whereas there is, he says, a preponderance of evidence against monotheism, such a preponderance of counterevidence is lacking in the case of Buddhism. We have already seen the inadequacies of Ducasse's description of the evidence against monotheism; let us now briefly examine some of the arguments he offers to support his contention that there is not a preponderance of evidence against this form of Buddhism and consequently to support his Right to Believe this doctrine:

(i) Behind many objections to belief in the survival-of-death part of this doctrine, Ducasse says, is the assumption that to be real is to be material, "and to be material . . . is to be some process or part of the perceptually public world." But, he continues, "the conception of the nature of reality that proposes to define the real as the material is not the expression of an observable fact to which everyone would have to bow, but is the expression only of a certain direction of interest." [20] In his metaphilosophical doctrine of "ontological liberalism" Ducasse has argued that 'real' is a value term and consequently no ontological position can be refuted by any other. [21] Such an ontological liberalism, to be sure, makes possible belief in an ontological realm independent of the material, namely, a realm in which mind can survive without a body. However, critics of Ducasse may point out that such an ontological liberalism is such a skeptical doctrine that it undermines Ducasse's entire critique of monotheism.

(ii) Ducasse's analysis of mind as a set of capacities is a second argument he uses to support the possibility of survival. As we shall explain in the next chapter, psychical research often suggests the survival, not of a complete personality, but of isolated capacities. Since, for Ducasse, an incarnate mind is understood as a collection of capacities without an underlying substance (physical or nonphysical), there is no absurdity in supposing that some capacities belonging to a mind, when discarnate, become separated from other capacities. As we have seen in Chapter IV, this analysis of mind is very controversial indeed. Many philosophers would suppose that we have no Right to Believe in this theory of mind, much less a Right to Believe in a religious doctrine which assumes, among other things, this theory of mind.

In short, Ducasse bases his defense of the Right to Believe in an Eastern form of polytheism on controversial philosophical doctrines, and many philosophers would insist that since a preponderance of counterevidence denies us the Right to Believe in each of these philosophical doctrines, much more does a preponderance of counterevidence deny us the Right to Believe in a religious doctrine which relies on the truth of all of them together, though of course no one denies that both the philosophical and religious doctrines are logical possibilities.

A further reason to suppose that Ducasse uncritically permits a Right to Believe in non-Western beliefs while prematurely denying that right to monotheism is his proposal of Karma as the most attractive form of reincarnation.

It has often been pointed out that we have little, if any, memory of earlier lives, and reincarnation cannot insure the punishment and reward so important to the function of religious belief unless earlier lives are remembered and we can appreciate our present suffering or happiness as punishment or reward for deeds in earlier lives. It is to escape this difficulty in the religious significance of reincarnation that Ducasse proposes belief in Karma.

An act of which we retain no memory may nevertheless have the remote effect of placing us eventually in a situation conducive to the acquiring of the wisdom, virtue, or ability, lack of which made us act as we did in the forgotten past. If as the Karma doctrine of the Hindus asserts, our conduct in one incarnation automatically tends to have this very sort of consequence in one or another of our later lives, then lack of memory of those past lives does not prevent our growing morally and spiritually in this indirect manner, owing to the nature of our conduct in unremembered earlier lives. [22]

The doctrine of Karma implies that the cosmos regularly promotes what human beings consider to be moral growth. However, a cosmos so regulated to promote moral growth in spite of the obvious inability of the world of ordinary experience to promote moral growth regularly seems extremely unlikely, though of course logically possible. Ducasse has himself noted that "if unseen spiritual beings exist . . . it would be natural to suppose that, as in the case of men" they are good and bad in varying degrees. [23] Would it not be equally "natural to suppose" that, if there is rebirth, it promotes moral *degeneration* as often as it promotes moral growth?

But let us suppose that Ducasse can find in Eastern thought or in psychical research some other belief that we have an epistemic right to adopt. What reason do we have to suppose that such a belief, once cognitively sanitized, will perform the social and personal functions that ordinary religious dogma performs? Ducasse assures us that he is "a deeply religious person," [24] but he has not presented a belief that is cognitively meaningful, epistemically legitimate *and* capable of performing (for some people at least) the functions performed by ordinary "viscous" religious dogma. Ducasse himself says that the efficacy of religious beliefs is enhanced by their vagueness. He rightly points out that vagueness shields from the believer's sight "the contradictions and incongruities which may infect the belief and which, if it were not vague, would be too glaring to make belief possible." [25] Ducasse is fond of quoting Michelet's characterization of theology as "the art of befuddling oneself methodically," but he nowhere considers the important question of whether methodical self-befuddlement and vagueness are essential ingredients of any belief that is capable of performing the social and personal functions he describes as the proper functions of religion. Although in his analyses of monotheism and the ethics of belief Ducasse often shows himself to be a brilliant player in what he says is the "game called Pursuit of Knowledge" wherein the rules are those of "observational, experimental, inductive, deductive, circumstantial, and testimonial evidence," [26] we cannot in good conscience, as fellow players of that "game," avoid suggesting that Ducasse's own religiousness may have been made possible only by methodical self-befuddlement, albeit a unique befuddlement, influenced by Eastern thought and psychical research and very different from the befuddlement found in Western monotheism.

NOTES

[1] C.J. Ducasse, "Are Religious Dogmas Cognitive and Meaningful?" in *Academic Freedom, Logic and Religion*, symposium at the 1953 meeting of the Eastern Division of the American Philosophical Association (Philadelphia: University of Pennsylvania Press, 1953), pp. 89–97; and Ducasse's response to comments at the same symposium, *Journal of Philosophy* 51 (1954), 169–70.

[2] Raphael Demos, *Journal of Philosophy* 51 (1954), 171; cf. Patrick Romanell's comment on "Mr. Ducasse's Denial of Cognitive Significance to Religion," *ibid.*, 154.

[3] C.J. Ducasse, "What Has Science Done to Religion?," *Centennial Review of Arts and Science* 3 (1959), 115–25.

[4] *Ibid.*, p. 124.

[5] C.J. Ducasse, "Philosophical Liberalism," in *Contemporary American Philosophy*, Vol. 1 (London: Allen and Unwin, 1930), pp. 309–10; *Philosophy as a Science* (New York: Oskar Piest, 1941), pp. 217–38; *Nature, Mind, and Death* (LaSalle, Illinois: Open Court Publishing Company, 1951), pp. 51–61.

[6] C.J. Ducasse, *A Philosophical Scrutiny of Religion* (New York: Ronald Press, 1953), p. 135.

[7] *Ibid.*, p. 144. Ducasse recognizes that religion also has its "debit side," that is, that religious belief can have harmful effects; but he likens the possibility of harmful effects to the possibility of ill effects of medicine or of a knife if they are misused (*ibid.*, pp. 168–94).

[8] *Ibid.*, p. 4.

[9] *Ibid.*, pp. 352–79.

[10] *Ibid.*, pp. 333–50.

[11] See Edward H. Madden and Peter H. Hare, *Evil and the Concept of God* (Spring-

field, Illinois: Charles C. Thomas, 1968), pp. 20–36 for a detailed discussion of this evasion tactic in recent theology and philosophy of religion.

[12] *Ibid.*, pp. 140–46, contains a discussion of modifications of monotheism in Edgar Brightman, Alfred North Whitehead, Charles Hartshorne, Josiah Royce and others.

[13] *A Philosophical Scrutiny of Religion*, p. 350.

[14] *Ibid.*, p. 233.

[15] Letter to Professor H.H. Price, June 1, 1966.

[16] Letter to Mrs. Roberts, April 4, 1956.

[17] Letter to Dr. Corliss Lamont, March 28, 1964.

[18] Letter to Professor Ralph Tyler Flewelling, May 28, 1947.

[19] In a letter to Professor Dale Riepe (March 5, 1968) Ducasse gives an account of his first contact with the idea: "[T]he idea of reincarnation, which immediately commended itself to me, was first brought to my attention by a lady who . . . in I think 1903 . . . showed me a little book that had been published shortly before in that year. The book's title was *La Sagesse Antique à Travers les Ages*, and its author was a Dr. Th. Pascal . . . It acquainted me with the views of the Theosophists, which appealed to me, . . . and when I returned to New York I joined the Theosophical Society and was for some time in charge of the library of its New York branch. There I read a book, *Esoteric Buddhism*, by A.P. Sinnett, which sets forth the theosophical doctrines as being esoteric Buddhism."

[20] *Nature, Mind, and Death*, pp. 458–59.

[21] C.J. Ducasse, "A Defense of Ontological Liberalism," *Journal of Philosophy* 21 (1924).

[22] C.J. Ducasse, *A Critical Examination of the Belief in Life After Death* (Springfield, Illinois: Charles C. Thomas, 1961), p. 226. Cf. *Nature, Mind, and Death*, pp. 491–502.

[23] *A Philosophical Scrutiny of Religion*, p. 204.

[24] *Journal of Philosophy* 51 (1954), 169.

[25] "What Has Science Done to Religion? ," pp. 122–23.

[26] "Are Religious Dogmas Cognitive and Meaningful? ," p. 94.

CHAPTER XI

PARANORMAL PHENOMENA

Few have done as much as Ducasse to make possible clear and unemotional discussion of paranormal phenomena. While we do not accept some of his conclusions, we have the greatest respect for his painstaking and illuminating analyses of the relevant concepts, arguments and evidence.

I

From the earliest stages of his career Ducasse had an interest in paranormal phenomena. For example, he reports (1961) that more than fifty years before he was present at what was purported to be the gradual materialization of a man's body.[1] But it was not until the 1940's that he devoted himself to the demanding task of determining what, in the entire field of psychical research, he was obliged to believe (justified in believing) or what he at least had a *right* to believe. Before we discuss the various contributions Ducasse made to psychical research as a means of establishing his epistemic obligations and rights, let us make clear what Ducasse's own conclusions were, i.e., what he actually considered his epistemic obligations and rights to be.

The situation is complicated both by the fact that Ducasse changed his conclusions between his earlier and later work and by the fact that he thought he had different epistemic rights in relation to different areas of psychical research. We shall first give an account of his later (1961) view of his epistemic rights in relation to the different areas and then indicate how he changed his mind.

In the area of paranormal phenomena not involving survival (where extensive experimental work has been done) Ducasse could not see "how any person who is at once open-minded, intelligent, and adequately conversant with the evidence, can fail to regard as established the reality of extrasensory and psychokinetic functions in certain persons."[2] The evidence for these paranormal phenomena he calls "practically conclusive."[3] He thinks, in other words, that he has a *justified* belief in these phenomena, not just a *right* to believe, and that to believe otherwise would be irrational.

In his later work he thinks he also has a justified belief in survival of death, though it is clear that he does not consider the preponderance of evidence for survival to be anything like as great as that for paranormal phenomena that have been *experimentally* demonstrated. He considers that "the balance of the evidence so far obtained is on the side of the reality of survival and, in the best cases, of survival not merely of memories of the life on earth, but of survival also of the most significant capacities of the human mind, and of continuing exercise of those." [4]

Finally, as regards reincarnation as a particular kind of survival, Ducasse also concludes that there is a preponderance of evidence in its favor, though it is a slim preponderance considerably weaker than the preponderance supporting *some* sort of survival, discarnate or embodied. "[I]f — as there is reason to believe — the facts of these cases are correctly reported in the records of them we have, then they are strong evidence that their cases are truly cases of reincarnation; and hence that reincarnation, whether general or not, occurs at least sometimes." [5]

The simplest way to describe Ducasse's change of view between his earlier and later work is to say that, as he studied the literature more and more, his confidence both in survival, and in reincarnation as a particular kind of survival, increased, while his virtually complete confidence in experimentally demonstrated paranormal phenomena remained unchanged. His earlier view that there is no clear preponderance of evidence and that we have *only* a right to believe in survival and reincarnation can be found in the following quotations from "Is a Life After Death Possible?" (1948), *Nature, Mind and Death* (1951) and *A Philosophical Scrutiny of Religion* (1953):

[W]hether or not such survival is a fact, it is at least coherently thinkable and not incompatible with any facts empirically known to us today ... [I]t does seem that if survival is a fact, then the most plausible form it might take would be rebirth on earth ... [6]

[N]o contradiction appears to be involved in the supposition that some parts or capacities of man's mind survive the death of his body, and therefore that such survival is quite possible. As to whether it is actually as well as theoretically possible, there is strong *prima facie* evidence that in some instances *something* survives, which appears to be some part or some set of capacities of the mind whose body has died. But the demonstrated reality and occasional functioning of the paranormal capacities mentioned above — in particular, telepathy, clairvoyance, and retrocognition — so complicate the interpretation of the facts ordinarily adduced as empirical evidence of survival that, with our present very meagre knowledge of the latent paranormal capacities of the human mind, and with the rather drastic revision of the ordinary ideas of our relation to *time* which the fact of precognition would appear to require, nothing both definite and well evidenced can yet be concluded concerning the actual, as distinguished from theoretical, possibility of partial survival.[7]

[L]et it be emphasized again that no claim is made that this conception of survival [reincarnation] is known to be true, or even known to be more probably true than not ... but only ... that it is possible ...[8]

[T]he belief in a life after death, which so many persons have found no particular difficulty in accepting as an article of religious faith, not only may be true but is perhaps capable of empirical proof ...[9]

II

Let us now turn to the important contributions Ducasse makes to psychical research in the course of, and as a means to, establishing his epistemic rights. We shall summarize these contributions here and in later sections discuss them in detail.

(i) Since Ducasse believes that philosophy has the semantical task of analyzing key terms in philosophical discourse, it is not surprising that he attaches great importance to the clarification of the meanings of terms that play key roles in psychical research. To answer adequately the question of whether a mind survives death, it is necessary, for example, to give an adequate analysis of the meaning of 'mind'. Conveniently, many of Ducasse's analyses of terms used in psychical research can be taken over from the semantical analyses he has already performed in discussing other philosophical problems. Indeed, some may consider Ducasse's most significant contribution to psychical research to be a systematic set of carefully defined terms in epistemology and metaphysics that lends itself to the clear discussion of paranormal phenomena. However, Ducasse goes beyond the use of his epistemological and metaphysical concepts to the clarification of distinctions between the many types of paranormal phenomena — levitation, possession, etc. Furthermore, his analytic contribution is not limited to *concepts*; his characteristic clarity and precision is also found in his discussion of the vast array of *arguments* relevant to the discussion of paranormal phenomena. Clear formulation of issues and arguments is, after all, at least as valuable as the analysis of concepts.

Although others working in the area of psychical research may differ with Ducasse in the analysis of this or that concept or argument, there can be little doubt that Ducasse's work, like that of C. D. Broad, H. H. Price and

A. G. N. Flew, serves as a model of analytical rigor in a field often sadly lacking in such rigor, and it is quite possible that, in the long run, Ducasse's philosophical method, his analytical rigor, and not any of his conclusions or analyses of particular concepts, will be his most important contribution to the field.

(ii) Just as Ducasse's work in epistemology and metaphysics enables him to make important contributions to the analytical rigor of the discussion of paranormal phenomena, so his knowledge of the philosophy and history of science makes it possible for him to make useful suggestions concerning the methods of investigation to be used in psychical research.

Although Ducasse has great respect for experimental and statistical work on extrasensory perception, he believes that the scientific importance of spontaneous paranormal phenomena has not been sufficiently appreciated. He argues that rarity *per se* does not detract from the scientific significance of paranormal phenomena. It is, he thinks, genuineness, not frequency and repeatability, that gives paranormal phenomena their importance, and he explains in detail what methods of observation and reporting are necessary to establish such genuineness. An understandable desire for scientific respectability has given statistical work with cards and dice a considerable vogue in psychical research, and Ducasse makes an impressive attempt to show how comparable scientific reliability can be achieved in the investigation of spontaneous paranormal phenomena.

(iii) A sophisticated methodology even when combined with an adequate ethics of belief is not enough, however. If widespread rational belief about paranormal phenomena is to become a *practical* possibility, we must also, Ducasse thinks, have a thorough understanding of why people adopt the irrational beliefs about paranormal phenomena that they do. For that reason, Ducasse offers a psychology of belief to supplement his ethics of belief and methodology. Once it is clear to people what dogmatic assumptions, unconscious habits and parochial interests motivate those who either make sweeping allegations of fraud and malobservation or accept the marvelous uncritically, people will be able, Ducasse hopes, to guard against these tendencies and to follow the methodology and ethics of belief he proposes.

(iv) Not surprisingly, Ducasse has much of interest to say about the philosophical implications of paranormal phenomena. Although he deplores the fact that few philosophers take paranormal phenomena seriously, he also regrets that prominent psychical researchers, notably J. B. Rhine, claim for paranormal phenomena philosophical implications they do not have. Paranormal phenomena do not imply, as Rhine thinks, freedom of the will, but they do have other important implications. Like C. D. Broad, Ducasse believes that paranormal phenomena are clues to forces or dimensions of nature as yet unknown and unexplored. Paranormal phenomena force us to look critically at the principles that we believe limit what is empirically possible. To alter such basic "limiting principles" is to alter our entire conceptual framework, and Ducasse believes that philosophers can and should play an important role in revising our conceptual framework to accommodate the new dimensions of reality uncovered by psychical research.

(v) Ducasse's discussion of the question of survival of death is widely known and is perhaps the most comprehensive and philosophically sophisticated treatment ever presented, but it is important to notice the respects in which his treatment is distinctive both as philosophy and as psychical research and in what respects his work summarizes the work of others. Ducasse does not pretend to add substantially to the critical accounts of particular cases of paranormal phenomena relevant to survival. His detailed defense of the Bridey Murphy case appears to be the only account that goes substantially beyond the literature familiar to psychical researchers, if not to philosophers. Ducasse's distinctive contribution to the discussion of survival lies in three areas: (a) conceptual analysis; (b) systematic and precise analysis of the numerous objections to survival, especially those that are theoretical and *a priori* (here his dispositional analysis of mind is basic, and C. D. Broad and A. G. N. Flew have commented interestingly on this aspect of his work); and (c) defense of the survival hypothesis against those (e.g. F. C. Dommeyer) who claim that a more economical and plausible explanation can be given in terms of such paranormal abilities as clairvoyance, telepathy, retrocognition, etc. (in doing this Ducasse relies primarily on his analysis of skills and capacities).

(vi) Finally, Ducasse contributes to the field of psychical research an interesting discussion of precognition, including his "Theory Theta." The remarkable conclusion he reaches is that to say of a psychical event that it is "present" is to *mean* only that it is the object of a perception which is present to some percipient. Since no psychical event is "present" or "past" *per se*, it is, Ducasse argues, logically possible for one and the same physical event to be "present" on many different percipient occasions.

Obviously Ducasse's use of analytical techniques in the discussion of paranormal phenomena is too extensive for us to summarize the results here. Instead of attempting a summary, we shall give illustrations of his techniques as they are used on terms, issues and arguments.

As a first illustration, his analysis of 'paranormal' is appropriate. "By a 'paranormal' phenomenon," Ducasse says, "I shall mean any occurrence whose cause is neither that from which it ordinarily results, nor any other yet known to the natural sciences as capable of causing it." [10] This analysis permits Ducasse to distinguish between 'paranormal' and 'supernatural'. Supernatural phenomena he takes to be those which (theologians believe) violate the laws of nature whereas paranormal phenomena are "just as natural and capable of being eventually understood as are those parts of nature whose laws we happen already to have ascertained." [11] His use of 'paranormal' so defined also allows him to avoid an illegitimate implication of the more traditional "psychic." To speak of psychic phenomena implies that the observed phenomenon or its cause (or both) are parapsychological, and not paraphysiological or paraphysical. In short, Ducasse's analysis of 'paranormal' effectively delineates a subject matter within the field of scientific inquiry without commitment to the mental or physical nature of cause or effect.

Ducasse is equally adept in using his analytical techniques to separate issues. An illustration of this is his distinction between the issue of survival and the issue of religious belief. Although Ducasse thinks, as we have seen in the previous chapter, that belief in survival can be used to perform the functions of religious belief, he points out that the two issues are logically independent of one another.

If the survival hypothesis is purged of vagueness, is defined in a manner not involving contradictions or other demonstrable impossibilities, and is dissociated from the additional supposition commonly coupled with it that survival will be such as to bring reward or punishment to the surviving personalities according as they lived on earth virtuously or wickedly, then it is no more religious than would be the hypothesis that conscious beings live on Mars . . . No contradiction at all would be involved either in supposing that one or more gods exist but that there is no *post mortem* human life, or in supposing that there is a life after death but no God or gods. [12]

Finally, a good illustration of his analytic technique as applied to *arguments* is his distinction between empirical objections to survival and theoretical or *a priori* objections. The objection, for example, that a lesion of the cortex eliminates or impairs mental capacities is an *empirical* argument against the possibility of consciousness existing independently of a living organism whereas the claim that what we call states of consciousness are nothing but minute chemical or physical events that take place in the brain is an *a priori* or *theoretical* argument against such a possibility. Here as elsewhere, Ducasse takes pains to state precisely and to order systematically all the arguments relevant to an issue.

IV

Taking issue with Rhine's view that spontaneous or mediumistic paranormal phenomena cannot establish anything and can only suggest experiments which, if properly controlled, can establish that the phenomena occured, Ducasse submits that "earthquakes, hurricanes, eclipses of the sun and moon, or the fall of aerolites, are phenomena over the conditions of which we have not the slightest control; and yet . . . their occurence is completely established." [13] What is needed, Ducasse thinks, is not wholesale rejection of spontaneous or mediumistic paranormal phenomena but instead methods of observing and recording such apparently paranormal phenomena that will establish their reality. He stresses the importance of detail in reports and describes at some length the types of detail needed.

But who is to be trained to make such careful observations and records? How are we to train observers of paranormal events if we do not know in advance who will experience or witness them? Obviously a good bet is to train those who have already experienced such phenomena and also those who, though they have not had such experiences, at least have an interest in the subject and are likely to put themselves in a position to witness paranormal phenomena. Such prospective observers should be trained in the mechanisms of perceptual illusion, hypnotically induced illusions, tricks of conjuring, etc.

But the development of such critical powers should not, Ducasse emphasizes, be done in such a way that the trained observer intimidates the medium. "[I]t is methodologically imperative to learn to speak with them in *their* language, even if when so doing one would privately put between quotation marks some of the terms one was using; and imperative also to approach them [the mediums] in a manner that will not cause them to freeze up as soon as they see us coming, but will on the contrary enlist their good will." [14] Moreover, such an observer should not be so skeptical as to assume that, because a medium is sometimes found to be cheating consciously or unconsciously, *none* of his performances constitute genuinely paranormal phenomena. What is scientifically important is not how large a number of reports of paranormal phenomena we can get, but rather that we have *some* that are completely reliable.

Not only does Ducasse think it methodologically important that people be trained to observe and record carefully the performance of those who *already* have paranormal abilities. It is also important that those trained in scientific and philosophical modes of thinking *develop in themselves* paranormal abilities,[15] and he suggests that hypnosis may be one way to develop such abilities.[16]

V

A paranormal phenomena such as levitation is not, Ducasse thinks, inherently any more or less paradoxical than gravitation. Yet people (including Ducasse) who have carefully and sympathetically studied the reports of levitation find it hard to believe. Why? Because gravitation we experience every day whereas few people have witnessed levitation, and belief is largely a matter of habit. Belief and disbelief are comfortable states of mind. Doubt is disturbing, and this discomfort leads us to reject any idea that demands radical changes in our beliefs or disbeliefs.[17] While it is true that love of the marvelous leads many people to accept reports of paranormal phenomena uncritically, Ducasse never tires of driving home the lesson that, although

> the evidence offered by addicts of the marvelous for the reality of the phenomena they accept must be critically examined, it is equally necessary ... to scrutinize just as closely and critically the skeptics' allegations of fraud, or of malobservation, or of misinterpretation of what was observed, or of hypnotically induced hallucinations. For there is likely to be just as much wishful thinking, prejudice, emotion, snap judgment, naivete, and intellectual dishonesty on the side of orthodoxy, of skepticism, and of conservatism, as on the side of hunger for and belief in the marvelous. The emotional motivation for irresponsible disbelief is, in fact, probably even stronger − especially in scientifically educated persons, whose pride of knowledge is at stake − than is in other persons the motivation for irresponsible belief.[18]

But it is not just their threatened egos, Ducasse adds, that motivate scientists in their irrational rejection of the paranormal. An unconscious creed also prevents them from taking a rational attitude. A major reason why scientists regard paranormal phenomena as impossible is that unconsciously "they have made a metaphysical creed − a doctrine as to the nature of *all* of Reality — out of what in fact is only the description of the particular *part* of Reality they undertake to explore, namely, the material world." [19] Furthermore, this metaphysical creed is nothing more than an expression of *interest* in subject matter of a certain character, and there is no reason why an interest in some other subject matter cannot be just as legitimate as the undeniably legitimate interest the scientist has in what is material.

"[T]he truly scientific attitude," Ducasse concludes, "is neither the will to believe nor the will to disbelieve, but the will to investigate." [20] Only the will to investigate avoids both gratuitous incredulity and gratuitous credulity and is compatible with "the plasticity of opinion that permits altering previous conclusions readily if new items of evidence demanding it present themselves." [21]

VI

In discussing the philosophical implications of parapsychology, J. B. Rhine contends that it has been experimentally proven that the kind of energy involved in the occurrence of extrasensory perception and psychokinesis is non-physical — non-physical because, unlike any known form of physical energy, it is unaffected by distance, time, intervening material obstacles or spatial orientation of target. That the energy is not affected in the ordinary ways Ducasse does not deny, but he takes exception to Rhine's inference that it is non-physical, i.e., non-material. If one understands "matter" to be whatever is either publicly perceptible or a constituent of what is publicly perceptible, then Psi energy could be material in the same sense that sub-atomic particles are material — as constituents of publicly perceptible objects. However, Ducasse is not asserting that Psi energy *is* material; he is simply insisting that it is still an open question. "The reputation of parapsychology," he says, "can only be damaged by the . . . insistence on drawing a conclusion . . . which patently goes so far beyond what the experimental findings strictly establish." [22] We do not yet know whether Psi energy is mental or material, or sometimes mental and sometimes material, depending on the particular case. He makes the important philosophical point that Rhine's experiments, successful as they are, do not necessarily indicate an additional *non*-material dimension of Nature; they may indicate a paramaterial (e.g. parabiological) dimension.

Having made the erroneous claim that Psi energy must be non-physical,

Rhine goes on to argue (also erroneously in Ducasse's view) that since the energy is non-physical it can free human action from the deterministic constraints of the material world and make possible moral responsibility and values. Values, Ducasse points out, in no way depend for their existence on non-materiality. "[I]f ontological materialism is true, what follows is that even the noblest artistic, ethical, and spiritual achievements of man then were potentialities somehow latent in the particular kinds of matter of which human beings consist. For those achievements are facts of historical record, which would not in the least be obliterated or made less noble by the other fact, if it be a fact, that man has been all along a wholly material being." [23]

Neither does human freedom depend for its existence on the non-materiality of man. If a volition, whether it be a molecular event in the matter of the brain or a mental event, can cause me to raise my arm under certain circumstances, human freedom exists. In showing in detail why parapsychology does not have any implications for the freedom and determinism issue Ducasse summarizes the theory of human agency we have discussed in Chapter II.

Paranormal phenomena, Ducasse believes, have more than enough startling implications without Rhine's unfortunate philosophizing. They have important implications because they clash with one or another of what C. D. Broad calls "basic limiting principles." "For example, one of the most basic among those limiting principles is that an event cannot cause anything before it has actually occurred; and a phenomenon which would clash with this principle would be, not the inferring but the *ostensible perceiving* [i.e. "precognition"], as for instance in a dream or vision, of an as yet future event of some out-of-the-ordinary kind one had no reason to expect. For then the dream or vision would, paradoxically, be a present effect of an as yet future cause." [24]

Another example of a limiting principle is "that no person can come to know the thoughts or feelings of another except through perceived bodily signs of them — signs such as words, gestures, facial expressions, or the like. And this 'basic limiting principle', if it is valid without exception, obviously rules out the possibility of telepathy." [25] Believing that in some cases the evidence for paranormal phenomena that clash with our limiting principles is too strong to explain away, Ducasse thinks that "philosophers ought to take a hand in devising the needed new conceptual framework; as they did when, in the 17th century, a similar need resulted from the new facts which were then being discovered." [26]

He recognizes that paranormal phenomena, considered simply in themselves, are often trivial, and that many believe that scientists have more pressing tasks than the study of raps, tilting of tables, and chatterings of old women and curates.

What is not necessarily trivial, on the other hand, but potentially momentous, is what these phenomena signify. That a piece of amber when rubbed on wool or silk attracts small bits of stuff — which for centuries was all that the word "electricity" meant — was in itself just as trivial and useless a fact. Nevertheless, the very force which was responsible for that paltry little phenomenon was mightily at work all about man even then. And, notwithstanding the scientists of Galvani's time who laughed at him and his frogs, that force was capable of being understood and harnessed by man who, by means of it, has in the succeeding centuries radically transformed the conditions of life in all civilized countries. [27]

Although Ducasse says that science as it has been practiced and is presently practiced is not futile, and says, further, that "[n]o fact that science has really established would be in the least endangered or rendered insignificant by the genuineness of paranormal facts," [28] it is clear that he believes that there might be a good deal of reinterpretation or qualification of established facts. He suggests that the causal action of a volition on our own body may be "a psychokinetic effect in maximum degree" [29] and "sensation could be viewed as a special instance of clairvoyance." [30]

To "clinch" his case for what he takes to be the philosophical importance of paranormal phenomena, Ducasse remarks that reports of paranormal phenomena have philosophical implications whether the phenomena really occurred as reported, or not. "If they did *not* so occur, then the specificity and numerousness of the reports, and the fact that some of the witnesses, and some of the persons who accepted their reports, have been people of high intelligence and integrity, is exceedingly interesting from the standpoint of the psychology of perception, delusion, illusion or hallucination, of credulity and credibility, and of testimony." [31] Indeed, we would find it difficult to quarrel with someone who claimed *that* sort of significance for reports of paranormal phenomena!

VII

Since we cannot give here a complete account of the numerous and complex arguments Ducasse considers in discussing survival, we shall instead explain briefly the pattern of his treatment of the question and discuss in detail only those considerations that seem most crucial.

Relying on his subtle analyses of key concepts, Ducasse first attempts to show that survival is *theoretically* possible because it contains no contradiction and *empirically* possible because it is not inconsistent with any definitely known empirical facts. Having shown that survival is both theoretically and empirically *possible*, he next examines the positive evidence for it — the *probability* of survival. Although some of this evidence he finds ambiguous and inconclusive since it can be explained away in terms of paranormal abilities not involving survival, he believes that some of it cannot be so explained and constitutes a preponderance of evidence for survival.

As we noted in the previous chapter, a great deal of the force of Ducasse's argument for the theoretical possibility depends on his analysis of mind in terms of capacities. Although we have pointed out in Chapter IV many of the difficulties in this analysis of mind, we must here point out how these difficulties have special relevance to the survival question, and have, in fact, been emphasized by such critics as A. G. N. Flew.

Flew is critical of Ducasse's basic contention that a person can be identified with a disembodied mind so that if my incorporeal element survives death it is recognizably *me*. "Certainly," Flew says, "there are minds; just as there are grins. But this does not necessarily imply that minds are, in the philosophical sense, substances; that is, that a mind could significantly be spoken of as existing separately. This is no more the case than that there are grins gives any warrant for the Wonderland suggestion that there could be said to be the grin of a Cheshire cat without there being a face to grin it. Again, certainly we meet and are familiar with other people. But this is the very opposite of a reason for thinking that people are, or are essentially, the incorporeal occupants of man-shaped corporeal containers." [32] Although Flew is aware that in Ducasse's analysis a mind is an integrated set of capacities whose existing consists in a history of the actual exercise of those capacities, he is not persuaded that such a history of the exercise of capacities can count as a person. Flew also argues that people are what you *meet*,[33] and he does not see how such meeting is possible without embodiment.

Philosophical criticism of the theoretical possibility of survival as conceived by Ducasse has not been limited, however, to criticism of his attempt to make personality independent of body. There has also been criticism of his attempt to use his disposition-event ontology in giving an account of the theoretical possibility of a discarnate mind. On the one hand, C. D. Broad insists that at the back of any purely dispositional fact, there is a *categorical* fact of some kind which serves as the needed ground or basis for the dispositions, and he proposes a "psychic factor" as such a substantive base. On the other hand, Ducasse believes that no such substantive basis is needed and the surviving mind can be analyzed without remainder as an integrated set of dispositions whose existence is the history of the exercise of those dispositions.[34] Broad, however, thinks that a purely dispositional analysis does not provide a criterion for attributing a disposition to one substance rather than another and does not *locate* (i.e. individuate) stimulus-events or reaction-events.[35] Ducasse thinks that he can use a psychical analogue of physical place to locate psychical dispositions and events in terms of causal relations between events in the same way as he can locate physical dispositions and events.[36] In discussing Ducasse's ontology elsewhere we have indicated why his event ontology is inadequate, and we believe that Broad's criticism of Ducasse's analysis of mental substance is of the same type as our more general criticism of Ducasse's ontology.

Let us now consider a major objection of a different kind. Even if Ducasse can show that the concept of a discarnate surviving self as a set of mental capacities is a coherent concept, he still must show that the cases cited in support of the survival hypothesis cannot be more economically and plausibly explained in terms of telepathy, clairvoyance, retrocognition and the dramatizing power of the unconscious. This objection has been put very forcefully by F. C. Dommeyer.[37] Since only part of Ducasse's interesting assessment of Dommeyer's objection has been published, we can most usefully present Ducasse's way of dealing with this sort of argument by quoting at length from his manuscript.

He [Dommeyer] holds that the a priori arguments for an affirmative answer have not supplied it; and therefore that if such an answer is possible at all it has to be based on empirical evidence of survival. Such evidence, however, is not provided either by ordinary experience or by any of the natural sciences. Hence, if it exists at all, it has to be looked for among paranormal phenomena; and more specifically in the communications purportedly from particular minds surviving discarnate, who appear to be either themselves employing a medium's or automatist's organs of utterance, or to be conveying their thoughts telepathically to the medium, who then utters them.

Dommeyer considers such communications and concludes that an alternative and more economical explanation of their evidential features is that the recondite yet true facts communicated are obtained by the unconscious mind of the medium or automatist either telepathically from the minds of living persons who know them, or clair-voyantly from existing physical records of them, or possibly by retrocognitive percep-tion of the past facts themselves.

The difficulty, however, which ultimately stands in the way of explaining *all* com-munications in view in this manner is that, in order to account for certain of the occur-rences that invite most strongly the survival hypothesis, ESP would not be enough; nor even "super" ESP in the sense of capacity to perceive extrasensorily physical and mental facts more hidden, numerous, slight, detailed, or distant in time or/and space than ESP is yet independently known to be capable of doing. What would be needed in addition would be something different from ESP *in kind*, not simply in degree. For perception, whether sensory or extrasensory, is inherently of particular facts; and perception by one person that elaborate skills or special powers which he does not him-self have are being exercized by another person does not confer them on the perceiver. Hence the weakest point in Dommeyer's attempt to show that ESP would be adequate to make the survival hypothesis unnecessary in all cases that have seemed to call for it, is the much too cavalier manner in which he dismisses what are probably the two best cases of their respective kind on record: the case of the apparitions of Mrs. Butler, and the Watseka case of "possession." There will not be room here to consider his treat-ment of both, so I shall confine my comments to his remarks on the Watseka case.

The facts which he claims adequate to explain without need to postulate survival are . . . "the dramatizing power of the unconscious;" "power of retrocognition" possessed by the unconscious; and that if, as I have contended, a medium "cannot acquire a skill telepathically or by other ESP means from another living person" then "exactly the same problem is present for one who asserts that the skill comes from a discarnate mind."

But, to deal first with this last contention, it is not true that the same problem is present in the "possession" hypothesis. For this hypothesis is *not* that the medium acquires from the discarnate mind the skill concerned – let us suppose for the sake of concreteness, skill to converse responsively in a language *L* which the medium has never learnt.

Instead, the "possession" hypothesis is that the mind of the deceased, which did have the skill to converse in that language, takes temporary possession of the medium's *bodily instruments of communication*; that is, of the medium's organs of speech and of writing and of audition; and that *the mind of the deceased* then employs those organs to converse with the sitter in the language *L* which that mind knew and still knows, but which the medium still does not know. That the words of language *L* are uttered by *the vocal organs* of the medium's body does not presuppose that *the medium* has gained command of the language *L*, any more than does the fact that two persons far apart in space employ a telephone to converse together presupposes that *the telephone* has gained command of the language they use!

As regards Dommeyer's positive contention that a "skill or creative capacity" can be acquired telepathically by a person lacking it from another having it, it is crucial to realize that although a skill is a capacity, not every capacity is a skill. Dommeyer mentions – as having been present in, and exercized by both Leibniz and Newton independently – the capacity to discover . . . or create . . . the calculus. But although this capacity presupposes possession of certain skills, *it is not itself a skill:* One could *not* correctly say that a person P must be highly skilled at discovering or creating the calculus since he can do it successfully more than 9 times out of 10! On the other hand, one *could* correctly say that *P* is highly skilled at target shooting, since he can hit the bull's eye more than 9 times out of 10.

The reason why the second of these two capacities is a skill but the first is not becomes evident if only one keeps in mind just what is required in order that capacity to do something *D* be a skill; namely (a) that *D* be a *purposive* activity; (b) that it be *sightedly*, not blindly, purposive; (c) that the performer be *conscious of the form his activity is taking* at each of its steps; (d) that he be *then aware of the rightness or defectiveness* of the step just taken; and (e) that he *then regulate accordingly the next step he takes.*

I submit that, in the light of this analysis of what constitutes a skill, the contention that a skill can be acquired telepathically or retrocognitively by a person lacking it from a person who has it or did have it retains no plausibility at all: no evidence exists that a skill, properly so called, can be acquired otherwise than *through practice.* What is possible is only that the practise needed be shortened through coaching by an expert.

As regards the dramatizing power of the unconscious, such relevance as it can have to the question of survival is neither to the Watseka case nor to cases of xenoglossy or of other elaborate skills; but only to mediumistic communications purportedly from minds surviving discarnate. What that dramatizing power can produce is impersonations; i.e., imitations of sensorily or extrasensorily perceived behavioral peculiarities of the deceased — tone of voice, pet phrases, style of handwriting; and imitations of such verbal displays of technical mental skills of the deceased as he did give while living. But imitations of displays of a technical skill do not confer that skill on the imitator. His imitations are merely apings, only good enough to make uncritical spectators believe that the deceased is again displaying the technical skill he had.

Consider for example the case of a person who has no knowledge of theoretical physics. Irrespective of whether he be awake, or in hypnosis, or in mediumistic trance, he could not possibly enact convincingly the part Einstein would take in discussing with a theoretical physicist present some technical point in theoretical physics.

The crucial question as regards the Watseka case is whether it is possible, or not possible, for a person *P* to identify himself unmistakably to another person *Q* who had known him intimately for years, by means of his behavior and of the contents, style, allusions, and responsiveness of his conversation with *Q*. That it is not possible in only an hour or two is probably true. But in the Watseka case, the Roffs had three and a half months of day-long close observation of the behavior, tastes, skills, knowledge, and capacity to make and understand allusions to intimate family matters, possessed by the personality which was expressing itself through the body of Lurancy during those months. And the Roffs testified that those traits were the very same as those which had together been distinctive of their deceased daughter Mary, whom Lurancy had never known.

Let Dommeyer suppose that a young woman who remains constantly masked and muffled somehow comes and lives in his house; and let him ask himself whether he thinks it would be possible for that woman, through facts perceived extrasensorily, to enact for three and a half months convincingly to him the part of his own daughter, if that woman's personality were not really that of his daughter.

An affirmative answer would amount to saying that no way ultimately exists by which it would be possible for a person whose face and figure have been disfigured by acid or by fire, to prove his identity to another who had known him intimately for many years. And this, I submit, is virtually beyond belief. [38]

Ducasse's reply to Dommeyer is based on the assumption that paranormal powers of the familiar sorts, even if present in unlimited degree, do not make possible the acquisition of skills. He does not, however, give any reason for limiting paranormal abilities to the familiar types. Could there not be, as has been suggested,[39] an additional type of paranormal ability that makes possible the acquisition of skills?

We conclude that until at least the serious theoretical problems pointed out by Broad and Flew have been solved and the possibility of paranormally acquiring skills has been ruled out, we do not have an epistemic right to believe in the survival of death.

VIII

Ducasse's suggestion of how to deal with the causal paradox of precognition is as puzzling as it is simple. However, before we comment on his suggestion, we must state the paradox: precognition appears to be impossible because any case of it would be one where an event E is future and therefore as yet non-existent but nevertheless causes another event, a veridical ostensible perception of E, in the form of, e.g., a dream; but that a later event should cause an earlier one is impossible according to the principle that it is impossible that an event should begin to have any effects before it has happened.

It has sometimes been suggested that we deal with this paradox by postulating either a second spatial dimension or a second temporal dimension, but Ducasse proposes instead an additional dimension in which physical events are intrinsically ordered only by entropy. Although, as Ducasse notes, a suggestion similar to his was made by Broad, Ducasse appears to be the first to believe this proposal (dubbed "theory Theta") to be plausible.

The fact from which theory Theta starts is that no definition of the adjectives "past," "present," or "future," *simpliciter*, i.e., applied categorically, can be given in purely physical terms; and hence that physical events *in themselves*, i.e., apart from the psychological events which are percepts of them, are not categorically either past, present, or future.

To physical events considered independently of percepts of them, the predicates "past," "present," or "future" are therefore applicable not categorically but only conditionally. That is, one can say of a physical event E so considered, that it is future to (or temporally after or beyond) a certain other one D *from a certain third C*; but not simply that it is *future* ...

This state of affairs entails that the serial time order of physical events in themselves has *no intrinsic direction* ... [T]he relation 'temporally between', which determines the serial order of physical events, does not determine one rather than the other of two theoretically possible directions within that order. In terms of entropy, all that could be said would be that, in one of the two directions, entropy never decreases; whereas in the other direction it never increases, and this does not, *in itself*, i.e., independently of our perception of physical events, specify as 'real' one rather than the other direction in the series of physical events.[40]

The paradox is eliminated, Ducasse thinks, because the proposal makes it possible for one and the same physical event to be present an indefinite number of times because it is perceived (normally or paranormally) an indefinite number of times. Unfortunately, the notion of an event, whose temporal relations have no purely physical meaning, appears, to us at least, unintelligible. Ducasse deals with one paradox by creating a second paradox.

NOTES

[1] C.J. Ducasse, *A Critical Examination of the Belief in a Life After Death* (Springfield, Ill.: Charles C. Thomas, 1961), pp. 155–56. For other accounts of Ducasse's own encounters with paranormal phenomena, see *ibid.*, pp. 166–68, and 257–71.
[2] C.J. Ducasse, "A Philosopher Looks at E.S.P.," mss. p. 1. This is an address given at Duke University in April 1953; its contents except for the initial three pages (from which this quotation is taken) consisted of his "Some Questions Concerning Psychic Phenomena," *Journal of the American Society for Psychical Research* 48 (1954), 3–20.
[3] *A Critical Examination of the Belief in a Life After Death*, p. 141.
[4] *Ibid.*, p. 203.
[5] C.J. Ducasse, "Life After Death Conceived as Reincarnation," in *In Search of God and Immorality: The Garvin Lectures* (Boston: Beacon Press, 1961), p. 162.
[6] C.J. Ducasse, *Is Life After Death Possible?* (Berkeley and Los Angeles: University of California Press, 1948), p. 30.
[7] C.J. Ducasse, *Nature, Mind, and Death* (La Salle, Ill.: Open Court Publishing Company, 1951), pp. 482–83.
[8] *Ibid.*, p. 502.
[9] C.J. Ducasse, *A Philosophical Scrutiny of Religion* (New York: Ronald Press, 1953), p. 412.
[10] C.J. Ducasse, *Paranormal Phenomena, Nature, and Man: the First John William Graham Lecture on Psychic Science*, delivered April 29, 1951 at Swarthmore College, p. 2; this lecture is reprinted from *JASPR* 45 (1951).
[11] *Ibid.*, p. 2.
[12] *A Critical Examination of the Belief in a Life After Death*, pp. 14–15.
[13] C.J. Ducasse, "The Philosophical Importance of 'Psychic Phenomena'," *Journal of Philosophy* 51 (1954), 819.
[14] C.J. Ducasse, "Method in the Investigation of Spontaneous Paranormal Phenomena," an unpublished paper presented at the Conference on Spontaneous Cases,

organized by the (British) Soc. for Psych. Research, and held at Newham College,
Cambridge University, England, July 11 to 17, 1955; a summary of this paper was
published as "Method of Investigation," in *Proceedings of Four Conferences of Parapsychological Studies* (New York: Parapsychology Foundation, 1957), pp. 111–13.

[15] "The Future of Parapsychology: A Symposium," *International Journal of Parapsychology* 4 (1962), 16.

[16] C.J. Ducasse, "Hypnotism, Suggestion, and Suggestibility," *International Journal of
Parapsychology* 5 (1963), 15–19.

[17] *Paranormal Phenomena, Nature, and Man*, p. 7.

[18] C.J. Ducasse, "Paranormal Phenomena, Science, and Life After Death," in *Paranormal Phenomena, Science, and Life After Death* (New York: Parapsychology Foundation, 1969), p. 35.

[19] C.J. Ducasse, "Science, Scientists, and Psychical Research," *JASPR* 50 (1956), 146.

[20] *Paranormal Phenomena, Nature, and Man*, p. 20.

[21] C.J. Ducasse, "Some Questions Concerning Psychical Phenomena," p. 20.

[22] C.J. Ducasse, review of J.B. Rhine and J.G. Pratt, *Parapsychology, Frontier Science
of the Mind, Philosophy East and West* 7 (1957–58), 157.

[23] "The Philosophical Importance of 'Psychic Phenomena'," p. 816.

[24] *Ibid.*, p. 811.

[25] C.J. Ducasse, "Physical Phenomena in Psychical Research," *JASPR* 52 (1958), 3.

[26] "The Philosophical Importance of 'Psychic Phenomena'," p. 812.

[27] "Some Questions Concerning Psychical Phenomena," p. 13.

[28] *Ibid.*, p. 12.

[29] *Is a Life After Death Possible?*, p. 18.

[30] *Ibid.*, p. 19.

[31] "The Philosophical Importance of 'Psychic Phenomena'," p. 811.

[32] A.G.N. Flew, "The Platonic Presuppositions of the Survival Hypothesis," *Journal
of the Society for Psychical Research* 42 (1963), 58.

[33] *Ibid.*, p. 58.

[34] C.J. Ducasse, review of C.D. Broad, *Lectures on Psychical Research, Philosophy
and Phenomenological Research* 24 (1964), 565.

[35] C.D. Broad, "A Reply to My Critics," in P.A. Schilpp (ed.), *The Philosophy of
C.D. Broad* (New York: The Tudor Publishing Company, 1959), pp. 795–96.

[36] Review of Broad, *Lectures on Psychical Research*, pp. 565–66.

[37] F.C. Dommeyer, "Body, Mind, and Death," *Pacific Philosophy Forum* 3 (1965),
60–73.

[38] C.J. Ducasse, "Dommeyer and His Critics," mss., pp. 1–5; this paper was partly
published in "The Watseka Evidence," *Pacific Philosophy Forum* 3 (1965), 104–06.

[39] John Beloff, "C.J. Ducasse on Survival," *JASP* 64 (1970), 331.

[40] C.J. Ducasse, "Broad on the Relevance of Psychical Research to Philosophy," *The
Philosophy of C.D. Broad*, p. 388.

CHAPTER XII

META-PHILOSOPHY

Throughout his long career, Ducasse was concerned with the nature of philosophy itself. If the philosopher is to be clear about all else, he must be clear about the nature of his own enterprise.

[T]he question, what is philosophy, has given me no rest throughout my philosophical life. It may well be that I am wrong in the answer to it I propose, but if so, then I wish someone could lead me to the right one, for I shall have no peace 'till I get it.[1]

We find his meta-philosophy already adumbrated in *Causation and the Types of Necessity*, presented in detail in *Philosophy as a Science*, and refined and corrected in his Howison Lecture (reprinted in *Truth, Knowledge, and Causation*) and in *Nature, Mind, and Death*.[2] We must pay close attention to Ducasse's meta-philosophy because it is easily misunderstood and sometimes has prevented full appreciation of his work on specific philosophical issues. There are various strands in Ducasse's analysis of the philosophical enterprise, and some of them, as we shall see, are important and widely accepted, while others are peripheral, misleading, and in fact not worthy descriptions of what Ducasse himself does by way of philosophical analysis. In his later meta-philosophical writings, Ducasse happily stressed the crucial factors, though the misleading ones were still present.

I

According to Ducasse, the subject matter with which the philosopher should work is the group of statements in ordinary language where the philosophically interesting word being considered is actually used. The word may be "real," "cause," "capacity," "probable," "right," "beautiful," or whatever, but in each case examples of the uses of that word in ordinary discourse must be assembled, and this group of statements constitutes the data of philosophical investigation. The method of such investigation should be semantical analysis, where by 'analysis' Ducasse means finding a definition for the given term which is not arbitrary but in fact fits the way it is used in the assembled predicative uses of the word. The test of the adequacy of any definition that is proposed consists in the possibility of replacing the term defined by the proposed definition and then noticing whether the truth values of the original statements are changed. If they are, then the proposed definition is faulty; if not, it is acceptable. The proposed definition is adequate if the replacement "shall not result in making false any of the statements that were true, nor in making true any that were false, nor in altering the truth or the falsity of any other statement implying or implied by the given ones." This test of adequacy "will be met automatically if a definition expresses a genuine equivalence, and will not be met unless it does." [3]

Ducasse stresses that semantical analysis in his sense is essentially scientific in nature. First, he views the enterprise as scientific because the philosopher seeks real and non-arbitrary definitions of key terms just as the scientist does. Second, and more surprisingly, he believes that philosophical "theories" explain and predict in the same sense scientific theories do. He emphasized this latter point in *Philosophy as a Science*, though it is never wholly absent from any of his work in meta-philosophy.

Ducasse's notion that philosophical analysis produces theories like any science arises in the following way. The raw data available to the philosopher for analysis is the denotative application of a given word. The intension or meaning of the term, however, will be vague, inexact, and imprecise — the way it is with most terms in ordinary discourse. The task of the philosophical analyst is to construct a theory about what *precisely* and *exactly* that term must mean in order to explain the denotative applications already examined and to predict what other applications can be made consistently with those already existing. When there is conflict in such applications, the user of the language must choose which application is to constitute the definition-by-type of that word.

To his general description of what he takes to be proper philosophical procedure, Ducasse always adds an example of its use. All his analyses of specific issues presumably constitute extended examples of his method, but he nevertheless always provides a sample analysis in his meta-philosophical discussions. His favorite example in such contexts is "the problem of the nature of reality," or the use of the "ontological predicate" and its cognates.

The data to be assembled in this case are statements of everyday discourse in which the word "real" or one of its cognates is used predicatively. As soon as such listing begins, however, it becomes clear that this word means one thing in some sentences and different things in certain others. So the sample statements must be separated into several groups, and the following meanings of 'real' emerge. First, there are various uses of the word which have a special, purely technical, sense. Such senses include, for example, real property as contrasted with personal or portable property, real numbers as contrasted with imaginary ones, and real definitions as contrasted with nominal ones. These technical uses of 'real', and others like them, may be dismissed from consideration, since it is clear that they give rise to no problem involving "the nature of reality."

The first significant group consists of descriptive statements in which the word real has an epistemic function and does not refer to some species of existence. We say that a dog seems or appears ferocious but is not really so; or that an apparently valid argument is really fallacious; or that the stone in the ring is a real diamond though it looks like glass; or that a certain substance seems to be paper but in reality is asbestos. In all such cases some entity (E) is cited and the hypothesis is offered that it is of a certain kind (K). Whatever K may be there is always a set of characters, a, b, c, d, such that E is K if and only if it possesses all the characters. The occasions which give rise to the question of whether a given E really is or only appears to be K are those where only some of the characters of E are manifest, though they are precisely the characters E would have were it K. On such occasions, then, we say that E appears to be K and upon subsequently discovering that E possesses the remaining characters we say that E really is K. If E subsequently fails to manifest the remaining characters then we say that although E appears to be K it is not really so. The function of 'E seems to be K', then, is to qualify the truth claim that E is K — there is still a chance for mistake. Correspondingly, the function of 'E really is K' is to say that 'E is K' is *true* in spite of some evidence to the contrary.

The next group of ordinary assertions about reality are existential in nature; they constitute answers to the question "Are there any so-and-so's?" in contrast to the previous ones that are answers to the question "What is this?" Instances of existential assertions in which the nature of reality enters would be that mermaids do not really exist; that the man called Hamlet by Shakespeare did not exist in reality; that Utopia is an imaginary land but Spain is real; that there is really such a mental state as hypnosis; or that black swans really exist but not green ones.

In some of these statements it seems that 'is real' is equivalent to 'exists', while in others the notion of reality again has the epistemic function. 'Mermaids do not really exist' would be an example of the latter. The occasion for saying this rather than simply "no mermaids exist" might, for example, occur when a child who has been reading about mermaids or had seen a picture representing one came to the simplest explanatory conclusion that mermaids exist. Then one says mermaids do not *really* exist, and the import of this statement would be that the evidence is misleading – that, in spite of it, the truth is that mermaids do not exist. In such cases, "realness" is again an epistemic qualifier and not a character differentiating one species of existence from another. "In both groups of examples alike, what the word 'really' or either of its cognates qualifies is the statement itself in which it occurs, and its force is the same as that of the adverbs 'truly' or 'certainly'."[4]

In cases where 'is real' is synonymous with 'exists' (Spain is a real country; there is really such a state as hypnosis) the task is then to analyze the meaning of 'to exist'. To say that a given kind K exists, where K is limited to physical existence (a kind of substance, property, activity, state of affairs, change in a state, and so on) is exactly synonymous with the assertion that something of that kind is *somewhere*; that is, occupies some place in space at some time. The assertion of such existence may be more or less determinate or specified, as *some* place, somewhere within a specified region, or here *now*. These specifications make it clear that in the phrases "there is" or "there are," the word "there" is not being used idiomatically but as a literal indicator. With existence other than physical, say mathematical, the analysis is clearly analogous. The difference is only that the place concerned is a location in some other order than space-time. To say that a square root of 9 exists, but no square root of 3, means that 'being square root of 9' characterizes a certain place in the order of whole numbers, namely, the determinant place called 3, while 'being square root of 3' characterizes no place in the series. In any assertion of existence, then, whether physical, mathematical, or psychological, two components are always involved, a *what*, or kind, and a *where*. And generically any *where* or place in a system is the sort of thing specifiable in terms of *ordinal* relations.

There is another use of 'really' and its cognates significantly different from those so far described. In this use of the word, real indicates what is of most importance or value to the user of the word. An example would be the statement that the trees on the distant hillside seem blue but are really green. Neither property is illusory, since the trees truly display both properties from different vantage points. Which property is called real is determined by what interest or purpose is at the time dominant. Given the interest of the landscape painter the hills are "really" blue, while given the practical purpose of most other people they are "really" green.

The four types of statements about reality so far considered have dissimilar features, to be sure, but they all agree in formulating something either true or false and are therefore susceptible of being more or less fully confirmed or refuted. Since the predicate "real" is the ontological predicate, these statements may be called *ontological hypotheses*. Contrasted with such statements are *ontological positions* which state the only thing or character which, for the time, one will accept as real. The statement of such a position always has the form 'to be real is to have such-and-such a character'. Anything not having this character automatically is not basic or primary and has to be explained, construed, or defined in terms of the basic character. Such a position is not an assertion at all but a rule about what is to count as "real"; hence it is not an expression which is true or false. Positions are simply occupied and rules accepted – all by virtue of some purpose or interest. An example of an ontological position would be the one occupied by natural scientists when they say that to be real is to be perceptually public or implicit in what is so. It is evident "that these words do not formulate a hypothesis as to properties empirically discoverable in some concretely given entity called reality; for no empirical facts one might adduce could prove or disprove what those words expressed, or render it probable, doubtful, or improbable."[5] Clearly they express only "the criterion by which the things in which the natural sciences interest themselves are distinguished from the things these sciences ignore."[6]

II

The account so far given of the problem, or problems, of the nature of reality, Ducasse continues, might seem like a discussion of *Hamlet* without any mention of the Prince of Denmark! Idealism, materialism, voluntarism, and so on, all supposedly constitute statements about the "ultimate nature" of reality, and yet they have not even been mentioned. They all purport to be statements about reality which are true, and presumably the big problem is to decide which one *is* true since they are mutually incompatible. However, as it turns out, he says, none of them is acceptable, and the whole enterprise they represent is misguided. This conclusion arises from the following considerations.

Consider the claim that ultimately reality is exclusively mental. (Any other ontological "ism," of course, is subject to identical criticisms.) It may be understood or construed in either of two ways. First, it may be interpreted as stipulating what is to count as real — 'to be real is to be either a mind or a mind's ideas'. In this case, it is the statement of an ontological position and is by its nature neither true nor false. "It only declares the primacy, for the idealist, of minds and their ideas, and his intent to construe everything in terms of them."[7] Second, the claim may be understood descriptively — that is, as the claim that there is nothing else in the universe except minds and ideas. In ordinary usage, however, the adjective "mental" is applied only to things like feelings, thoughts, or memory images, or to minds comprising them, while the adjective "material" is reserved for such other things as the wood of the table which also clearly exist. Descriptively (or denotatively) then, the claim would be simply mistaken, though the idealist (like the proponent of any other ism) avoids this outcome by forcing *ad hoc* some new meanings onto the old terms that are at variance with their customary senses.

The idealist may say that what he contends is that nothing which is not mental has *real* existence. This qualification of 'exist', however, again amounts to a declaration of what he is willing to accept as basic and primary, a declaration of what is to count as real, and hence is a stipulative position that is neither true nor false. Or he might say that what he contends is that everything which exists is *really* mental, notwithstanding appearances to the contrary. This qualification of 'mental' (by stretching its meaning), however, is clearly mistaken, since it is impossible that wood should only appear to be material but really be mental. To suppose this is equivalent to supposing that wood lacks the properties that ordinary language denominates "material" and has instead those it denominates "mental," while the fact is that properties such as those of the wood are the very ones 'material' is intended to denote. That wood is material is a definition-by-type of what we mean by the word material.

Under the circumstances, to assert nonetheless that wood is really mental — a primitive sort of mind, perhaps — is not to voice a new insight into its nature. It is not to mention a hitherto undetected but observable character of wood. It is, I submit, only to elect *arbitrarily* to employ the word "mental" to denote not only the things it is customarily intended to denote, but also those customarily denoted by the word "material." *To do this, however, is exactly the same logically, and just as futile, or indeed, semantically perverse, as would be electing to say henceforth that members of the white race are really Negroes, or that Negroes are really white.* Obviously, this would not be revealing any hitherto unnoticed fact about the color of their skins. It would only be tampering wantonly with established language.[8]

From the fact that all efforts to turn mind into matter, or vice versa, or either into something else, are gratuitous it does not follow that there are no genuine philosophical problems connected with the concepts of mind and matter. The genuine problem has for its datum that certain things are in fact called material and not mental and that certain other things are in fact called mental and not material. The task, then, is to establish exactly what these terms, as respectively denotative of the ones and not the others, mean, imply, or connote. Any hypothesis advanced about their meaning must be tested by seeing whether the character which is supposed to constitute the meaning of one is in fact possessed by all the things language denominates by the other. The further problem then arises "as to how, in the light of that result, mind and matter are or can be related." As to this, "the preceding discussion has shown only that their relation cannot be identity."[9]

III

There are numerous strands in Ducasse's meta-philosophy, and they seem to have varying degrees of merit. The task is to separate and briefly evaluate the elements, and to place Ducasse in the general analytic movement.

Ducasse's opening remarks, plus part of his example, constitute the major strand. The crucial point is that the data of philosophical analysis must be examples of the actual use of the philosophically interesting words in ordinary discourse. The job of the philosopher, then, is to articulate precise, non-arbitrary, and adequate definitions of these key terms. The major criterion of the adequacy of any such definition is that the substitution of the definiens for the definiendum leave the truth values of the sentences in which the latter originally occurred unchanged. Since the definitions of 'mental' and 'physical' given by idealists and materialists violate the way in which these words are actually used, these definitions, and the enterprise they represent, must be rejected as misguided. Not all definitions of key terms offered by metaphysicians involve such violations, however, and may in fact constitute an adequate analysis of common usage.

It should be noted at the outset that this concept of analysis is different from the one advocated either by ordinary language philosophers or logical positivists. For Ducasse, ordinary discourse raises philosophical issues, and sets a requirement for a proposed analysis, but does not solve such issues. Hence he differs from the ordinary-language analyst. For him, moreover, there are legitimate metaphysical issues remaining after the spurious ones have been eliminated. Hence he differs from the positivist. Ducasse's concept in fact is closely allied to the classical philosophical enterprise that has come to be called descriptive metaphysics as distinct from speculative metaphysics. The former is the effort to discover the general traits of being implicit in the many things we do in fact experience, while the latter is the effort to discover the nature of reality behind or beyond what we experience. Ducasse is simply formulating this concept of descriptive metaphysics in a characteristically modern fashion — that is, linguistically. His formulation, we submit, is the one held or followed by the majority of philosophers who are themselves analytical but reject the notion that all metaphysical issues are misguided. The important fact is that Ducasse was not reporting what he found on the philosophical scene but was himself a pioneer in both the advocacy and practice of this sort of analysis.

There are, however, a number of problems that would have to be solved before Ducasse's concept of analysis could be said to constitute an adequate meta-philosophy.

To begin with, the criterion of adequacy proposed by Ducasse is wholly extensional in nature, and this seems unsatisfactory. No proposed definition is acceptable, according to the extensional requirement, if it entails the falsity of ordinary sentences in which the definiendum is correctly used. There may be some philosophical claims eliminated by this requirement, but not many. If the claim made by absolute idealists that spatial and temporal relations are illusory entails the falsity of ordinary sentences in which spatial and temporal concepts are applied correctly, then such a claim is eliminated by Ducasse's requirement. However, it is clear that most metaphysicians of the speculative variety do not intend to clash with the truth value of common usage. A Berkeleyan idealist, for example, as a result of his epistemic dialectic, defines a material object as a collection of sensations given a common name. But he believes that he can make all the distinctions

commonly made — between illusions and reality, between the meanings of
'mental' and 'physical', and so on — within his system, and hence that he
does not change the truth values of assertions in ordinary discourse. He
believes the same is true for science. Kepler's laws hold whether the planets
are conceived in terms of realistic sub-strata or in terms of clusters of
sensations. There are, however, crucial differences between the *meanings* of
idealistic definitions and the *meanings* of the ordinary concepts they
purport to define. Certainly the ordinary meaning of 'chair' is quite at odds
with the analysis of sensation clusters, and the meaning of 'atom' in science,
unless heuristically interpreted, is quite different from the Berkeleyan
analysis of the concept. Hence, if speculative metaphysics, or the redefining
of ordinary terms, is to be excluded from the philosophical enterprise, the
extensional requirement must be supplemented by an intentional one to the
effect that philosophical meanings that go against ordinary meanings are just
as unacceptable as analyses that go against the truth values of ordinary assertions. But we do not find Ducasse making this crucial amendment. Indeed,
he looks upon the meanings of concepts in ordinary discourse as too vague,
inexact, and imprecise to be useful as a check against unbridled speculation.

   Another crucial question to be answered is why ordinary language has any
privileged status at all whether it be extensional or intensional. Ducasse has
a kind of answer, though it is not really very satisfactory. He believes that if
one accepts the privileged status of ordinary language as far as the extensional criterion is concerned, then one can avoid the useless arguments and
counter-arguments of traditional metaphysics and, if careful enough in
analysis, produce knowledge results that are cumulative in nature. But it is
not clear how such an answer as this would satisfy a speculative philosopher
who would insist that while such knowledge is achievable, it is not the *sort*
of knowledge that the philosopher is seeking.

   A different sort of defense of the privileged status of ordinary language is
made in some quarters to the effect that ordinary language, and its scientific
extension, constitutes a linguistic frame of reference which reflects com-
munity or shared meanings of words and that an idiosyncratic language is a
self-refuting notion. Ducasse, however, has no sympathy for this line of
defense. As far as he is concerned his notion of analysis would be just as
applicable to a "private" language as to the shared language of science and
ordinary life. "I take it that what we are interested to analyze is examples
which, like those given, illustrate commonly accepted usage; but it is worth

noticing that if examples of some freak usage of those same words were given instead, then, if it interested us to do so, we could analyze equally well the meaning those words had there."[10] Ducasse continues by saying that "the essential point is that either *no* applications of these words are given us, and then we can make them mean anything we please; or else concrete examples of *some* applicative usage of them are furnished, and then we have data by which to test empirically the soundness of any proposed definition of what they mean in that particular sort of context."[11] On Ducasse's view, however, it remains a mystery why the philosopher should be interested in ordinary usage rather than freak usage. He assumes that in fact philosophers are interested in ordinary usage, but he fails to give any justification for this interest. The reason presumably is that analyzing ordinary usage will produce real definitions while analyzing freak usage would produce arbitrary definitions. Ducasse believes that the job of the philosopher is indeed to produce real rather than arbitrary definitions, but he never insists that only by analyzing ordinary, common, or shared applications of concepts can this goal be realized.

There are, finally, certain difficulties in Ducasse's specific criticisms of idealism and materialism as examples of philosophical claims that fly in the face of ordinary usage. According to Ducasse, the idealist claims that ultimately reality is exclusively mental and that this claim can be interpreted either as a stipulation of what is to count as real or as a statement to the effect everything that exists in fact is mental. The first, he says, is an ontological *position* and so neither true nor false, and hence can safely be ignored. The second, literally interpreted, is simply false since it contradicts ordinary usage. To avoid this clash, Ducasse says, the idealist (or materialist) forces *ad hoc* meanings onto old terms at variance with their customary senses. These redefinitions occur either by stipulating again what is to count as "real" or by qualifying 'mental' or 'physical' so it turns out that everything is "really mental" (or "really physical") – both of which maneuvers Ducasse again rejects for the same reasons above.

To begin with, Ducasse's description of the idealist's (or materialist's) position does not seem wholly convincing. The idealist does not begin with a claim that reality is exclusively mental and then redefine 'mental' and 'physical' in an *ad hoc* way to sustain this claim. Rather he purports to show by certain a priori arguments that these words must be interpreted in the way he specifies, and it is from these necessary redefinitions of ordinary terms that his claim about reality being exclusively mental *analytically* follows. One might object to this procedure in two crucial ways, one by showing the arguments to be faulty and the other by rejecting out-of-hand any view that violates the *sense* of ordinary assertions even though it mediates their truth value. Ducasse does not try the first sort of response, but he is using the second when he writes that the idealist's new sense of old words *is at variance with their customary senses.* Since this is the case he should supplement his meta-philosophy by admitting intensional as well as extensional criteria of the adequacy of a philosophical analysis. Such a procedure, however, involves taking the meanings of ordinary concepts more seriously than Ducasse seems prepared to do; he never relinquishes his notion that such meanings are vague, obscure, and inexact and hence useless for philosophical analysis. In fact, even if one accepts Ducasse's exaggerated emphasis on the deficiences of ordinary language, it does not follow that such usage can provide *no* intensional criteria of adequacy.

In addition, Ducasse's concepts of *ontological hypothesis* and *ontological position*, insofar as they are clear, seem open to certain difficulties. The former is characterized as a use of ontological predicates that does not fly in the face of ordinary usage but rather is a statement about either linguistic or extra-linguistic fact, while the latter is a stipulation, reflecting some purpose or interest, about what is to count as real. In discussing his concept of onto-logical position Ducasse seems to assume that only expressions capable of empirical testing qualify as true or false. If X is not an expression which is testable, then X must be interpreted as a stipulation and not a proposition. The very dichotomy between "hypothesis" and "position" as mutually exclusive and exhaustive concepts implies this conclusion, and Ducasse frequently comes close to saying it explicitly. However, this assumption is the very foundation of any *positivistic* metaphilosophy, and reflects a commitment to the verifiability view of meaning, and Ducasse explicitly rejects such a position in other places. Moreover, it is incompatible with his own explicit view that certain metaphysical assertions are legitimate. For example, as we have seen, to defend mind-body dualism, as Ducasse does, is to make a claim that is neither empirically testable nor a mere stipulation.

One strand in Ducasse's meta-philosophy that seems unfortunate, and has kept some readers from a just appreciation of his philosophy, is his insistence that the analytical procedure of philosophy as he describes it is scientific in nature.[12] If all Ducasse meant was that philosophical analysis is like scientific procedure in certain respects, though unlike it in others, there would be no great problem. But Ducasse means literally that philosophy is a science in the sense that physics or anything else generally called science is. Philosophy is scientific, he writes, both because it seeks non-arbitrary, precise, and real definitions, and because philosophical "theories" about the meanings of words are explanatory and predictive. They explain the denotative applications so far encountered and predict what other applications can be made consistently with those that have already occurred.

There are grave difficulties confronting this view, though there seems no point in pursuing very many of them. We shall consider only one particularly glaring difference between science and philosophical analysis as Ducasse conceives it. In science, if there is a conflict between theory and new data, the theory is given up or modified but the data are not ignored or changed in some fashion to conform to theory. In semantical analysis, however, if there is a conflict between the meaning of a word as it covers past denotative applications and the use made of that word subsequently, the new use must be changed to conform to previous meaning (provided, of course, that the user of the language wishes to act consistently). Here the "new data" rather than the "theory" are abandoned.

One reply Ducasse makes to this criticism shows the lamentable lengths he is willing to go to preserve his claim that philosophical analysis *is* a science and not simply like a science in such-and-such-a respect (and hence, by implication, quite unlike it in other respects). He says that scientists in fact sometimes do "paint the black swan white" — that is, alter the fact to fit scientific theory. They insist the contradicting event was "impossible," and what must have occurred was trickery, hallucination, or mal-observation. Thus Gassendi in 1627 "explained" the fall of an aerolith in Provence by ascribing it to some unobserved volcanic eruption; and, over a century later, Lavoisier argued in a report to the French Academy that stones cannot possibly fall out of the sky since there are not any up there!

This sort of reply seems to miss the point of the criticism. The point is that it is always illegitimate for the scientist *once the data have been agreed upon* to ignore or alter them, while it is always legitimate in the interests of consistency to alter new usage to fit the semantical theories governing previous usage.

Instead of strained defenses of his strong view, Ducasse might better, on our view, simply claim that theories about meaning are like scientific theory in some respects but unlike them in others. He should admit that in the case of altering facts to fit theory, and, no doubt, in innumerable other ways, there are great differences. He can still, if he wishes, claim that semantical theories are like scientific theories in reaching real and non-arbitrary definitions, and he can still claim that philosophical inquiry, like science, "yields knowledge, not just dogmas, guesses, wishful beliefs, articles of faith, or irresponsible opinions," but it is not clear how much is to be gained by this claim from Ducasse's own viewpoint. It is a minimal similarity, and the comparison adds no great clarification to the nature of semantical analysis. On the other hand, to make such comparisons at all puts off many readers and leads them to think, erroneously, that there is some basic confusion in Ducasse's meta-philosophy.

Ducasse's straining after analogies between science and philosophy has another unfortunate consequence. Having insisted that philosophy closely resembles science in *method*, he is obliged to find some important respect in which they differ since they are obviously not identical. The difference he naturally hits on is one of *subject matter*. The distinctive subject matter of philosophy is "appraisals" — that is, the use of such value-predicates as 'cogent', 'erroneous', 'real', 'beautiful' and 'immoral'. Those problems of philosophy that do not *appear* to be about values he calls derivative in the sense that they arise in the attempt to clarify these "primitive" predicates used in appraisals. However, a difficulty immediately arises. A problem as basic as the nature of causality he must consider derivative despite the fact that when he is *doing* philosophy (as opposed to talking about its nature), he treats the analysis of causality as the most basic analysis in relation to which other philosophical analyses are derivative. If Ducasse had been content simply to claim that philosophy, like science, is knowledge-yielding, and had not strained to find additional resemblances between philosophy and science, he would not have felt obliged to make this dubious claim concerning the subject matter of all philosophy.

Another strand in Ducasse's meta-philosophy, and one in harmony with all brands of current analytic thought, is his insistence on the need to separate the various uses of a single word in ordinary discourse and to give an appropriate analysis of each one of them. Ducasse expertly illustrates the need and the procedure in his analysis of the various uses, and different senses, of "the ontological predicate" and its cognates. His skill in separation and definition will be admired by any analyst, however he might disagree on certain points. Unfortunately, however, the skill shown by Ducasse in disentangling the various senses of a word in ordinary contexts exhibited in his standard discussion of meta-philosophy does not always carry over into the contexts where he is actually doing philosophy. As we have been, he is insistent that there is only one legitimate sense of 'cause' and so on.

V

What unity does Ducasse's metaphilosophy give to all aspects of his philosophy? Although his theory of the *subject matter* of philosophy does not unify his philosophy since so often in treating specific philosophical issues he is not discussing value predicates at all, his semantical *method* does tie together the many strands of his thought. In more than forty years of discussing topics as diverse as causation, perception, the mind-body relation, ethical values and religious belief he has always had as his primary concern the analysis of key terms.

Unity of method is not, however, the only kind of unity to be found in Ducasse's work. Within his philosophy there are a number of overlapping themes. Perhaps the most important of these themes are his adverbial analysis of perception, his dispositional analysis of properties, and his ethics of belief. His adverbial analysis recurs whenever perception is discussed, and there are not many philosophical issues in which the concept of perception does not play a significant role. He carefully distinguishes between sensory terms which refer to ways off experiencing and property terms which require causal-dispositional analysis. This dispositional analysis he extends to many contexts. Human agency, he argues, is a matter of the causal dispositions of beliefs and desires; mental and physical substances and their interaction are to be understood in terms of the capacities to cause mental or physical events; the truth of a proposition is its disposition to cause belief; the meaning of a sign is a disposition to cause certain private mental events; value is the capacity to cause pleasure; education is an activity that causes the acquisition of certain capacities; and artistic expression is the capacity to arouse feelings. Underlying these analyses, of course, is his own triadic definition of the basic concept of cause. The discerning reader no doubt will also have noticed various overlapping themes in his discussion of religion and paranormal phenomena — themes which presuppose the same commitments on the ethics of belief.

It would have been a major accomplishment to have ably defended any one of these themes. It is Ducasse's greatness to have advanced them all in what remains an outstanding example of traditional system building in a careful, analytical way.

NOTES

[1] Letter to Brand Blanshard, January 5, 1944.

[2] *Causation and the Types of Necessity* (Seattle: University of Washington Press, 1924), pp. 119–130; *Philosophy as a Science: Its Matter and Its Method* (New York: Oskar Piest, 1941); "The Method of Knowledge in Philosophy," The Howison Lecture for 1944, in *Truth, Knowledge and Causation* (London: Routledge and Kegan Paul, 1968), Chapter 15; and *Nature, Mind, and Death* (La Salle, Ill.: Open Court, 1951), Chapters 1–6.

[3] *Truth, Knowledge and Causation*, p. 244. Cf. *Nature, Mind and Death*, pp. 62–87.

[4] *Truth, Knowledge and Causation*, p. 247. The same example of metaphilosophical analysis is treated at length in *Nature, Mind, and Death*, pp. 62–67.

[5] *Truth, Knowledge and Causation*, pp. 251–52.

[6] *Ibid.*, p. 252.

[7] *Ibid.*, p. 253.

[8] *Nature, Mind, and Death*, p. 84. Cf. *Truth, Knowledge and Causation*, p. 254.

[9] *Nature, Mind, and Death*, p. 86. Cf. *Truth, Knowledge and Causation*, p. 255.

[10] *Truth, Knowledge and Causation*, p. 243.

[11] *Ibid.*

[12] This emphasis is the main theme of *Philosophy as a Science*. This book does not rank nearly as high as the rest of his work in our opinion. It has been well criticized. For some of these criticisms and Ducasse's replies see: J.E. Ledden, "Questions Concerning the Metaphilosophy of C.J. Ducasse," *Philosophy and Phenomenological Research* 6 (1946), 410–17; Ducasse, "The Subject-Matter Distinctive of Philosophy," *P. and P.R.* 6 (1946), 417–21; Arthur E. Murphy, "Ducasse's Theory of Appraisal," *P. and P.R.* 13 (1952), 1–14; Ducasse, "Scientific Method in Ethics," *P. and P.R.* 14 (1953); F.C. Dommeyer, "A Critical Examination of C.J. Ducasse's Metaphilosophy," *P. and P.R.* 21 (1961), 439–55; Ducasse, "Some Comments on Professor Dommeyer's Criticisms," *P. and P.R.* 21 (1961), 552–55; R.E. Santoni, "Comments Regarding the Dommeyer-Ducasse Disagreement," *P. and P.R.* 23 (1962), 125–26; and Ducasse, "Concerning the Logical Status of Criteria of Morality," *P. and P.R.* 23 (1962), 127–30. Also cf. Ducasse's "Correctness vs. Occurrence of Appraisals — A Reply," *Journal of Philosophy* 39 (1942), 119–23.

BIBLIOGRAPHY OF THE WRITINGS OF C.J. DUCASSE*

BOOKS

Causation and the Types of Necessity. Seattle: University of Washington Press, 1924. Reprinted by Dover Publications with an introduction by Vincent Tomas and four papers added, 1969.

The Philosophy of Art. New York: The Dial Press, 1929. Reprinted by Dover Publications with revisions and a paper added which replies to critics of the book, 1966.

The Relation of Philosophy to General Education. General Education Board of the Rockefeller Foundation, for private circulation, 1932.

Philosophy as a Science: Its Matter and its Method. New York: Oskar Piest, 1941.

Art, the Critics and You. New York: Oskar Piest, 1944. Reprinted in 1948 by Hafner and in 1955 by Bobbs-Merrill.

Nature, Mind, and Death. The Carus Lectures, Eighth Series, 1949. LaSalle, Ill.: Open Court Publishing Co., 1951.

A Philosophical Scrutiny of Religion. New York: The Ronald Press Co., 1953.

A Critical Examination of the Belief in a Life after Death. Springfield, Ill.: Charles C. Thomas, 1961.

Truth, Knowledge and Causation. London: Routledge & Kegan Paul, 1968. A collection of fifteen previously published papers with a preface by Ducasse.

Paranormal Phenomena, Science, and Life after Death. New York: Parapsychology Foundation, Inc., 1969. A collection of three papers with a foreword by Ducasse and an introduction by J.M.O. Wheatley, the title essay unpublished, the remaining papers previously published.

ARTICLES

"The Retina and Righthandedness" (in collaboration with H.C. Stevens). *Psychological Review* 19, No. 1, 1912.

"A Defense of Ontological Liberalism," *Journal of Philosophy* 21, No. 13, 1924.

"R.M. Blake, Sceptic," *Journal of Philosophy* 21, No. 19, 1924.

"The Non-Existence of Time," *Journal of Philosophy* 22, No. 1, 1925.

"Explanation, Mechanism, and Teleology," *Journal of Philosophy* 22, No. 6, 1925.

"A Liberalistic View of Truth," *Philosophical Review* 34, No. 6, 1925.

"Liberalism in Ethics," *International Journal of Ethics* 35, No. 3, 1925.

"Significant Form," *The Nation* 122, Febr. 3, 1926.

"On the Nature and the Observability of the Causal Relation," *Journal of Philosophy* 23, No. 3, 1926.

"A Neglected Meaning of Probability," *Proceedings of the Sixth International Congress of Philosophy*, 1926.

---

* Reviews, translations and reprints of articles have been omitted.

"Words of Cheer for Worms," *The Nation* 123, Sept. 8, 1926.

"Seven Popular Dialogues on Various Questions in Aesthetics," *The Providence Journal* (newspaper), Jan. 5, 19, Feb. 2, March 2, 30, April 20, June 15, 1927.

" 'Mind and Its Place in Nature'," *Philosophical Review* 36, No. 4, 1927.

"Terminological Anarchy," *Philosophical Review* 37, No. 2, 1928.

"What has Beauty to do with Art? ," *Journal of Philosophy* 25, No. 7, 1928.

"Is Art the Imaginative Expression of a Wish?," *Philosophical Review* 37, No. 3, 1928.

"Six Discussions of Current Art Exhibits," *The Providence Journal* (newspaper), 1930.

"The Place of Philosophy in an University Education," *Brown Alumni Monthly* 30, No. 6, 1930.

"A Philosopher Considers the Price of Liberty," *The Providence Evening Bulletin*, Jan. 25, 1930.

"Of the Spurious Mystery in Causal Connections," *Philosophical Review* 39, No. 4, 1930.

"On our Knowledge of Existents," *Proceedings of the Seventh International Congress of Philosophy*, 1930.

"Philosophical Liberalism," *Contemporary American Philosophy*, vol. I, 1930.

"What Should Pembroke Girls Study? ," *The Record* (Pembroke newspaper), May 16, 1931.

"Art History, Criticism, and Esthetics," *Creative Art* 9, No. 1, 1931.

"Some Questions in Aesthetics," *The Monist* 42, No. 1, 1932.

"Graduate Work at Brown," *Brown Alumni Monthly* 32, No. 6, 1932.

"Of the Nature and Efficacy of Causes," *Philosophical Review* 41, No. 4, 1932.

"The Aim and Content of Graduate Training in Ethics," *International Journal of Ethics* 43, No. 1, 1932.

Untitled address, *Symposium in Honor of the Seventieth Birthday of Alfred North Whitehead.* Cambridge: Harvard University Press, 1932.

"On the Attributes of Material Things," *Journal of Philosophy* 31, No. 3, 1934.

"Is Scientific Verification Possible in Philosophy?," *Philosophy of Science* 2, No. 2., 1935.

"A Dialogue on the Fine Arts," *The Town Crier* (newspaper, Providence, R.I.), 1935.

"Mr. Collingwood on Philosophical Method," *Journal of Philosophy* 33, No. 4, 1936.

"The Meaning of Probability: Discussion," *Journal of the American Statistical Association* 31, No. 193, 1936.

"Introspection, Mental Acts, and Sensa," *Mind* 45, No. 178, 1936.

"Verification, Verifiability, and Meaningfulness," *Journal of Philosophy* 33, No. 9, 1936.

"Are the Humanities Worth Their Keep? ," *American Scholar* 6, No. 4, 1937.

"The Animal with Red Cheeks," *American Scholar* 7, No. 3, 1938.

"The Esthetic Object," *Journal of Philosophy* 35, No. 12, 1938.

"Symbols, Signs and Signals," *Journal of Symbolic Logic* 4, No. 2, 1939.

"Conditions of Social Progress," *The Providence Evening Bulletin*, 1939.

"Has Science Increased Race Happiness?," *The Providence Evening Bulletin*, April 14, 1939.

"Philosophy and Natural Science," *Philosophical Review* 44, No. 2, 1940.

"Concerning the Status of So-called 'Pseudo-Object' Sentences," *Journal of Philosophy* 37, No. 12, 1940.

"The Nature and Function of Theory in Ethics," *Ethics* 51, No. 1, 1940.

"Some Critical Comments on a Nominalistic Analysis of Resemblance," *Philosophical Review* 49, No. 6, 1940.

"Propositions, Opinions, Sentences and Facts," *Journal of Philosophy* 37, No. 26, 1940.

"Truth, Verifiability, and Propositions about the Future," *Philosophy of Science* 8, No. 3, 1941.

"Some Observations Concerning the Nature of Probability," *Journal of Philosophy* 38, No. 15, 1941.

"Objectivity, Objective Reference, and Perception," *Philosophy and Phenomenological Research* 2, No. 1, 1941.

"Art Appreciation and the Curriculum," *The Association of American Colleges Bulletin* 27, No. 3, 1941.

"Moore's 'The Refutation of Idealism'," *The Philosophy of G.E. Moore*, The Library of Living Philosophers, ed. by P.A. Schilpp, vol. IV. Evanston, Ill.: Northwestern University Press, 1942.

"John Herschel's Philosophy of Science," *Studies in the History of Culture*. Menasha: George Banta Publishing Company, 1942.

"Is a Fact a True Proposition?," *Journal of Philosophy* 39, No. 5, 1942.

"Correctness vs. Occurrence of Appraisals," *Journal of Philosophy* 39, No. 5, 1942.

"Concerning Professor Bogholt's Criticism of My 'Disposal of Naturalism'," *Philosophical Review* 51, No. 2, 1942.

"Some Comments on C.W. Morris's 'Foundations of the Theory of Signs'," *Philosophy and Phenomenological Research* 3, No. 1, 1942.

"Esthetic Contemplation and Sense Pleasure – A Reply," *Journal of Philosophy* 40, No. 6, 1943.

"What is the War Doing to Our Morals?," *The Providence Sunday Journal*, August, 1943.

"Liberal Education and the College Curriculum," *Journal of Higher Education* 15, No. 1, 1944.

"Propositions, Truth and the Ultimate Criterion of Truth," *Philosophy and Phenomenological Research* 4, No. 3, 1944.

"On Our Knowledge of the Meaning of Words," *Proceedings of the Congres International de Philosophie Consacré aux Problemes de la Connaissance*, Port-au-Prince, Haiti, 1944.

The Method of Knowledge in Philosophy (The Howison Lecture for 1944), *University of California Publications in Philosophy* 16, 1945.

Philosophy in American Education (co-authored with Brand Blanshard, Charles W. Hendel, Arthur E. Murphy and Max C. Otto). New York: Harper's, 1945.

"Facts, Truth and Knowledge," *Philosophy and Phenomenological Research* 5, No. 3, 1945.

"Some Comments on Professor Nagel's Latest Remarks," *Philosophy and Phenomenological Research* 5, No. 3, 1945.

"Some Comments on Professor Sellars' 'Knowing and Knowledge'," *Philosophy and Phenomenological Research* 5, No. 3, 1945.

"The Subject-Matter Distinctive of Philosophy," *Philosophy and Phenomenological Research* 6, No. 3, 1946.

"Aesthetics and the Aesthetic Activities," *Journal of Aesthetics and Art Criticism* 5, No. 3, 1947.

"Some Comments on Professor Wild's Criticism of My Views on Semiosis," *Philosophy and Phenomenological Research* 8, No. 2, 1947.

Science: Its Nature, Method, and Scope. David Wight Prall Memorial Lecture, 1947. Piedmont, California: The Prall Memorial Foundation, vol. III, No. 1, 1947.

"Some Comments on Professor Wild's Preceding Remarks," *Philosophy and Phenomenological Research* 8, No. 2, 1947.

Is a Life After Death Possible? (The Agnes E. and Constantine E.A. Foerster Lecture on the Immorality of the Soul, 1947), Berkeley: University of California Press, 1948.

"Discussion" (comment on M. Dynnik's "Contemporary Bourgeois Philosophy in the United States"), *Modern Review* 2, No. 2, 1948.

"C.I. Lewis' Analysis of Knowledge and Valuation," *Philosophical Review* 57, No. 3, 1948.

"Aiken's 'Criteria for an Adequate Aesthetics': Discussion," *Journal of Aesthetics and Art Criticism* 7, No. 2, 1948.

"Graduate Preparation for Teaching," *Journal of Higher Education* 19, No. 9, 1948.

"Some Observations Concerning Particularity," *Philosophical Review* 58, No. 6, 1949.

"Causality," *Collier's Encyclopedia* 4, 1950.

"Cynicism," *Collier's Encyclopedia*, 6, 1950.

"The 'Introductory' Course in Philosophy," *Philosophers' Newsletter*, No. XL, 1950.

"Reality, Science and Metaphysics," *Synthese* 8, Nos. 6–7, 1950–51.

"Qu'est-ceque la Philosophie?," *Synthese* 8, Nos. 6–7, 1950–51.

Untitled contribution, Chapter VI, *Democracy in a World of Tensions.* A symposium prepared by UNESCO, ed. by Richard McKeon. Chicago: University of Chicago Press, 1951.

"Francis Bacon's Philosophy of Science," *Structure, Method and Meaning: Essays in Honor of Henry M. Sheffer*, ed. by Paul Henle, H.M. Kallen, and S.K. Langer. New York: Liberal Arts Press, 1951.

"Whewell's Philosophy of Scientific Discovery," *Philosophical Review* 60, Nos. 1 and 2, 1951.

"Paranormal Phenomena, Nature, and Man" (The First John William Graham Lecture on Psychic Science, 1951), *Journal of the American Society for Psychical Research* 45, No. 4, 1951.

"Mr. G.N.M. Tyrrell's 'Man the Maker'," *Journal of the American Society for Psychical Research* 46, No. 4, 1952.

"The MacDonald 'Spook' Collection," *Bulletin of the Hartford Seminary Foundation*, No. 14, 1952.

"Philosophy, Education, and the Nature of Man," *Journal of the Phi Beta Kappa Society* 31, No. 4, 1952.

"Causality, Creation, and Ecstasy," *The Philosophical Forum* 2, 1953.

"Patterns of Survival," *Tomorrow* 1, No. 4, 1953.

"Deductive Probability Arguments," *Philosophical Studies* 4, No. 2, 1953.

"Scientific Method in Ethics," *Philosophy and Phenomenological Research* 14, No. 1, 1953.

"A 'Terminal' Course in Philosophy," *Journal of Higher Education* 24, No. 8, 1953.

"Demos on 'Nature, Mind, and Death'," *Review of Metaphysics* 7, No. 2, 1953.

"Are Religious Dogmas Cognitive and Meaningful? ," *Academic Freedom, Logic and Religion* (the symposia at the 1953 meeting of the Eastern Division of the American Philosophy Association), University of Pennsylvania Press, 1953. Untitled comment on Raphael Demos' contribution to the same symposium, *Journal of Philosophy* 52, No. 5, 1954.

"Some Questions Concerning Psychical Phenomena," *Journal of the American Society for Psychical Research* 48, No. 1, 1954.

"How Does One Discover What A Term Means?," *Philosophical Review* 43, No. 1, 1954.

"International Conferences of Parapsychological Studies," *Journal of the American Society for Psychical Research* 48, No. 4, 1954.

"The Philosophical Importance of 'Psychical Phenomena'," *Journal of Philosophy* 51, No. 25, 1954.

"Knowing the Future," *Tomorrow* 3, No. 2, 1955.

"On the Function and Nature of the Philosophy of Education," *Harvard Educational Review* 26, No. 2, 1956.

"The John William Graham Collection of Literature of Psychic Science," *Books at Brown* 18, No. 1, 1956.

"Concerning the Language of Religion," *Philosophical Review* 65, No. 3, 1956.

"On the Whole Beneficial to Serious Studies" (contribution to a Symposium on Seven Questions concerning "The Search for Bridey Murphy"), *Tomorrow* 4, No. 4, 1956.

"Science, Scientists, and Psychical Research," *Journal of the American Society for Psychical Research* 50, No. 4, 1956.

"What Could Survive?," *Tomorrow* 5, No. 1, 1956.

"On the Analysis of Causality," *Journal of Philosophy* 54, No. 13, 1957.

"Method of Investigation," *Proceedings of Four Conferences of Parapsychological Studies.* New York: Parapsychology Foundation, 1957.

"Determinism, Freedom and Responsibility," *Determinism and Freedom in the Age of Modern Science*, ed. by Sidney Hook. New York: New York University Press, 1958.

"Christianity, Rationality, and Faith" (A John Hershel Morron Lecture, Hamilton College, 1954), *Review of Religion* 22, Nos. 3–4, 1958.

"Physical Phenomena in Psychical Research," *Journal of the American Society for Psychical Research* 52, No. 1, 1958.

"The Guide of Life," *The Key Reporter* (Phi Beta Kappa Newsletter) 23, No. 2, 1958. "Mr. Ducasse Replies," No. 3, a reply to a letter from a reader to the editor concerning "The Guide of Life".

"What Can Philosophy Contribute to Educational Theory?," *Harvard Educational Review* 28, No. 4, 1958.

"Sanity in Education," *Educational Summary*, Crofts, Sept. 12, 1958.

"Broad on the Relevance of Psychical Research to Philosophy," *The Philosophy of C.D. Broad*, ed. by P.A. Schilpp. New York: The Tudor Publishing Company, 1959.

"Psychoanalysis and Suggestion, Metaphysics and Temperament," *Psychoanalysis, Scientific Method, and Philosophy*, ed. by Sidney Hook. New York: New York University Press, 1959.

"What Has Science Done to Religion?," *Centennial Review* 3, No. 2, 1959.

"Causality and Parapsychology," *Journal of Parapsychology* 23, No. 2, 1959.

"Philosophy Can Become a Science," *Revue Internationale de Philosophie* 13, 1959.

"How Good is the Evidence for Survival After Death?," *Journal of the American Society for Psychical Research* 53, No. 3, 1959.

"Life, Telism, and Mechanism," *Philosophy and Phenomenological Research* 20, No. 1, 1959.

"In Defense of Dualism," *Dimensions of Mind*, ed. by Sidney Hook. New York: New York University Press, 1960.

Chapters 3, 7, 8, 9 and 10, *Theories of Scientific Method: The Renaissance Through the Nineteenth Century*, by R.M. Blake, C.J. Ducasse, and E.H. Madden. Seattle: University of Washington Press, 1960.

"How the Case of *The Search for Bridney Murphy* Stands Today" (a pre-publication of a chapter of *A Critical Examination of the Belief in a Life After Death*), *Journal of the American Society for Psychical Research* 54, No. 1, 1960.

"The Doctrine of Reincarnation in the History of Thought" (a pre-publication of a chapter of *A Critical Examination of the Belief in a Life after Death*), *International Journal of Parapsychology* 2, No. 3, 1960.

"What Metaphysics is Good for," *Self, Religion and Metaphysics: Essays in Memory of James Bissett Pratt*, ed. by G.E. Myers. New York: The Macmillan Company, 1961.

"Life After Death Conceived as Reincarnation," *In Search of God and Immorality* (The Garvin Free Lectures, Vol. II). Boston: The Beacon Press, 1961.

"The Sources of the Emotional Import of an Aesthetic Object" (comment on Hayner's "Expressive Meaning in Art"), *Philosophy and Phenomenological Research* 21, No. 4, 1961.

"Some Comments on Professor Dommeyer's Criticisms" (comment on Dommeyer's "A Critical Examination of C.J. Ducasse's Metaphilosophy"), *Philosophy and Phenomenological Research* 21, No. 4, 1961.

"Concerning the Uniformity of Causality" (comment on Gale's "Professor Ducasse on Determinism"), *Philosophy and Phenomenological Research* 22, No. 1, 1961.

"Concerning the Logical Status of Criteria of Morality" (comment on Santoni's comment on Dommeyer's criticisms), *Philosophy and Phenomenological Research* 23, No. 1, 1962.

"What Would Constitute Conclusive Evidence of Survival after Death?," *Journal of the Society for Psychical Research* 41, No. 714, 1962.

"Early History of the Association for Symbolic Logic" (co-author Haskel B. Curry), *Journal of Symbolic Logic* 27, No. 3, 1962.

Contribution to "The Future of Parapsychology: A Symposium," reported in *International Journal of Parapsychology* 4, No. 2, 1962.

"Comments by C.J. Ducasse" (on A.G.N. Flew's criticism of Ducasse's "What Would Constitute Conclusive Evidence of Survival after Death?"), *Journal of the Society for Psychical Research* 42, No. 716, 1963.

"Hypnotism, Suggestion, and Suggestibility," *International Journal of Parapsychology* 5, No. 1, 1963.

"Addendum to 'Early History of the Association for Symbolic Logic'" (co-author Haskel B. Curry), *Journal of Symbolic Logic* 28, No. 4, 1963.

"Substants, Capacities, and Tendencies," *Review of Metaphysics* 18, No. 1, 1964.

"Art and the Language of the Emotions," *Journal of Aesthetics and Art Criticism* 23, No. 1, 1964.

"Broad's Lectures on Psychical Research," *Philosophy and Phenomenological Research* 24, No. 4, 1964.

"Causation: Perceivable? or Only Inferred?," *Philosophy and Phenomenological Research* 26, No. 2, 1965.

"Minds, Matter, and Bodies," and comments on contributions by others, *Brain and Mind*, ed. by J.R. Smythies. London: Routledge and Kegan Paul, 1965.

"The Watseka Evidence" (comment on Dommeyer's "Body, Mind, and Death"), *Pacific Philosophy Forum* 3, No. 3, 1965.

"Taste, Meaning, and Reality in Art," *Art and Philosophy: A Symposium*, ed. by Sidney Hook. New York: New York University Press, 1966.

" 'Cause' and 'Condition' " (comment on Gorovitz's "Causal Judgments and Causal Explanation"), *Journal of Philosophy* 63, No. 9, 1966.

"Concerning Berofsky's 'Causality and General Laws'," *Journal of Philosophy* 63, No. 18, 1966.

"How Literally Causation is Perceivable" (comment on Ranken's "A Note on Ducasse's Perceivable Causation"), *Philosophy and Phenomenological Research* 28, No. 2, 1967.

"Intrinsic Value" (comment on Beardsley's "Intrinsic Value"), *Philosophy and Phenomenological Research* 28, No. 3, 1968.

"Philosophy and Wisdom in Punishment and Reward" and "Reply to Comments," *Philosophical Perspectives on Punishment*, ed. by E.H. Madden, M. Farber and R. Handy. Springfield, Ill.: Charles C. Thomas, 1968.

"Naturalism, and the Sense and Nonsense of 'Free-Will'," *Phenomenology and Natural Existence: Essays in Honor of Marvin Farber*, ed. by Dale Riepe. Albany: State University of New York Press, 1973.

UNPUBLISHED WRITINGS*

"The Principles of Universalism (The Program of a Metaphysics)," an earlier version of his doctoral dissertation, 1911.

"The Fallacy of Counteraction and Its Metaphysical Significance," a thesis submitted for the degree of doctor of philosophy, Harvard University, mid-year, 1912.

"The Nature and Number of the Categories," October 26, 1912.

"The Lovestone and Other Dream-Spun Tales," ca. 1920.

Letter to the Editor of the *Journal of Philosophy*, December 11, 1928 ("I believe that the correct answers to the questions raised by Mrs. Ladd-Franklin in the Dec. 6 issue of the Journal, would be . . .").

Lecture notes for course in philosophy of science given in 1930's, transcribed by Roderick M. Chisholm (as an undergraduate) from Ducasse's own notes.

"Conference Reports, No. 4, Literature of Psychical Research, a few suggestions from Prof. C.J. Ducasse," undated.

59 Aphorisms, undated.

"Design Relationships and Emotional Import," ca. 1943.

Lecture notes for Philosophy 1, 2 (Philosophy and the Types of Human Experience), 1945–46.

Lecture notes on morality, undated.

Lecture notes for course in philosophy of education (Philosophy 54 or 154), given in 1952 and for some years before and after.

"When is There a Problem as to What a Term Means?," ca. 1954.

* These unpublished papers are in the archives of Brown University, John Hay Library.

"Method in the Investigation of Spontaneous Paranormal Phenomena," presented at the Conference on Spontaneous Cases, organized by the (British) Society for Psychical Research and held at Newham College, Cambridge University, July 11–17, 1955.

"Does it Make Sense to Say that Death is Survived?," undated.

"Biographical Notes Concerning C.J. Ducasse," undated.

"What Reality Have the Past and the Future? ," presented to the New York Philosophy Club, Columbia University, Jan. 17, 1958.

Notes of remarks made May 3, 1964 at conference on psychedelics at New School for Social Research, New York City.

Analytical Philosophy of Knowledge. A comprehensive restatement of his theory of knowledge on which he was working in the last years of his life. The substance of several of the chapters were published as articles in the 1960's.

Voluminous correspondence with many philosophers, unclassified by topic, of much importance for the study of the philosophy of C.J. Ducasse.

INDEX OF NAMES

INDEX OF SUBJECTS

Feeling
  adverbial analysis of 51
  in expression theory of art 122–36
Feeling images, in art 126, 129

Hedonism 103–14

Images, of feelings in art 126, 129
Integration of capacities 85f.
Interactionism 78–85
Introspection 47f.

Language 96–98
Language of feeling, art as 124, 132f.

Meta-ethics ‾101–03, 110–11
Meta-philosophy 1f., 185–99
Method, philosophical 1f., 185–99
Mind-body relation 78–85
Monotheism 159–61

Necessity
  etiological or nonlogical 23–33
  natural 32–33

Objective reference 52–55

Paranormal phenomena 167–83
Parapsychology 167–83
Perception
  of etiological necessity 27–29
  theory of 46–63
Philosophy as a science 196f.
Pleasure, adverbial analysis of 113f.
Polytheism 162–65
Precognition 182f.

Properties, dispositional analysis of
  48–51
Propositions 88–91

‘Real’, analysis of 186–91
Realism
  adverbial 46–63
  new and critical 55–59
  in aesthetics 134f.
Reference, objective 52–55
Reincarnation 162–65
Relativism, in artistic criticism 136–43
Religion, definition of 157–59
Religious assertions, as cognitively mean-
  ingless 156f.
Religious belief, in Ducasse-Miller cor-
  respondence 144–54
Right to Believe, in Ducasse-Miller cor-
  respondence 144–54

Science, philosophy as a 196f.
Semantic analysis 185–99
Sensing
  adverbial theory of 46–63
  indubitable or incorrigible 59–63
Signs and symbols 96–98
Substance, mental and physical 65–78
Substants, and substances 42f.

Truth 91–96

Volitions, as causes 35–44

Will to Believe, in Ducasse-Miller correspondence 144–54
Wisdom 114f.